ALPHA DOGS

THE AMERICANS WHO TURNED
POLITICAL SPIN INTO A GLOBAL BUSINESS

JAMES HARDING

D0071426

Farrar, Straus and Giroux

NEW YORK

Farrar, Straus and Giroux
18 West 18th Street, New York 10011

Library of Congress Cataloging-in-Publication Data
Harding, James, 1969–
   Alpha dogs : the Americans who turned political spin into a global
business / James Harding.— 1st ed.
      p.   cm.
   Includes index.
   ISBN: 978-0-3745-3175-1

   1. Sawyer Miller (Firm)—History.   2. Political consultants—United
States—History—20th century.   3. Media consultants—United States—
History—20th century.   4. Sawyer Miller (Firm)—Biography.   5. Political
consultants—United States—Biography.   6. Media consultants—United
States—Biography.   7. Public relations and politics—United States—
History—20th century.   8. Political campaigns—United States—History—
20th century.   9. Campaign management—United States—History—20th
century.   10. Globalization—Case studies.   I. Title.

JK2281 .H365 2008
324.7092'273—dc22

                                                            2007047953

Designed by Robert C. Olsson

www.fsgbooks.com
P 1

ALPHA DOGS

For my parents

From this we can deduce a general rule, which never or rarely fails to apply: that whoever is responsible for another's becoming powerful ruins himself.

—Niccolò Machiavelli,
The Prince

CONTENTS

Introduction: "What's in the Bag?"   3

PART ONE

ONE: "The Loner in Love with the City"   15
TWO: "Democracia con Energía"   37
THREE: "The Real Thing"   61
FOUR: "A Dangerous Combination for Israel"   82

PART TWO

FIVE: "Stand Up and Fight Like a Woman"   113
SIX: "No"   143

PART THREE

SEVEN: "It's Time for a Great Change"   169
EIGHT: "What Is a Junk Bond?"   196
NINE: "Quit and Move"   216

Epilogue: "Vote Different"   225

A Note on Sources   233
Acknowledgments   235
Index   237

ALPHA DOGS

INTRODUCTION: "WHAT'S IN THE BAG?"

THIS IS THE STORY of three drop-outs who changed the world's politics. They didn't mean to do it. One had hoped to be an actor; one dreamed of playing American football; the third was a disenchanted spy. They stumbled into the election business because it paid well, because it seemed meaningful, because it was more fun than real work. They had a knack for television, the new medium of politics. They had an ability to read the public mind. They recruited a handful of other canny men, each with insuperable egos and the gift of the gab. And together they built a short-lived but influential little company that sold American politics to the world.

The firm was called the Sawyer Miller Group. The people who worked there were not politicians, even less political thinkers. They were political consultants, the campaign trail's crossbreed of roadies and impresarios. Starting out in the early 1970s, they cut ads and they wrote speeches, they polled voters and they devised strategies, they planted yard signs and drove candidates around. They learned their low-brow science running election campaigns for presidents, senators, governors, and mayors. They then sold the lessons of America's television spots and battleground states around the world: the men from the Sawyer Miller Group helped Cory Aquino to lead the People Power revolution in the Philippines and advised democrats in Chile on the removal of General Pinochet; they led their clients to victory in Bolivia, Colombia, and Ecuador, as well as to defeat in Greece and Peru; they worked pro bono for Tibet's Dalai Lama, and they got paid in sweaty bundles of hundred-dollar bills in Nigeria.

In its prime, Sawyer Miller worked in dozens of countries around the world, touching the lives of more than a billion people. Their headquarters was a discreet little office on East Sixtieth Street in Midtown Manhattan. Next door was the famed Copacabana nightclub, a frisky place that was packed every Friday and Saturday night and described in song by Barry Manilow as the "hottest spot north of Havana." Up on the top floor of Sawyer Miller's building, the great entertainer Sammy Davis, Jr., had his apartment. And halfway in between, David H. Sawyer rented a floor of the neoclassical office block. He furnished it with matte black desks, wide leather sofas, and vogueish deep purple walls. He built a bank of TV screens into the wall of his office and a wet bar from which he offered candidates advice and a scotch and soda. Against the prime-time glow of the Reagan presidency, Sawyer Miller became a discreet political powerhouse.

The forty or so people in the firm set out to sway elections across Latin America, Africa, Europe, and Asia, working on every continent, they used to boast, where the people outnumbered the penguins. "At its best, Sawyer Miller sat around the conference table and walked around the world and talked about our clients and it was like the National Security Council," remembers David Morey, who worked there for a couple of years in the mid-1980s and then spent a decade trying to get Kim Dae-Jung elected in South Korea. "In fact, we were more armed with facts. Probably more accurate intelligence than most of the agencies. It was that well penetrated. There was so much talent. You could have run the country out of that conference room."

The firm was never short of such boosterish self-confidence. Still, there's more than an echo of the truth in there: in its day, Sawyer Miller had a bigger global reach than McDonald's.

They all started out as idealists. They wanted to do good and make money. They were generally antiestablishment and anti-intellectual. They were smart, entertaining, and, most of all, passionate. They believed that politics and politicians could make a difference. They believed that democracy—in particular, the new "electronic democracy" made possible by televisions, telephones, and computers—challenged elites and empowered common people.

For all that, they ended up with a decidedly mixed record. On the one hand, their clients included five Nobel Peace Prize winners—the Dalai Lama, Shimon Peres, Kim Dae-Jung, Oscar Arias, and Lech Walesa. On the other, the firm was also named by a Washington think tank as part of the "Torturers' Lobby," blamed for working on behalf of governments, such as Colombia's, that had ugly records of human rights abuses. In the United States, Sawyer Miller worked almost exclusively for Democrats; internationally, they were more promiscuous. They worked on the left and the right, and sometimes both. In the 1970s, they worked against and then for Carlos Andrés Pérez in Venezuela. They worked for and then against Manuel Noriega in Panama. In the early 1990s, they helped campaign to get Václav Havel elected in the Czech Republic; they advised Lech Walesa in Poland.

Very often, they lost. Sawyer Miller's clients lost every time they ran for the U.S. presidency. They lost congressional races from North Carolina to Florida, Illinois to Utah. They lost in Argentina, they lost time and again in Israel, and they lost most spectacularly in Peru. When Mario Vargas Llosa, the Peruvian novelist, invited the firm to come down to Lima to help his presidential campaign in 1990, he looked like a shoo-in: more than half the people of Peru were preparing to vote for him, while his rivals languished in single digits in the polls. Still, he lost—brought down by colossal misjudgments, allegations of racism, high-pitched shouting matches, feuds within a family-run campaign, and an embarrassing episode with an incontinent monkey. It was a humbling defeat. But, as they say in the industry, there are only two kinds of political consultants: those who never lose and those who cannot lie.

Sawyer Miller was in the vanguard of innovation, when television gave birth to the modern era of politics. Many people then feared an Orwellian future, a world of electronic political propaganda in which Big Brother controlled public thought. Others hoped that TV would create a new kind of dialogue, bringing substantive debate into the living room, pulling politicians down from their pedestals, and cutting out the rotten corruption of the party machine. Neither of those things happened. Instead, the men at the Sawyer Miller Group and a whole new breed of political professionals realized that the power of television was more profound, but less ennobling: they grasped the supremacy of image. They told their clients to "go negative"; they peddled "spin"; they placed their faith in continuous polling; they championed the permanent campaign; they put greater emphasis on character than on policy; they sliced and diced the electorate into myriad little targeted constituencies. They did all this because it worked.

Their intention was to engage voters. The irony is that they helped to usher in a political culture that has turned ordinary people away in droves. More than a third of voters seem to have deserted the ballot box for good. There is more to this, of course, than slippery PR: access to information has eroded the authority of government and loosened the hold of the political party; ideological differences have narrowed, prosperity has increased, the isms of the twentieth century have been superseded by pragmatism, and politics, thankfully, does not shape and twist human lives as it did a generation or two ago. The education system and the media have failed to nurture civic involvement; the power of the nation-state has, increasingly, seemed dwarfed by the multinational corporation, the electronically empowered individual, the asymmetry of modern warfare. Still, the backdrop to the Sawyer Miller story is the disenchantment with democracy. The march of freedom in the past thirty years has brought hundreds of millions of people to polling stations for the first time, but disillusionment with politics has driven nearly as many away. Spin reinforced a vicious circle of suspicion in politics, while a calculating politician, a cynical media, and a distrusting public reinforced one another to hollow out the national conversation.

The men from Sawyer Miller were not the only ones to fashion a new style of politics. And they were not the only, or even the first, American professionals to whisper in the ears of the world's presidents and politicians. They were the servants of change as much as they were the agents of it. The world's politics has been governed by the defining forces of our times: the triumph of capitalism's argument with communism; the transforming power of technology; the spread of democracy. But Sawyer Miller understood quicker than most that the information revolution lay at the root of all three. They harnessed the power of television. They learned to apply the wisdom of psychology and the verve of advertising to winning elections. They seized upon the opportunity of taking the American campaign ethic overseas and became the progenitors of a discreet international industry in American political know-how. At the same time, even as they pioneered the Americanization of world politics, they were pulled back home by the politicization of U.S. business. They found that what they had learned in New Hampshire and Iowa, Venezuela and Israel—that to communicate was not just to "inform," but to "relate"—applied just as much to Apple and Coca-Cola, Goldman Sachs and Continental Airlines.

Together, David Sawyer and Scott Miller did for international political consultancy what Andrew Lloyd Webber and Tim Rice did for the world of musicals. They did not invent the art form, but they helped forge a massive modern industry.

They proved that, language, history, and national pride notwithstanding, the ballot box is as susceptible to the forces of globalization as the box office. Since Sawyer Miller, "political communications" has become an international business. American advisers have been behind the scenes when a dancing Boris Yeltsin ran for office in Russia, when a modernizing Tony Blair remade the Labour Party in Britain, and when Silvio Berlusconi swept to power promising a "Contract with the Italian People" (drafted by the same pollster who helped draw up Newt Gingrich's "Contract with America" a few years earlier). One of the more subtle expressions of the Pax Americana has been the triumph of U.S.-style politics and the ubiquity of American political consultants.

Mark McKinnon was one of several Sawyer Miller men who went on to help get a man elected to the White House. A hip Texan who used to show up for work in Washington, D.C., dressed like a country-western singer minus the hat, McKinnon ran the advertising campaigns for George W. Bush in 2000 and again in 2004. In the run-up to the 2008 election, he worked for John McCain. During his time at Sawyer Miller, he advised candidates and parties in Ecuador, Colombia, and Nigeria. "There is a parochial notion that elections are different everywhere. They are not. They are the same everywhere," McKinnon says. "The things that drive elections are the same in Nebraska as they are in Ghana."

Politics in country after country has become as similar as Starbucks— and about as surprising. The assumption underpinning the international consultancy business is that the same principles apply everywhere, that a foreign country is just like another swing state, just like Ohio. Elections are carnivals. Message discipline has supplanted ideological debate. Parties have been in long decline, with personalities taking their place. Politics is estranged from policy-making. The battle is ever more for hearts, not minds: America's winning and irresistible formula has been to repackage an intellectual argument inside an emotional appeal. We are all fans of *The West Wing* now.

The world increasingly speaks in the same terms. London sounds more than ever like Washington: John Major tells the BBC he does not want to play "Monday-morning quarterback"; *The Daily Telegraph* has a front-page story on the Conservative Party courting the "religious right"; Labour heckles the new Tory leader David Cameron for being a "flip-flopper," an echo of the Republican attack on John Kerry in 2004. For the rest of the world, the U.S. presidential election is not just a spectacle. It is a preview.

The Sawyer Miller Group accounts for just one twisted strand in the curiously underreported story of the globalization of politics. The office on East Sixtieth Street was a chaotic and sometimes farcical place: the company travel agent generally had a better idea of where the partners were going and what they were doing than David Sawyer. But the firm made an enduring difference. It epitomized how U.S. politics has become a global business. Its experience helps makes sense of the political world we live in now—and the new one we are on the threshold of entering. This book is the story of the life and times of the Sawyer Miller Group. At its most banal, it is the biography of a soon-forgotten PR company; in its more ambitious moments, it is an archaeology of the present, an investigation into the crime scene that is modern political culture, a short and selectively edited history of how political spin became a global business— all told through one New York office drama.

Like many political stories, it did not end well. Not for its founders, at least. Not, you might say, for any of us.

ALTHOUGH I didn't know it at the time, I started writing this book on a humid summer morning in Troy, Ohio, the kind of deliberately retro town where you wouldn't be surprised to bump into Jimmy Stewart walking down the street. That morning, thousands of people had thronged into the town square to cheer George W. Bush. The president was setting off on that modern political pilgrimage, the whistlestop bus tour through Middle America. I was standing on the sidelines, deeply involved in the groaning buffet of barbecue and fried chicken that gets laid on for the White House press corps at every stop, because I was covering the 2004 U.S. presidential election.

Quite unusually, Karl Rove wandered over. Rove was, at this point, a man of mythical proportions. He was the singular commander of the Bush-Cheney '04 campaign. He was the most intriguing man in American politics, the master of modern micro-politics, and the man entrusted with making the big strategic decisions. Bush called him his "Boy Genius," "Turd Blossom," and his "architect."

As the president headed over to the podium to give his standard stump speech, we hacks descended upon Rove. He was peppered with questions—about the state of the race, the state of Ohio, the state of John Kerry's campaign . . . the usual. After about half an hour, people started to peel away to jot down notes or listen to Bush. Soon there were only a handful of us standing around Rove, and the gaps between the questions and answers grew longer. The journalists, addled by too many consecutive predawn starts or simply too unimaginative, seemed to have run dry of things to ask the closeted mastermind of the Bush campaign.

After another pause, a Japanese journalist pointed to Rove's canvas shoulder case bulging with papers and manila folders and asked him, half question, half small talk, "What's in the bag?"

"Secret shit," Rove said, letting out a laugh and putting a hand protectively on the case.

"The codes," he went on, making his own silly mockery of the Myth of Rove. "I have the codes . . . name any city you want." He chortled and I, being well brought up and English, politely chortled back at this joke about nuclear Armageddon.

Then Bush was done; Rove hurried back to the president's bus to head to the next town hall meeting. The press scrambled to get on the buses that follow in convoy. Sitting on the coach as it rolled through the small towns of western Ohio; the fields of corn, potatoes, and soybeans; the streets of the small towns lined with people cheering the presidential motorcade or brandishing their own homemade Kerry banners, you couldn't help wondering: What is in that bag? If you like, this whole book is an attempt to find out what was in that bag.

The Bush-Kerry race, much like the Bush-Gore contest in 2000, was not about a fundamental ideological choice. It was not a watershed in public opinion. It was about personality, perception, and organization. In the noisy blur of the election year, at least one thing was clear: the campaigns mattered. The Swift Boat ads, the evangelical vote, the online fund-raising and the get-out-the-vote operation all really counted. The election seemed to exemplify the primacy of tactics, the special place of a master tactician like Karl Rove, the sense that real power lies today in the hands of the political consultant, the modern Machiavelli. That intriguing, disheartening realization lies at the heart of this book: it is about politics in a tactical age, not an ideological one. It is also about how technology can transform politics. The Sawyer Miller Group flourished thanks to television, a new medium that a generation ago had an impact that was as profound as it was unpredictable. Today, the Internet is just beginning to have an impact on elections and the exercise of power, promising to rewrite the rules of the political game in ways that are, if anything, more sweeping and less certain. Part of the fascination in going back to the original innovators of modern political communication has been trying to come to grips with the election business on the brink of another information revolution. After two perplexing elections in America, and before the frenzied caravan starts barreling across the United States once again, the antics of the people at Sawyer Miller can help explain how the modern election machine works.

Television has simplified politics. It has done the same for history. We are seduced by the neat historical narrative, the idea that history is made by great men: the lone statesman in a political wilderness, the solitary inventor in the laboratory, the courageous soldier willing to confront the military establishment. The fact is, though, history is generally a team effort. It is not a soliloquy; it is a chorus line. And nowhere is this truer than in politics, a field that needs committees of people to agree to a new picture on a postage stamp and a congressional hearing to ascertain that American sportsmen take steroids. The "swarm theory" of history applies here: the idea that groups of people, not one or two individuals, change the course of our lives and the culture in which we live. The story of Sawyer Miller is much more than the story of the two men whose names were on the door.

But they were not *all* men at Sawyer Miller. There was one woman. Mandy Grunwald came straight out of Harvard and joined the firm in the late 1970s. When it came to putting together a political ad, she could make a silk purse out of a sow's ear. She was also difficult, abrasive, and rude. Seen as one of the guys, she was the kind of woman with a booming laugh and a sewer mouth who liked a bloody steak and a strong martini. She started as an intern, and after working on more than a hundred campaigns, she left New York a dozen years later to work in Little Rock for a no-hope presidential candidate named Bill Clinton.

Sawyer Miller was a place that relished its machismo; where people worked through the night on takeout, coffee, and cigarettes; where men found their wives—and lost their wives—in office romances and chance encounters on international flights; where every new candidate meant a gladiatorial battle that would ultimately end in victory or defeat. It hummed to the electronic pulse of television and thrilled at its own proximity to power. In 1986, Sidney Lumet made a movie about a successful political consultant that was based on the character of David Sawyer and played by Richard Gere. The film was called *Power*. (The catchline read: "More seductive than sex . . . More addictive than any drug . . . More precious than gold. And one man can get it for you.")

"It was," in the words of Mark McKinnon, "a damn mean business. All alpha dogs."

It was the same phrase Ned Kennan used when he described the firm to me a few months later. Kennan had been a pivotal figure in Sawyer Miller, the pioneering pollster who had delved deeply into the public mind and provided the voter research that dictated the political message. When I spoke with him he had long retired from Sawyer Miller and moved out of New York City to live in the New England countryside. He was exploring Buddhism. Over a burger in Taylor's, a dank downstairs bar in the faded town of Greenfield, Massachusetts, Kennan looked back at Sawyer Miller and the "alpha dogs." He explained: "The alpha dog is the one who calls the shots. It comes from watching dogs. There's always a dog in the pack who controls things." It's a curious boast, but several other of Sawyer Miller's alumni have used the same term to describe their breed. "Alpha dogs" makes them sound like a crack troop of guerrilla forces who parachute behind enemy lines, sleep rough, and live off woodland berries, which is ironic for a bunch of guys who used to fly business class and write memos by the hotel pool. It is also a name that is ambivalent, hinting at both the brilliant and the dastardly, the inspiring and the manipulative. It is a name that fits.

PART ONE

As for the little lean, shrivelled, paunchy old man, of five feet two, in a jacket and breeches, there is no majesty in him at any rate . . . Put the wig and shoes on him, and he is six feet high:—the other fripperies, and he stands before you majestic, imperial, and heroic! Thus do barbers and cobblers make the gods that we worship.

—W. M. Thackeray,
"Meditations at Versailles"

ONE

"THE LONER IN LOVE WITH THE CITY"

ON A BRIGHT WINTER'S DAY in late 1978, Kevin White, the mayor of Boston, breezed into the grand reception room at his official residence, the Parkman House. He had come for a meeting to discuss the prospects of his reelection, nearly a year away, and he was trailed by the people he liked to call his "political family"—his chief of staff, his press secretary, his diary scheduler, a clutch of local Democratic grandees, and a couple of Beacon Hill pals. White stood broader and taller than most of them, a thickset, handsome man with a smile as wide as the Charles River. That afternoon, Ned Kennan would be responsible for wiping that smile off White's face.

"The people of Boston really do not like you," Kennan said in his thick, guttural Israeli accent. "In fact, they hate you." He grinned, and paused for effect. "They view you as an aloof, arrogant, son-of-a-bitch bastard." Kennan beamed at the mayor like an insolent child goading a teacher. "You don't give a damn about people. You are seen as the boss of a huge political machine. You are . . . not liked."

White's entourage of aides had scattered themselves across the plush sofas and Italianate furniture of the reception room in the Parkman House. Now they sat silently, watching the blood rise in the mayor's cheeks. They volunteered nothing. They were not used to seeing anyone address the most powerful man in Boston and one of America's most successful politicians in such a way. They were deferential to his authority, afraid of his temper. Worse, they knew it was all true: Kevin H. White's long rule had achieved nothing quite so much as the distrust of Bostonians.

In the words of White's own chief of staff, the people of Boston thought that he had become "an emperor." By the late 1970s, the mayor's hopes of a historic fourth term were in danger. He was under threat from a clean-cut, handsome young challenger. White had drafted Kennan and a little-known team of political consultants from New York because, at some instinctive level that operates in even the haughtiest of politicians, he could sense his imminent extinction.

Kennan continued: "The people of Boston think you are inside the temple, they are outside the temple. They think you are selfish." He explained to the mayor that the pollster has one question that counts more than the rest, one that serves as a weathervane for any campaign: "Does he care about people like me?" It is a simple, elemental test that asks not just if the candidate has a caring image but if the electorate cares for him. The favorable responses to Kevin White were near zero. " 'Does he care about people like me?' " Kennan asked again. "No. They say no. They think you don't care for anybody."

White, a trim, handsome Irishman, stared back at this short, scruffy Israeli. "On the other hand," Kennan said, "you are seen as a good mayor of the city. Not a nice person, but doing a pretty good job."

Night after night in the previous few weeks, Kennan had gathered with small groups of people from across the city. In long, rambling conversations with them, he brought his curious collection of skills to bear: he was born in Jerusalem and his first job had been as an intelligence analyst for the Israeli intelligence service, Mossad. He then went to college in California, where he studied psychology. In the previous ten years, he had developed new methods of understanding popular attitudes toward such everyday products as Listerine mouthwash and Dentyne chewing gum. He was one of a new, innovative breed of public opinion researchers who were trying to put the entire American public on the couch. In Boston, he had been developing a relatively new technique in politics: it was called the "focus group."

The mayor listened to Kennan's jumble of expletives, the biblical deconstruction of his character, and the painstaking explanation of his unpopularity. With admirable restraint, he asked: "So, how do we change my image?" "I don't believe we can," Ned said, "because, frankly, Kevin, I've only met you a couple of times, but you appear to me to be someone who is an aloof, arrogant son-of-a-bitch bastard who doesn't care for anybody."

Kennan explained that people do not change. More important, the public does not believe people change. It would be pointless to try to manage, let alone manufacture, White's image. Over the past twelve years, the people of Boston had come to know the mayor for what he was: uptight, opinionated, and superior. They liked his record, but they most decidedly did not like him. You could not suddenly dope them into thinking he was an all-around nice guy.

"Does it mean I'm going to lose the election?" White asked.

"No, I believe you are going to win the election." Kennan said. Then he offered his prescription: "Tell the truth. Say, 'I'm Kevin White, I'm a selfish, aloof, son-of-a-bitch bastard. I run a big political machine. But I love this city, Boston, and I'm using all of that machine politics and power to make the city prosper.' " Kennan stood by his flip chart looking at White's family of political advisers. He paused to admire his handiwork. It was as if a man had given a master class in wallpaper hanging to a wisdom of blinking owls.

"I want to be liked," White said, an afterthought.

Kennan smiled again, sympathetically this time: "Not everyone can like a person like you, Kevin."

KENNAN—part shrink, part show-off, part statistician—was an exceptional pollster. He viewed the body politic much the way a psychologist judged a human individual, as a mixture of competing sexual impulses and social prejudices, emotional needs and value judgments. He also had an essential gift for anyone who has to inform a politician of public opinion: he presented unwelcome truths with relish. Anyone who has worked in politics for any period of time will tell you that the trick in polling is not just setting the questions or analyzing the answers. The difficult bit is convincing the average, insulated politician that the polls are, actually, true. Ned was a brilliant storyteller. He could bring numbers to life. When he spoke, he blended the voice of God with a Borscht Belt comedy routine. And, of course, Kennan was used to unwelcome truths: he had grown up in Israel.

His boyhood was spent by the radio, the herald that announced the birth of the new state of Israel in 1948. Ned—or, to use his Israeli name, Nadav Katznelson—was born on Mount Scopus and into a family of well-known Zionists. He made his contribution to the Zionist cause in short trousers, as a bicycle courier during the War of Independence.

When he finished school in Jerusalem, like all other boys, he was drafted straight into the Israeli military. By the age of seventeen, he was working in Israeli intelligence.

One night in 1957, Kennan crossed the border to meet one of his informants in Jordan. He started out on the long walk back a few hours before dawn. Just before sunrise, a man jumped him. Kennan took out his knife, but his assailant kicked it from his hand. The man pulled his own knife and swiped at Kennan. Kennan remembers grabbing the man's arm and twisting the knife back in on him. With the man bleeding on the ground, Kennan reached for one of the large rocks that litter the Judean hills and killed him. As the day began to brighten, he crossed back over into Israel. He did not mention the incident for five years. (His attacker's knife—a beautiful one with a carved handle—today lies in a drawer in Kennan's Massachusetts home.)

When he got the chance, he quit the Israeli intelligence service, severing ties with the army, his family, and his homeland. It was 1960. He and his new wife, a physical education instructor in the Israeli army, took a boat called *The Jerusalem* to New York. From there, they headed to the West Coast, where, a little late in life, Kennan started his studies. He brought a contrary intellect to his understanding of social psychology and a frisky libido to the UCLA campus. He did his master's dissertation on Friedrich Nietzsche and European nihilism; he did his Ph.D. on "Classification of Juvenile Delinquents Based on Their Psychological and Behavioural Attitudes"; he peppered discussion with his thoughts on priapism and the female orgasm. When his studies were done, he had to get a job.

Kennan moved into the research wing of the consumer goods industry just as the relationship between corporate America and the public psyche was changing. The polling industry had already been around for decades. Gallup had become a household name even before the war. Lou Harris had made a reputation for himself in the 1950s, sealed in 1960 by his work for John F. Kennedy. But in the 1960s, a second generation of pollsters was developing a much more penetrating form of market research. During World War II, the U.S. military had begun developing the precursor to the focus group: sociologists were asked to assess the American audience's reaction to military propaganda films. They realized that when viewers were questioned and probed smartly and repeatedly, they could identify which lines in the film, which images, and which ideas chimed most deeply and which had no effect. America's big consumer goods companies, the sellers of soaps and shampoos, who rely so heavily on effective advertising, were quick to seize on the business potential of the focus group. While the Gallup generation of pollsters was driven by politics, Kennan and his colleagues were driven by commerce. They did not want to find out only how many people liked the product but also how to sell more of it. That meant they did not want just to know what people were thinking, but to understand, too, what drove those opinions. To do this, researchers needed to develop new ways of understanding how the public thought—better yet, how it felt. They replaced the blank questionnaire with the in-depth interview and the focus group.

One of Kennan's first projects was working on Listerine, the mouthwash. The company had run a bunch of studies, and the findings had been utterly predictable: people with higher incomes used Listerine; there was more usage among smokers; there was less usage among blue-collar workers; people gargled with it after meals of garlic and onions. Kennan pointed out that the executives at Listerine could probably have worked this out without leaving the office. More important, this information told them where the market was, but not what drove the market, which were the levers on consumer behavior. At a meeting of the board, the directors were discussing plans that might add two, perhaps three, percentage points in sales. Kennan announced grandly that he had a plan to increase sales by exactly 25 percent. He had conducted what he called, pseudo-scientifically, a series of FGIs and IDIs—focus group interviews and in-depth interviews—with Listerine users. And what he had found over hours and hours of conversation was that they tended to be work-hard, play-by-the-rules kind of people, the types who would never run a stop sign and would help an old lady across the road, the sort of people who buy an appliance and follow the instructions in using it. In short, the kind of people who read the label. Kennan's point was that the vast majority of Listerine users did what they were told to do by the instructions on the side of the bottle: they poured the concentrated mouthwash into the cap, added water, gargled, and spat it out. Kennan's proposal was to make a 25 percent bigger cap.

Kennan was an impish young man in the body of an old hippie: he was short and fattening, a man with a round face, a bushy prematurely gray beard, a bulbous nose, and a wicked glimmer in his eye. He was into Off-Broadway theater and smoking weed, and he carried his lunch—a sandwich in waxed paper—in the pockets of the one sports jacket he owned. Nonetheless, he soon found himself ushered into the boardrooms of corporate America and, very quickly, the offices of American government. For he was one of the leading figures in a changing of the guard in public opinion research.

The pioneers of quantitative polling were being superseded by a new generation of researchers who were harnessing the power of the computer as well as the science of psychology. They were going beyond traditional demographics, which divided people by age, gender, and income, and slicing and dicing the population into groups defined by their behavior. At the same time, they were delving more deeply not just into what people thought but *how* they thought. One of Kennan's mentors was Seymour Lieberman, who had developed new methodologies for differentiating groups within the broader population that built on the original segmentation studies and motivation research done by the likes of psychologist Ernst Dichter in the 1940s and 1950s. The group psychology approach appealed to Kennan's fascination with popular attitudes, private sexual appetites, and public values. It was also new, experimental, and unconventional.

KENNAN'S JOB in the Parkman House that afternoon in the winter of 1978 was not just to tell the mayor he was unpopular, but to tell him why. White needed a dose of unwelcome reality. The mayor was twenty-six points behind. As White's tenure in city hall had rolled on, his popularity had slipped further.

Boston born and bred and the son of Irish Catholics, Kevin White had started out in city politics on a populist platform. When he first ran for mayor in 1967, one of his slogans was "When landlords raise rents, Kevin White raises hell!" He quickly came to be seen as one of the most charismatic politicians in America. He was dubbed, in those early years, "Kevin from Heaven," and was described in the same breath as John Lindsay of New York, a mayor who treated city hall as a national stage. White had adapted Lindsay's idea of "little city halls," creating neighborhood organizations that decentralized power. He seemed able to cut across the communal lines that had so long hemmed in Boston politics. And he liked to play to the gallery: when the Rolling Stones were arrested on the way to Boston, the mayor released them into his own custody. He told the awaiting audience at Boston Garden: "The Stones have been busted, but I have sprung them!"

In 1972, White was being bandied about as the "Mayor of America." He was five years into the job in Boston—spurring development; speaking out against the Vietnam War; holding together the fractious constituent parts of the Democratic Party; straddling communities of Italians, Irish, and Jews, labor and business, black and white. He not only commanded the begrudging respect of the people of Boston but also was making a name for himself nationwide.

That year, George McGovern chose White as his running mate to mount the Democrats' challenge to Richard M. Nixon. He was on the ticket for about four hours. McGovern called White to tell him he wanted him to be the vice presidential candidate, but he still had to square it with that dynastic force in Democratic politics in New England, the Kennedys. As ever in politics, the opposition is the other party, but the enemy lies in wait within your own. The Kennedy Democrats would have none of Kevin White. They nixed his candidacy. McGovern was steered away, and the mayor of Boston, who had been told he was on a shortlist of one, was dropped. White got the call from McGovern asking him to join his presidential ticket; he never got a second call inviting him down to the Democratic convention in Miami.

Having hoped for higher office, White more than made do with Boston. Through the 1970s, he presided over the revival of the city, throwing up skyscrapers downtown and attracting shops and restaurants to Quincy Market. Following the federal drive to integrate neighborhood schools, White struggled to keep a lid on the racial tensions in the city. (The violence that erupted during the busing crisis included the unforgettable image of an African-American man, Ted Landsmark, being attacked by a white man with an American flag.) There was also the whiff of corruption about the White administration, a scent that has filled the noses of the voters of Boston for so long that they smelled it whether it was there or not. (This was, after all, the town that had elected James Michael Curley, the "last hurrah" mayor who brought not just charisma but also a criminal record to the job.) White—or "Mayor DeLuxe," or "King Kevin," as he was sometimes known—was another in a long line of Boston officials getting a reputation for enjoying the discreet indulgences of the mayor's sumptuous public residences and extensive entertainment account.

Over time, he seemed to grow more embattled, more dictatorial. The "little city halls" were scrapped, and by the late 1970s, White was being criticized for running a network of ward henchmen who gave city jobs and contracts to those people who supported the mayor. As White seemed to slip further out of touch, Joe Timilty, a local state senator and a good-looking neighborhood candidate with the backing of the lunch-bucket Democrat crowd, stepped up once again to challenge haughty Kevin White and his rarefied friends from Beacon Hill.

White was bitter that, having done so much for Boston, he still had to fight so hard for its approval. He had forged an extraordinary coalition of Italians, blacks, and liberals, winning the mayor's office without banking on the Irish vote. Increasingly, though, he was being cast by his opponents as a wheeler-dealer politician, not a presenter; a master of the backroom bargain not cut out for life at the front of the house. This was a time when television was cleaving the unsuspecting world of politicians in two: on the one hand, there were those who knew how to wield power but who looked distinctly uncomfortable asking for it—Lyndon B. Johnson, for example, or Richard Nixon; on the other hand were the natural perform-ers, the likes of John F. Kennedy and Ronald Reagan, who seemed to know instinctively how to campaign in front of the cameras but who sometimes looked out of depth behind the big desk. Kevin White was be-ing painted, he thought quite unfairly, as a politician from the old school, a Democrat in the LBJ mold. His talent, as his political biographer George Higgins later put it, was "in holding office, not in seeking it."

He was, though, grudgingly aware of the problem, as his responses to Kennan later made clear. As the 1979 election loomed into view, White sent Micho Spring, his chief lieutenant, to New York to find some profes-sional political help. Spring had been given a bunch of names of these so-called "political consultants." (The term was still relatively new.) Many of them, she found, were unimaginative or unconvincing. After a long day in Manhattan, she was weary of being told things she already knew and was tempted to cancel the last appointment with one little-known political shop that had come highly recommended but that she had never heard of. Out of politeness, she stayed to hear their pitch. She headed back to Boston convinced that she had found the two smartest guys around. One was really a copywriter in the advertising business; the other was a docu-mentary filmmaker. At the time, politics was for them much more than a hobby but still a little less than a business. They were called Scott Miller and David Sawyer.

ALTHOUGH NO ONE IN THE ROOM at the Parkman House appreciated it then, they had all seen Scott Miller's work countless times before. He was the most sought after creative talent at the advertising firm of McCann Erickson, where he was responsible for, among other things, the Coca-Cola account. As a result, more people in America had seen his work than watched any single movie, listened to any particular song, tuned in to any one TV program. "Have a Coke and a smile!" was Miller's line. "Coke is it!" was his, too. While Ned Kennan practiced the art of telling the truth bluntly, Scott Miller was a subscriber to H. K. McCann's philosophy of advertising: "The truth well told."

Dressed in blue jeans and sneakers, Miller looked—as he so often did—as though he had just come from the gym. His first and enduring love was sports. During the 1960s, that tumultuous decade for America, he mostly thought about football. In 1960, when John F. Kennedy was beating up and down the campaign trail, Miller was running laps. He was fifteen and a receiver for the Pioneers, the football team at his school in Hudson, Ohio, where he harbored dreams of playing professional football. In that pivotal year in politics, when Kennedy met Nixon in the first televised debate and America was witness to a revolutionary new technology in politics, Scott Miller was aware of only one news event outside Ohio: the Ole Miss football team won its second national championship in a row.

Miller's family was all-American but not upper-class. His father was a shoe salesman, selling wholesale to department stores across the Midwest. He knew he would be on the road much of the time, so he could choose where to live. He settled the family in Hudson, which back then was a small farming town, halfway between Cleveland and Akron. Miller's father had come from the boot heel of Missouri, the southeastern corner of the state, where his own father had run a hunting lodge. Before that the Millers had been in Texas, cattle-ranching. The family was at home more or less anywhere in America. They had a blue-collar history and white-collar aspirations—not wealthy, but affluent enough to send their sons to private school and to college.

Washington and Lee, a small private men's college in Lexington, Virginia, was a blithely happy place in the 1960s. College campuses elsewhere were in open revolt. Demonstrations against the Vietnam War drew thousands of people, not to mention tear gas and riot police, at other colleges, but not at Washington and Lee. Miller's friends on the football team were not dodging the draft; they were volunteering to fight. America was losing 1,200 men a month, but boys at Washington and Lee wanted to be forward observers. Miller and one of his other roommates were disqualified from serving because of knee injuries; his two other roommates went to Vietnam. Of course, being pro-Vietnam was no way to get laid, which, other than football, baseball, and track and field, was Miller's preoccupation as a graduating senior in 1967. So he was pro-war with the guys, antiwar with the girls. Deep down, Vietnam was not the battlefield he was interested in.

That summer, he went for a tryout with the New England Patriots. He arrived strong and quick and hoping to make it through the morning's passing drills and fitness tests to join the team for preseason training at Amherst. Within minutes, he found himself lying on his back on finely manicured grass, looking up at the sky, wondering who was the sixteen-wheel linebacker who had sideswiped his left knee. The coaches told him to go see the doc. He did not need to. He lay there, crystal clear in the knowledge that his sporting career was over.

Miller stayed in Boston, trying his hand at any odd job. He worked in a bar, he played in a band, he took up rugby, and he tried out acting. He felt as though he had been given a free pass in life, because even though his football dreams had been shattered with his knee, he had not been drafted to go to Vietnam. Still, he needed a job. He had come up with a few headlines for *The Southern Collegian*, the rag that passed for a humor magazine at W&L, and he thought he might have a crack at advertising. He put together some ideas and went through the phone book—ABC, Acme, Apex—and got a job in the Bs somewhere.

The advertising industry was going through its own rebellious, inventive adolescence just as Miller was growing up. The 1950s and 1960s witnessed a revolution in advertising, as commercials got chatty, funny, and oblique. David Ogilvy not only put a new premium on consumer research; he was also ripping up the rules of copywriting. Gee-whiz statements of the obvious were out. Advertising was getting clever. Ogilvy's 1958 ad for Rolls-Royce was accompanied by this copy: "At 60 miles an hour, the loudest noise in this new Rolls-Royce comes from the electric clock." This was a new golden age of advertising, the heyday of firms like Doyle Dane Bernbach, which came up with a new kind of irreverent, counterintuitive ad for the Volkswagen Beetle in 1959: the "Think Small" campaign that inspired a generation of postwar Americans to think the "ugly" little German car was hip.

It was Doyle Dane Bernbach, too, that conspicuously applied advertising's newfound wit to politics. A DDB executive, Tony Schwartz, came up with the daisy election ad, still the most famous political commercial of all time. It was made for Lyndon B. Johnson, and although it aired only once—to much criticism—it dominated the news agenda and helped Johnson defeat Barry Goldwater. The ad showed a girl picking petals off a daisy, counting them off one by one. A heavy voice is then heard counting down as the girl turns toward the camera. It zooms in until her pupil fills the screen, blacking it out. The countdown reaches zero. A mushroom cloud fills the screen.

The voice-over from Johnson follows: "These are the stakes. To make a world in which all of God's children can live, or to go into the dark. We must either love each other, or we must die." "Vote for President Johnson on November third," another voice said. "The stakes are too high for you to stay home."

Writing advertising copy came naturally to Miller. He had a gift for marrying images with an emotive phrase and—perhaps thanks to his family's peripatetic past, perhaps because he saw life through the lens of football, perhaps because he stayed at home when other men his age went to war overseas and lost faith in their country—he had an unsullied instinct for finding the high, providential symbolism of America in the life of everyday Americans. These were the post-Vietnam, post-Watergate years, when Madison Avenue was trying to remind the nation of its strengths and its positive values, when companies such as Coca-Cola were launching the "Look up, America" campaign: "From sea to shining sea . . . no matter what you're doing or where you are, look up for the real things."

The young Scott Miller had a sunny disposition and channeled into his work that most American of qualities, hope. He won his first industry award within a matter of years, for a spot about a kid who wrote a poem to his shoes, his Converse All-Stars, which he called "limousines for the feet." Later, Julius "Dr. J." Erving, the basketball player, became known for the phrase. For Coca-Cola, Miller condensed all the optimism of an American consumer icon into a single slogan: "Have a Coke and a smile." For Miller Lite, he ran a campaign designed to try to bring women into the beer-drinking fold: "Great taste, less filling." He started in Boston but was quickly noticed in New York, and in 1975 he was hired by Mary Wells, then the best-known copywriter and most famous businesswoman in America, to join her firm, Wells, Rich, Greene.

On Miller's second day in what was then the General Motors Building on Fifth Avenue, an elegant man in a Dunhill suit walked into the office. He had a high forehead and thin dirty-blond hair swept back as if he had just stepped off a yacht in a strong wind. No sooner had he arrived than he seemed to be in a hurry to leave. He started the conversation politely, without pleasantries, as if he were apologizing for having just interrupted Miller in midstream. He said his name was David Haskell Sawyer and he asked Miller if he wanted to do some campaign work with him.

SAWYER'S TALENT was not for telling the truth bluntly or well, but for telling it like it is. He had fallen into a life of political image-making after his early success in cinema verité, a genre of documentary filmmaking that sought to portray life on-screen as rough as it was offscreen.

At Princeton University Sawyer had fallen in love with the theater. He was president of Theatre Intime, the student-run theater that originally opened in a dormitory bedroom. Born into a family that could trace its history back to Plymouth Rock, Sawyer lived his life in a tug-of-war between establishment conformity and individual expression. Dave, as he was known to the other men of the class of '59, was accepted into Cap and Gown, a Princeton eating club, and then chose not to eat there. Sawyer had been born into a dysfunctional but wealthy family that derived its fortune from the United Shoe Machinery Corporation. (The Sawyers were at the other end of the shoe business from the Millers: while Miller's father was going from town to town wholesaling shoes, Sawyer's father was heir to a company that liked to boast that nearly every shoe made in America had passed through one of its machines.) And, like many men with his class and wealth, Sawyer went on a grand tour of the world after college; but unlike others, he chose to travel by cargo ship. In what he wore, how he spoke, where he spent his summers, Sawyer forever sought the affirmation of the East Coast establishment. In his work, he was forever drawn by those outside it. As Oren Kramer, a Democratic rainmaker steeped in the fund-raising industry of New Jersey, said years later, "David was arguably the most creative and charming preppy I met in my whole life. If preppies were more like David, they wouldn't have such a bad name."

After graduating, Sawyer went to New York to study acting with Lee Strasberg, then the doyen of the Method school of acting, as exemplified by Marlon Brando. But he came to terms quickly with the fact that he was not going to succeed as an actor: he was too awkward and self-conscious. He was good-looking, for sure, but he couldn't disguise the fact that he was a restless, impatient man who fidgeted and ground his teeth in his sleep. He switched from a life in front of the camera to a life behind it. He started studying filmmaking at City College in New York, weaving back and forth on his motor scooter to film classes uptown.

By then, the young Boston Brahmin had started stepping out with a short, smart, and high-strung Jewish girl from the Upper East Side. Iris Michaels was a sparky, opinionated intellectual hooked into the New York scene. She bumped into Truman Capote at parties. She worked as an assistant on the "People Are Talking About" column at *Vogue*. She moved on to work for the photographer Richard Avedon at his studios. Iris would be seen by Sawyer's family, Sawyer told his friends, as "the most unacceptable woman he could find." In 1960 he married her.

It is a measure of how far removed from politics David Sawyer was that the wedding was held in the middle of the Democratic National Convention of 1960. It was a crucial week in the year when John Kennedy and Richard Nixon ushered in a new era of American politics—the television era that Sawyer would do so much to define. On the same day that Adlai Stevenson was getting up to address the delegates in Los Angeles, Sawyer was half a world away, stepping into a small chapel inside St. Thomas's, the giant gothic church on Fifth Avenue in New York.

The wedding was, as Iris remembers it, "a nightmare." David's parents were divorced and bitterly divided, so much so that David's mother chose to sit with Iris's mother rather than with her former husband on the groom's side. There were only about twenty people there. Iris wore a short white dress from Henri Bendel, David, a dark suit. The ceremony had been organized in a hurry. Iris wanted to get married quickly, worried that if they didn't do it then, they never would. The ceremony was also unusual: Iris was Jewish, but she had always wanted a church wedding.

After the service, the newlyweds went for an early dinner with a few members of the family. Then they drove back to spend the summer in Princeton, as the speeches from the convention in L.A. played on their car radio.

Politics continued to serve as background noise for most of the 1960s, as Sawyer pursued a career in film. He soon fell in with a crowd of people trying to film "life as it is." He got a job working for Richard Leacock and D. A. Pennebaker, who had set up a small studio of their own in 1963 and were in the vanguard of what was known in America as "direct cinema." In 1967, Frederick Wiseman made *Titicut Follies*, an exemplar of the new style of documentary, recording with a handheld camera the experiences of patients at Bridgewater State Hospital in Bridgewater, Massachusetts.

Titicut Follies had a profound impact on Sawyer, as it did on so many other budding documentary filmmakers of the time. For Sawyer, who had discovered that he was dyslexic and, perhaps because of it, more versatile with the moving image than the written word, the film seemed to capture life from behind the viewfinder, which was the way he framed the world. It transformed the idea of cinema verité from an intellectual import from Europe into an American genre that recognized the intelligence of the audience, the power of unvarnished footage, and the extraordinary drama of ordinary life. The film came just as Sawyer had been asked to come down to Bucks County, Pennsylvania, to do some filming to help raise funds for the Delaware Valley Mental Health Foundation. A one-day visit to the institution expanded into an eighteen-month project and, eventually, a full-length documentary: *Other Voices*.

Sawyer's first full-length film charts the progress of five apparently hopeless mental patients. The film is rough and ready, the camera work choppy, and the editing disjointed. But it is an unforgiving exploration of mental illness, culminating in the suicide of one patient and the beginning of redemption for another. In 1970, it was nominated for an Oscar.

Other Voices turned out to be the last full-length film Sawyer would ever make. At the close of the 1960s, he started fielding calls from people in public life who wanted a little less "voice of God" in their infomercials and a touch of the vogueish, gritty realism of cinema verité. He was hired to do some work for the U.S. Army, making short factual spots for soldiers on topics such as how to clean an M16. (This came at an uncharacteristically ideological time for Sawyer, who had just read the sayings of Chairman Mao and, inspired by them, taken a short swing to the far left.

He was not a radical for long. But the late 1960s was his one short period of flirtation with the life of a socialist peacenik.)

In 1970, a Jewish businessman named Milton Shapp was running for the governorship of Pennsylvania and commissioned Sawyer to create a half-hour, grainy biopic. The film softened public suspicions of Shapp, helped him find a place in Pennsylvanians' hearts, and set him on the road to victory. Soon, politicians everywhere wanted their own cinema verité biopic. After his near miss at the Oscars in 1970, Sawyer was hired by Bobby Kennedy's adman to help him work on Governor Frank Licht's campaign in Rhode Island. Then he was hired to produce a biographical film for a candidate for governor in Illinois. It was Sawyer's first significant political work in the United States, but it quickly gathered momentum. Working with Bob Keefe and Maurice Sonnenberg, two young guys who had been staffers on Capitol Hill, Sawyer established a little business in 1972 specializing in the half-hour biopic. "That sort of was David's niche," Keefe remembers. "He did not know how to spell 'politics.' We did not know how to spell 'film.' " D. H. Sawyer and Associates was run out of Sawyer's one-bedroom Manhattan apartment, a hand-to-mouth operation that picked up work for people such as Thomas Eagleton, the Missouri senator who was briefly the Democratic vice presidential nominee in 1972. The firm was not making much money, but in the tiny circle of professional political operatives, it was beginning to get noticed. Peter Hart, one of the most prolific pollsters of modern American politics, was one of the first to spot Sawyer's talent: "His genius was, as a dyslexic, he never saw things backward, he really saw things forward. He had a visionary sense of . . . how to translate a message." Hart brought Sawyer into several campaigns in the early 1970s, all for political outsiders.

Ella Grasso, for example, was a Democratic congresswoman from Connecticut. In 1974, with the help of Hart and Sawyer, she became the first woman elected governor of any U.S. state in her own right. (There had previously been other women governors, but they had succeeded their husbands or served as stand-ins.) Grasso won by defeating the profound suspicion of a woman's capacity to lead a male-dominated government. At the time, one popular bumper sticker read: "Connecticut Needs a Governor, Not a Governess!" Sawyer cut an ad that showed Grasso at the head of a long library table, surrounded by men, sounding them out on the issues. Ostensibly, the ad was a way of voicing Grasso's policy ideas; subliminally, it pictured a woman in command.

From the start, Sawyer seemed to have a penchant for underdogs. As his reputation and his firm grew, he became known for his knack for getting women elected. The new media would prove to be the best possible means of challenging the men of the old political machine.

By the time David Sawyer walked into Scott Miller's office in the GM Building, he was beginning to see a new kind of business take shape. He knew that he did not have the resources or the skills to meet the demand from a growing list of potential political clients. Here and there, he had heard of Scott Miller, who had worked in his spare time in Boston on a couple of campaigns. Sawyer would prove in the years to come that he had the two signal qualities needed to recruit great people: an eye for talent and a lot of patience. When Sawyer and Miller walked into the Parkman House that winter's day in 1978, they were still working together only on a haphazard, campaign-by-campaign basis. They were three years into a professional courtship; it would take Sawyer another four years to share a name with Miller on the company door.

AS KENNAN KEPT DELVING into the focus group findings and further insulting their potential client, Mayor White, Sawyer smoked and fidgeted. Immaculately turned out as ever, he wore a worsted pinstripe suit, a striped blue-and-white shirt, a silk tie with a slender knot, and a handkerchief in the breast pocket of his suit. But regardless of the country-club tan and the air of refinement, Sawyer was anxious to get on to the next stage: the message.

Miller, meanwhile, was quietly enjoying Kennan's show. He had spent a few years in Kevin White's Boston and he knew well enough that even those in town who admired White didn't necessarily like him. The mayor was in trouble, and this was no time to be treading on eggshells. There was also no point trying to convince people that White was really a sweetheart. Instead, Miller liked Kennan's thinking: *"Tell the truth. Say: 'I'm Kevin White, I'm a selfish, aloof, son-of-a-bitch bastard.'"* Miller liked the contrariness of it; he liked the fact that it had a ring of truth; he liked the simplicity of it: Kevin White doesn't care about you, but he cares about the city.

Both Sawyer and Miller were learning the fundamentals of a new communications industry as they went along. In the case of Kevin White, they lit upon principles that would serve them well in the years ahead.

White, Sawyer said, had to "control the dialogue." This was to become his mantra: David Sawyer's pitch to every client, whether the president of a country or the head of a tobacco company, was simply that you had to define yourself or you would be defined by your opponent. There was not enough time to turn around Kevin White's arrogant image; they were better off trying to make his arrogance an essential element of his record of achievement as mayor.

At the same time, they did what they would do time and again: they went negative. Joe Timilty, White's challenger, had run against White four years earlier, and after a long, bitter campaign, he had come tantalizingly close to pushing White out of city hall. Timilty was a little-known state senator back then, a thirty-six-year-old former marine who was fresh, good-looking, and well liked. He challenged Kevin White over allegedly irregular campaign contributions and fancy dinners for big-money donors at the Ritz. It was a charge that reinforced both Boston's suspicion of corruption in the mayor's office and White's reputation for indulging in the high life on the city's dollar. White had given as good as he got: he rolled out the chief of police to denounce Timilty and suggest that the Mob was out to smear White because they knew that their business interests were getting squeezed by the mayor. (The neat implication was that the Mob wanted Timilty to win.) White won in 1975, but he was chastened. His support in Back Bay and Beacon Hill was ebbing. He had played on his years of experience in office, but he knew that his long tenure was generating disenchantment. He had also allowed Timilty to control the debate.

This time, Sawyer and Miller were determined that White be in charge of the conversation. They sent the mayor a memorandum: "We must define the issues, and take the battle to Timilty. We've got to score early and often." The strategy, as they set it out, focused entirely on the perceived personalities of White and Timilty. There was not a mention of a policy issue, a budget priority, an urban problem, or a tax proposal in there. The memo said: "We want to begin negative advertising on Timilty as soon as possible."

David Sawyer and Scott Miller were both early champions of "going negative." Maurice Sonnenberg, one of Sawyer's first partners, remembers a conversation years after they set up D. H. Sawyer and Associates. "David had got a call. The guy said he wanted to run a nice clean campaign. David and I looked at each other because we both agreed that if you're going to run a campaign, the candidate has got to agree to a negative campaign," remembers Sonnenberg, who left political consulting for a life as a dapper New York banker, an expert in the U.S. intelligence services, and a sometime actor in Woody Allen movies. (At the time of writing, he was well into his seventies and, he said, had many girlfriends.) "David used to say that it is an irony that negative campaigns are more honest than positive campaigns. Positive campaigns, you're saying how wonderful you are. Negative campaigns, you're doing some research and finding out some things about the candidate."

Scott Miller developed a whole body of thought around going negative. He heard many candidates and clients complain that people do not like negative advertising, but the truth is that people like a good fight. Negative ads are so commonplace because they are so effective. Miller's view was that there are three circumstances in which negative advertising doesn't work: if the ad is not true, then it will hurt the accuser more than the accused; if the ad is personal, voters may well sympathize with the individual being attacked; if it is irrelevant, it will be considered an attempt to misdirect the voter and will be resented. Otherwise, negative advertising worked.

In the White campaign, Sawyer and Miller sought to toy with latent public doubts about Timilty. "Timilty carries the lightweight image . . . we must help form that image," they told Kevin White. They would tease Timilty for being fresh-faced, for having tried and failed twice before to be elected as mayor, for coming up again and again with new pet issues. "We will be willing to say that Joe Timilty is an okay guy, but Joe Timilty is a lightweight. He doesn't understand the tough job of running this complex city."

The tone of the negative advertising was very important to Sawyer and Miller. It needed to have style and wit. It had to be entertaining in its own right, not part of a painful political dogfight. So Miller put together a parody of a long-running show called *The Bickersons*, which starred Don Ameche and Frances Langford, and was the archetype of the bickering husband and wife—" 'matrimony' is not a word, it's a sentence"—radio comedy. For the mayor's reelection campaign, the couple were the Bixbys and they quarreled about White and Timilty. Mrs. Bixby had her reservations about the mayor; Mr. Bixby would respond with a funny but belittling one-liner about the challenger. Mrs. Bixby would ask about Timilty: "He's the guy who's for law and order, isn't he?"

"No, that was when he was running for city council . . . I think he's anti-something," Mr. Bixby would reply.

"Oh, no. That was when he ran for mayor the first time. Now it's something else . . . I'm not sure what."

"I know . . . it's, uh, classification."

"Right."

"Yeah."

"Wrong . . . classification was when he ran for mayor in seventy-five."

"He wasn't Tippicanoe and Tyler too, was he?"

"Be serious, he's for something . . ."

Miller's view was that people did not want to be told what to think, but they could be led. The negative ads ended with a doubt-inducing inflected question: "Joe Timilty—for mayor?"

At the same time, Sawyer and Miller wanted to offer a positive spin on Kevin White, but fight the battle on the basis of his real strengths rather than the qualities they wished he had. It would have been easy to succumb to the pressure from some of the people in White's political family, who wanted the image makers from New York to "soften" Kevin White. Instead, Miller and Sawyer decided to use Kennan's research as the template: "White's crazy, but he loves the city and makes it work."

A few days after the Parkman House meeting, they outlined their strategy: "This will show that elements of his style (he's a consummate politician, he's forceful, he's opportunistic, he's fiery, he's wily) which are perceived as vaguely negative will be portrayed as necessary talents to run this complex city . . . He *has* to be complex. He *has* to be tough." Miller liked the cognitive dissonance at the heart of the Kevin White problem, the challenge of selling a product that was unpopular but effective, the difficulty of getting people to vote for someone they did not like but whom they respected. Over the weeks that followed Miller toyed with catchphrases that might fit.

One evening, reading a bunch of newspaper clippings he had been sent by Micho Spring, the mayor's deputy, he stumbled across a phrase that Mike Barnicle, the *Boston Globe* columnist, had used: "The loner in love with his city." Miller read it over a few times. "That just captured Kevin for me," he recalled years later. He appropriated it, with a tweak: "The loner in love with the city" worked on a number of levels. It portrayed Kevin White as vulnerable rather than arrogant, a sole warrior rather than a machine boss, and a man who had Boston at his heart.

The New York consultants brought in the best commercial filmmakers to cut the spots in Boston: Joe Hanwright, who had done a lot of work with Miller on Coca-Cola, was on camera; and Alan Blevis did the voice-over, something he would do for countless Democrats up to and beyond Bill Clinton. The films that Sawyer and Miller made of Kevin White were all shot in documentary style. They were romanticized versions of hard work.

There were other ads, reinforcing the same theme. One showed Kevin White at work, with the tagline "Knowing which arms to twist and hands to hold: that's what it takes to be the mayor." Another showed White in his office at 2:00 A.M., tired and alone and still working the phone. The slogan: "The Mayor." A third spot showed White poring over plans to expand the airport, mediating a neighborhood dispute, listening to the arguments over the busing crisis, bringing new business into the heart of downtown. "It's been tough," he says, "but I love that job." The ad concluded with Kevin White standing alone on the bridge over Mystic River, looking out over Boston: "The loner in love with the city."

Still, there were missteps, too. White was not too pleased when he read an interview with Ned Kennan in *The Boston Globe* in which the pollster said that "selling Kevin White is like selling cottage cheese." Then again, the White team also got lucky: Joe Timilty never mounted the challenge that Sawyer, Miller, and Kennan had most feared, the most simple and powerful platform in any democracy: "It's time for a change."

Election Day, November 6, 1979, represented the high-water mark of public participation in Boston politics. In 1975, 156,846 people cast mayoral ballots—or 81 percent of those who had voted in 1967. In 1979, 141,337 people went to the polls—or 73 percent of the 192,673 voters of 1967. The campaign may have been more sophisticated, but for a whole host of reasons the voters were less interested.

Still, the trio of Sawyer, Miller, and Kennan had dragged White back into contention because they had defined the debate, making it a vote not for change but for competence. And nearly a year after Kevin White had breezed into the Parkman House to be told, in no uncertain terms, why he was twenty-six points behind in the polls, the mayor of Boston won a fourth term. That night, the smile as wide as the Charles River was back.

THE PARKMAN HOUSE has seen moments of greater drama than the planning meeting for Kevin White's reelection campaign in the winter of

1978. For a start, George Parkman, the wealthy Harvard benefactor, was bludgeoned to death there by a Harvard professor in the middle of the nineteenth century. But that afternoon marked the first occasion that Sawyer, Miller, and Kennan clubbed together, an accidental collaboration that, unbeknownst to them at the time, opened an extraordinary and generally unexplored chapter in the Age of America—the remaking of politics in America's image. Starting with the 141,337 people who voted in Boston that winter, Sawyer, Miller, and Kennan would go on to touch the lives of well over one billion people in more than twenty-six countries.

White's victory had an immediate impact on their careers. "The loner in love with the city" was held up as an instant classic of political story-telling. By the time Kevin White's next election rolled around and the mayor prepared for a historic fifth term, Sawyer and Miller had a national and internationally expanding roster of political clients.

In 1983, it once again fell to Ned Kennan to set out the mayor's predicament, which had only deteriorated. While White's own pollster, Dick Dresner, was telling him the numbers looked good for his reelection, Kennan's focus groups were suggesting that White faced an even steeper uphill battle. "You are Jehovah, and in order to win this election you have to be willing to become Jesus Christ," Kennan told White, as he considered whether to run again. "You have to be able to change a little of your persona." White knew that he could neither change nor convince the people of Boston that he had changed. His triumph in 1979 had, at the very least, taught him that. Over the weeks that followed, White explored how he might repeat his triumph against Joe Trimilty, how he could fight and win this battle without massaging his image—by being unrepentantly the man he was.

As spring gave way to summer in 1983, White's decision to run for office came to dominate the political conversation in Boston. The mayor had been giving mixed signals. In March, he told a local TV station that he was a candidate; then, within hours, a press aide said the comment was "inoperative." A few weeks later, he declared that he planned to defend his record.

On the last Sunday in May, White headed down to New York to prepare his announcement with his media advisers, David Sawyer and Scott Miller. The mayor had been through months of soul-searching, intense public speculation, and secretive planning. In order to minimize the chance of a leak, they filmed him in front of the fireplace in the living room of David and Iris Sawyer's apartment on East Sixty-sixth Street. The tapes were sealed and hand-delivered to three television stations and nine radio stations for simultaneous broadcast at 6:55 on the evening of May 26, 1983. The Boston media had been determined to breach the security of the New York City taping, and on the morning of the announcement, *The Boston Herald* ran a page-one story: "Herald Exclusive: White Will Run."

For the first few minutes, White left his audience guessing. He had been the longest-serving mayor of a big American city, having taken over the same month of the Tet Offensive in Vietnam and still in office when the space shuttle *Challenger* made its maiden voyage the previous month. Back in 1968, "American cities were in trouble," he said, but "today, people are moving into the neighborhoods of Boston, not out of them. So, we've come a long, long way . . . As mayor, I have felt the glory and the pain." After sixteen years in office, White seemed determined to eke out a few more moments of well-choreographed drama, a couple of minutes of political suspense. And then, in what *The Boston Globe* described as the most dramatic local event since game six of the 1975 World Series, the mayor took Boston by surprise: "I have decided not to be a candidate in this election, but to seek new horizons and challenges here in Boston and beyond. There will be no Last Hurrah for this city. No, Boston, this is just a beginning."

TWO

"DEMOCRACIA CON ENERGIA"

SIX YEARS AFTER DAVID SAWYER strolled into his office at Wells, Rich, Greene, he had still not quite managed to lure Scott Miller away from the advertising industry and into his business.

They had worked together on a freelance basis on dozens of campaigns. Before Boston, they had already tried their hand at a presidential bid: they briefly advised Henry "Scoop" Jackson on his short, doomed run at the White House. They had also been signed up on a number of state races. They helped Bruce Babbitt's campaign for the Arizona governorship, and they worked with Jane Byrne, who became mayor of Chicago and the first woman to run a big U.S. city. After their success with Kevin White, they were recruited to work on even more campaigns. In the 1980 election cycle, they tried, pointlessly, to help the addled, alcoholic Warren Magnuson, by then a representative of Washington state for thirty-six years, win yet another term in the U.S. Senate. The same year, they headed to Connecticut and ensured the safe elevation from the House to the Senate of the young Christopher Dodd. (They worked there with a young Yale academic named Stan Greenberg, who was trying his hand as a professional pollster for the first time.) And they had stood in Boston's Faneuil Hall to hear Ted Kennedy announce his decision to challenge Jimmy Carter and seek the Democratic nomination for the presidency: "This country is not prepared to sound retreat. It is ready to advance. It is willing to make a stand. And so am I." Just ten months later, they stood at the Democratic National Convention in New York and heard the Kennedy insurgency draw to a close. "For me, a few hours ago, this campaign came to an end . . . For all those whose cares have been our concern, the work goes on, the cause endures, the hope still lives, and the dream shall never die."

(It was a speech drafted by Bob Shrum, then a Kennedy staffer who himself would go on to be a political consultant, sometimes collaborating but more often competing with Sawyer and Miller.) But as much as Sawyer and Miller had become a double act on the Democratic Party circuit, they were still not a partnership.

Scott Miller was the toast of Madison Avenue, recently promoted to creative director, the youngest in the history of McCann Erickson. He had been given a huge apartment in an Upper East Side brownstone; he was ferried to and from work in a limousine; he had gotten married and divorced within the space of eighteen months, and after what he called his "practice marriage," he was a bachelor much in demand in New York City. Nonetheless, he also itched to get out of working for a big company. He was responsible for the day-to-day oversight of the firm's creative product, on-the-spot reviews of new people and new projects, monitoring the flow of work and managing the people. He didn't much like having to decide which staff member got a corner office or who should be entitled to a potted plant.

He was, however, developing a real fascination with an electronic revolution unfolding in every American home. In a memo to his colleagues at McCann in October of 1981, Miller was almost evangelical on the subject: "Television is one of those businesses that fails to understand the miraculous machinery that it is working with," he wrote. "This warm and friendly flickering light, we must not forget, is also capable of changing the world."

Sawyer and Miller had almost nothing in common except this missionary zeal. Miller was in awe of the lost world of the downtown boxing club, the journeyman fighters and the broken-nosed bums; Sawyer, who looked, dressed, and even sounded much like David Niven, the English matinee idol, loved the old world of the dock-shoe set, the fellow members of the yacht club in the Hamptons. Yet, the two men were bound by this sense that they "got it" when the rest of the world didn't, that they understood the widely underestimated power of television and how it was rapidly revolutionizing politics and business. The more they worked together, the more they developed a shared working philosophy that bordered on the ideological. As they used to tell people: "Nothing, other than war, has revolutionized the world like television."

Even as their ideas fused, however, Sawyer's efforts to recruit Miller

into a business to fulfill this shared vision of a new kind of political communications company had come to nothing. So he launched what he
considered a full-court charm offensive: he invited Miller for lunch at the
Knickerbocker Club.

Sawyer reveled in his membership at the Knickerbocker, a gentleman's
club on Fifth Avenue that is as conservative as it is prestigious. (It was
founded in 1871 by a group of men who had gotten wind of plans to re-
lax the rules at their existing club, The Union. Alarmed at the thought of
slipping standards, they set up an unrepentantly exclusive club of their
own.) The appeal of the place baffled Scott Miller: there was no gym, not
much of a bar to speak of, no women, and it was considered bad form to
discuss business over the lunch table. Sawyer, though, loved the place, delighted in hobnobbing with Wall Street financiers and old New England
money. Over lunch that day in 1981, he listed its virtues: the other members, the food, and the fact that the Knickerbocker had very nice rooms
upstairs. To this day, Miller remembers the conversation that followed:

"But you have a duplex apartment four blocks up the street," he said,
still bewildered.

"Well, it's very convenient if you ever separate from your wife," Sawyer
explained.

"Have you?"

"Nineteen times."

The conversation that day hinted at a couple of the leitmotifs of David
Sawyer's professional life: the Knickerbocker lunch routine became his
tried-and-tested way of bringing new blood into his business; it also suggested the blazing rows and long periods of mutual avoidance that made
for the tragicomic melodrama of his first marriage. But it also marked the
beginning of a new partnership. Within a few months, Scott Miller had
finally left McCann Erickson and gone into business with David Sawyer
to create what they hoped would be a discreet but hugely influential
little firm and reap the whirlwind of what they dubbed "electronic
democracy."

The formal creation of the Sawyer Miller Group in 1982 added to a
small but rapidly growing collection of American political consulting
firms. Sawyer Miller would end up reaching more widely into the world
of business than most of the others, it would prove to have more global
aspirations than its competitors, and, by contrast with the one-man

bands that dominated the industry, it traded off more than just the campaign scrapbooks of its founders. It became a firm of more than a dozen partners, men—and one woman—bound by the idea that technology was reinventing political communication.

Nonetheless, they were not the first people to see a business opportunity in the shortcomings of politicians. Campaign management is almost as old as U.S. democracy. John Beckley, who was born in London and settled in America in the late eighteenth century, drove voter turnout for Thomas Jefferson in Pennsylvania in 1796 by distributing pamphlets and handwritten ballots. (He was also one of the first to go negative: he claimed George Washington had stolen public funds, and called for his impeachment.) A century later, Mark Hanna famously hovered over the presidency of William McKinley. In 1922, the journalist and political commentator Walter Lippmann released his book *Public Opinion*, which foresaw the coming industry of political message management: he argued that powerful government was at odds with modernization, as politicians relied on a commonly held public view but the modern media world was fragmenting ideas and opinions of ordinary people. Lippmann predicted that a new breed of professional would be created to steer the public mind in a more confusing age. And in 1933, Clem Whitaker and Leone Smith Baxter, a husband-and-wife team, formed Campaigns, Inc., the first political consultancy in America. A year later, they made their name smearing Upton Sinclair, the Depression-era populist challenging for the California governorship. After he had been defeated, Whitaker concluded: "Every American likes to be entertained. He likes the movies, he likes mysteries; he likes fireworks and parades. So, if you can't put on a fight, put on a show."

Polling, too, had a long lineage. The first political poll in the United States was produced for a newspaper, *The Harrisburg Pennsylvanian*, which, in 1824, predicted the precise opposite of the outcome of the U.S. presidential election. The newspaper surveyed the voters of Wilmington, Delaware, and, according to the straw ballot, the electorate favored Andrew Jackson two to one over the eventual winner in the Electoral College, John Quincy Adams. The straw ballot was a polling technique ultimately abandoned after a spectacular humiliation in 1936: *The Literary Digest* mailed ten million Americans asking them to name their preferred candidate in the upcoming U.S. presidential election. The magazine then announced that Alf Landon, the Republican, was poised to unseat Franklin Delano Roosevelt. FDR won in a landslide and *The Literary Digest* never recovered. (Pollsters learned the lesson of the skewed sample—the mistake had been to poll only people with telephones and cars, overwhelmingly wealthier and more conservative than the population at large.) By then, though, a young man named George H. Gallup had already begun to use the developing technology of polling to help political candidates, starting with his mother-in-law, Mrs. Alex Miller, who, with his assistance, became the first female secretary of state in Iowa.

By 1952, Neil Staebler, the chairman of the Michigan Democratic Party, was telling congressional hearings that "elections will increasingly become contests not between candidates but between great advertising firms." And by the time Sawyer was recruiting Scott Miller into D. H. Sawyer and Associates and turning it into the Sawyer Miller Group, a clutch of other political consultants had made names for themselves on the U.S. campaign trail: Gerald Ford had lost in 1976, but his advisers Douglas Bailey and John Deardourff were admired for their candidate's surge in the homestretch; David Garth had made his name helping underdogs Ed Koch into the New York mayor's office and Brendan Byrne back into the New Jersey governor's office; Bob Squier was building up his reputation, hailed for his media campaign on behalf of John Y. Brown in a victorious off-year election; Tony Schwartz still had legendary status, thanks to the daisy spot for LBJ.

When Mandy Grunwald, then a young Harvard undergraduate, went looking in 1978 for a summer internship in the political consultancy business, her political science professor laid out her choices: "There's Tony Schwartz, who is crazy; David Garth, who is a son of a bitch; and if you're lucky, David Sawyer will hire you."

The other difference between David Sawyer and the rest was that he had not done his apprenticeship in politics traipsing the icy lanes of New Hampshire, or going from motel to motel in West Virginia, or working the church halls of Iowa. Other political consultants had earned their spurs in a race for the White House; Sawyer had undertaken his first serious professional work overseas. In 1968, he was asked to go down to Puerto Rico to help produce films for the Senate campaign of a young politician, Rafael Hernández Colón. In 1972, he was back in San Juan to work on Hernández Colón's successful race for the governorship. That same year, Sawyer learned the seminal lessons of a presidential campaign in Venezuela, fighting for a man he didn't know in a language he didn't speak in a country far from home.

TODAY, Caracas has sunk far beyond the realms of faded charm. Shantytowns spill out over the hills, encircling the city like the dirty rings of Saturn. The boxy apartment blocks downtown are grimy, caked in the soot of stagnant traffic belching out exhaust. From atop lush Avila Mountain, the view of the city below is clouded by a yellow mist of pollution. The center of town is dangerous—a place where taxi drivers tell visitors to take off their plastic digital watches to minimize the risk of a mugging. The tallest skyscraper is a charred skeleton, a building burned out and blackened by fire, which stands like a monument to urban paralysis, neither restored nor razed to the ground but stoking ever more elaborate suspicions of arson in a country where conspiracy theories are the only booming business. Across the road, peach-colored paint is peeling off the Caracas Hilton.

It is not the sparkling new hotel that David Sawyer and Iris checked into the week before Thanksgiving, 1972, and the city is not as he found it.

Venezuela in the early 1970s was a place brimming with fabulous new wealth. The country was blessed with vast oil resources. Thanks to the Arab oil embargo, Venezuela was about to be doubly blessed by the soaring price of crude. Caracas, the capital, was no oil painting: it had slums and clapped-out cars and Sovietski office buildings. But as the petrodollars began to gush into the country, Caracas was breaking records that made it the envy of Latin America. Venezuelans were quickly becoming the largest importers of Japanese electronics, the biggest drinkers of fine scotch whiskey, and the greatest collectors of modern art on the continent.

Venezuela had promise aside from the money: it was a young democracy where a two-party system was taking hold. So many other countries on the continent were stuck in a nineteenth-century time warp, still ruled by moustachioed dictators in military garb. Venezuela, though, had suddenly closed the door on a century and a half of caudillismo. In 1958, it embraced a pluralist, representative democracy. Power began to pass peacefully and relatively cleanly from one man to the next: Rómulo Betancourt, a new breed of president with a popular mandate, won power at the polls in 1958; Raúl Leoni, Betancourt's chosen successor, became president in 1963, in the first constitutional transition of power in the country's history; in 1968, Venezuela crossed another great political threshold when the opposition, Rafael Caldera's Social Christian Party, COPEI, defeated Betancourt's party, the Acción Democrática, or AD, and ushered the country into an age of competitive, two-party democracy. The West was impressed: Venezuela seemed to hold out the hope of a new Latin America of free markets and free men, a country that threw off the legacy of the presidential strongman, put its trust in the ballot box, and quickly created the party institutions of modern democratic politics.

For a tiny handful of Americans, Venezuela represented much more than that. It was a swing state in an off-year election. It had a tropical climate, big hotel swimming pools, and staggeringly large campaign budgets. Adventurous political consultants who were willing to chance their arm in foreign climes could make tens, even hundreds, of thousands of dollars, while enjoying smoky sirloin steaks, jugs of sweet sangria, and long evenings on leafy verandahs sucking on Havana cigars and playing the familiar game of presidential politics on an entirely different field. The Land of Grace, as Christopher Columbus called it, became an American battleground state abroad in the 1970s, as Venezuela became the first country that fully succumbed to the "politica Americana."

For David Sawyer, the Venezuela election of 1973 provided not just a much-needed income but also a handsomely paid education in some of the defining forces of modern politics—polarization of the electorate, voter mobilization, and the power of the telegenic candidate—and the chance to learn the rudiments of modern campaigning from half a dozen of America's most expert political consultants.

An election, in H. G. Wells's estimation, is "democracy's ceremonial, its feast, its great function," and Venezuela in the 1970s took Wells at his word. Within just four cycles, Venezuela's election cycle had become a carnival, a barrage of radio messages, full-page newspaper advertisements, mass rallies and marches, nationwide polling operations, vast get-out-the-vote efforts, television commercials and telethons, the carpeting of the country in placards, banners, and flags. Venezuelan elections were even longer and more expensive than the American elections on which they were modeled. In fact, Venezuela spent more per capita on its presidential election in 1973 than the United States had on its election the previous year. The political parties of Venezuela, one and a half times the size of Texas but with a population the same size as North Carolina's, spent about ten times as much per voter as the Democrats and Republicans did in the United States. (At a very conservative estimate, the two main Venezuelan parties each spent 160 million bolivares ($36 million), and the election, all told, cost well over 450 million bolivares ($103 million), the equivalent of 100 bolivares ($23) on each of Venezuela's then 4.5 million eligible voters. In today's terms, that is about $450 million on the election in total or $100 per voter. The U.S. presidential, House, and Senate races in 2004, all combined, cost $2.05 billion, roughly the equivalent of $10 per eligible voter in America.)

With oil money to burn, Venezuela could afford to shop in America for political advice. In the summer of 1972, Venezuela's political leaders sent scouts to the Democratic and then the Republican national conventions, which were held three months apart in Miami Beach. The unofficial Venezuelan delegates not only studied the latest in American election technologies, but they sounded out U.S. party strategists about coming down to Caracas to advise on the upcoming presidential election. Pretty soon, they had signed up the equivalent of the backroom all-stars, the best of the new breed of political consultants. The Acción Democrática party hired Joe Napolitan, F. Clifton White, and, later, Bob Squier. The *copeyanos*, the Social Christians in COPEI, hired Matt Reese and David Sawyer. After Caracas, each of these men would get a taste for working political campaigns abroad. They would prove to be the pioneers of an accidental American democracy corps, men who went out and found election battles to fight on foreign fields.

Matt Reese, for example, had worked for John F. Kennedy, running the ground game in the West Virginia primary that proved such a crucial milestone on Kennedy's road to the White House in 1960. Reese was a round, affable man who mined a rich seam of cynical humor: "My penchant for larceny is one of my greatest advantages," he once told Larry Sabato, author of *The Rise of Political Consultants*. "My skill is having the taste to know what is good enough to steal." F. Clifton White was a Republican consultant who had steered Barry Goldwater to the Republican presidential nomination in 1964. He would be one of the leading lights of the conservative movement in the United States for thirty years, and nearly a generation after drafting Goldwater, he would help carry Ronald Reagan to the presidency in 1980. The perpetually tanned Bob Squier was a *bon viveur* who had already worked Hubert Humphrey's 1968 campaign. In the years that followed, Squier would work across Latin America, although he never learned Spanish. It was said that he once promised a client that he would learn the language if the man won the election. The day after polling, his man had indeed won and was now the president. Squier was summoned to the palace, and when he proved unable to speak a word of Spanish he explained, "Mr. President, you above all people should have understood the value of a campaign promise."

They were, outwardly, different breeds of men, but they were of much the same spirit: raconteurs who preferred to make a point with a long anecdote rather than a short sentence; amateur psychologists who airily put a nation on the couch; card-carrying cynics who believed—or convinced themselves they believed—in the higher purpose of what they did; professional operatives who, with a knowing smile, straddled the lofty idealism and grubby compromises of politics.

Even within that Venezuela pack, Joe Napolitan was a breed apart. In 1968, Napolitan had come within a whisker of pulling off the political upset of a lifetime. He and his team of scriptwriters, media buyers, and producers almost turned the Hubert Humphrey campaign around. The candidate scraped back from twelve points behind to come within seven tenths of winning the White House. Nixon, of course, moved into the Oval Office, but Napolitan had made his name. Over dinner at the Metropolitan Club in New York in June the following year, he was asked to help President Ferdinand Marcos become the first man in the Philippines to be elected to a second term. It was the beginning of a long career parlaying American political know-how into overseas contracts: Napolitan advised Marcos in the Philippines in 1969 ("This was before he turned into a prick," according to the now frail Napolitan); Valéry Giscard d'Estaing in France, 1974 ("A terrible job. I had to fly from JFK to Charles de Gaulle, first class . . . [to] go have lunch with the president of France in the Elysée Palace. And I was getting paid for this"); Neil Kinnock in the United Kingdom in 1992 ("We knew it was a hopeless cause").

His influence on world politics was not, ultimately, as pervasive as that of David Sawyer and the Sawyer Miller Group, but Napolitan was the first to make a career of politics abroad, the man who had coined the term "political consultant" and written a how-to book for aspiring spin doctors: *The Election Game—and How to Win It*. He was not only a modern Machiavelli but also a globe-trotting, self-promoting one. He believed that "there was no reason why the political techniques and technology learned and developed in the United States could not be transferred to other countries." Looking back, Napolitan acknowledges that his first job abroad was a foregone conclusion: "Marcos was always a bullshit campaign. There was no way he was going to lose that election." But Caracas in 1973 was a real contest. The parties were neck and neck. Both candidates thought they were going to win. And for the first time, but not the last, there were two teams of American consultants squaring up against each other.

The fact, therefore, that Sawyer spoke no Spanish mattered little. He was surrounded by other American political consultants who all worked only in English. More to the point, he did not need the local language to understand a political conversation that, to an American, took such a familiar shape.

For one thing, the dialogue was being transformed by television. Rafael Caldera had been elected in 1968, and he was the first leader to lean heavily on the new medium: he hosted a weekly program, *Habla el Presidente* (*The President Speaks*). Venezuela had introduced television in 1952, but throughout the 1950s hardly anyone had a TV set. (Venezuela was in the first wave of countries to start TV broadcasting. The United Kingdom was the first, in 1936; the United States started in 1941; the USSR, in 1946; and Venezuela was the twelfth country to adopt the new technology. Countries such as Argentina, Brazil, and the Dominican Republic were also in the first wave of broadcasters—and all subsequently clients of Sawyer Miller.) By 1961, there were 250,000 TVs in Venezuela. By 1970, there were 822,000. And by 1978, *Time* magazine estimated that seven out of ten urban homes in Venezuela had television. The candidates for the presidency were planning a media blitz, the chief component being television spots, biopics, and talk shows. With little political experience to speak of, all of this played to Sawyer's one genuine expertise: filmmaking.

Venezuela was also in the process of "polarization." It was a country becoming more or less evenly divided in its political affiliations between two parties: the Acción Democrática on the one side, the Social Christian Party, known as COPEI, on the other. Some of the intellectual differences between the two may have been blurring, and many of the policy differences were hard to distinguish, but the partisan allegiances were getting more and more fierce. It was beginning to look like a fifty-fifty nation. And with both parties commanding a more or less even share of the vote, the margins of victory were slim. That meant that both sides were scrambling for new techniques to add those few crucial votes they needed to win.

Sawyer's candidate was Lorenzo Fernández, the favorite, one of those men whom destiny seemed to have chosen for the nation's highest office. He was a summa cum laude law student who soon became one of the founders of Venezuela's young democracy, helping to form the opposition, the Social Christian Party, and holding practically every public office other than the presidency: councilman, deputy, senator, and cabinet minister. Fernández was a portly man. He always seemed to be smoking a thin, hand-rolled Venezuelan cigar, a *cumanense*. He was a fatherly figure, which was not surprising, as he liked to be photographed surrounded by his ten children. He was also one of Latin America's patrician elite, a fading class of men who assumed the burden of national leadership with noblesse oblige.

The spirits in the Fernández camp were so high that his team was not concerned about whether or not their man would win, but by how much. The strategy was to rely on the government record and attack the personality of the challenger. There are, essentially, two basic strategies in a democratic election between an incumbent and a challenger. The challenger's gambit: "It's time for a change." The incumbent's defense: "Trust what you know." In the United States, William McKinley, FDR, and Ronald Reagan all swept to power on the promise of change; Abraham Lincoln, Woodrow Wilson, LBJ, and George W. Bush all stayed the course, stirring fears of change in difficult times. (All four, incidentally, were campaigning when America was at war, jittery times when "the devil you know" argument was at its most persuasive.) In 1992, the Conservative Party in the United Kingdom played to popular fears of change, scaring voters with the threat of "Labour's Tax Bombshell." At the next general election, Tony Blair's Labour Party appealed to the British people's yearning for change, its campaign theme song being the peppy "Things Can Only Get Better."

The Fernández plan was simply to see off a "time for a change" candidate with a "trust what you know" campaign. The strategy was based on two deeply held but untested assumptions. The first was that the Caldera administration was the finest anyone could remember. (The fact that Rafael Caldera was playing a key part in the Fernández campaign may have had something to do with this.) The second was that Carlos Andrés

Pérez, the challenger, did not have the caliber of a man worthy of the presidential sash. He struck the Establishment as a provincial thug who spoke Spanish with a thick Andean accent and had never been to university.

If the personalities were different, the policies were not. Fernández positioned himself to the center-left. He argued that the role of government was to help the poor. He promised to create a ministry of social development and a ministry of economic development. Carlos Andrés Pérez said much the same. But when all the little parties on the far left and right were included, the ideological spectrum in Venezuela was broad: there were the Communists, inspired by Castro's Cuba, on the far left, and on the far right were the hard-line iron-fisters, who admired the fascist order Rafael Trujillo had imposed on the Dominican Republic. But these people were at the fringes. The real contest was not among twelve parties but between the two in the middle, who were grappling with similar challenges. It was an argument, primarily, about the cost of living and unemployment. In Venezuela in 1973, it was clear what the election was about: in James Carville's unbeatable phrase, it's the economy, stupid.

Since both parties were cramming themselves ideologically into the middle ground, they did not expect that ideas would drive them to victory so much as organization. The Fernández campaign took over a drab, three-story building in Boleíta, an industrial suburb in eastern Caracas. There they established an electronic communications hub and staffed it with hundreds of radio technicians, computer operators, data analysts, pollsters, press officers, public relations advisers, and gofers. The atmosphere was busy and informal, but the operations were highly secretive. Poll numbers and get-out-the-vote plans were kept under lock and key. Operations were given code names. The men in Boleíta spoke of "Operación Delta, Operación Gama, Operación Arauca." The focus of these operations was mass mobilization. Operación Gama, for example, involved marshaling twenty-two thousand copeyano volunteers across the country to visit six hundred thousand homes in thirty towns and ten states. And there were more than a dozen other operaciónes, each marrying mass mobilization of volunteers, big computers, and volley after volley of new advertising. "The sheer cost of propaganda and publicity, multiplied by the exceptional length of the campaign," reported John D. Martz and Enrique A. Baloyra, "can only be regarded as extraordinary."

Unfortunately, all this was like putting chrome hubcaps and bull bars on a tricycle: Fernández was a lethargic, lackluster candidate. He believed that his credentials for the presidency were self-evident: his top-of-the-class law degree, his experience in government, and his promise to carry on the good work of Rafael Caldera. Such self-confidence, coupled with ill health, made him a halfhearted campaigner. Even Rafael Salvatierra, one of the young turks of the Social Christian Party charged with organizing the voter-mobilization effort, admitted years later, "Lorenzo Fernández was a great guy, but a very bad candidate." In August, just over three months from Election Day, Lorenzo Fernández made just two public appearances in two weeks, preferring to spend most of the time resting up behind the gates of his expansive home, La Muchachera. The man supposedly campaigning for president held only one major campaign event per day in the week before the election. In today's parlance regarding modern trust fund babies, he had an entitlement problem.

Fernández's campaign slogans were just as lazy, each belying the campaign's assumption that he somehow deserved the presidency: *Siga sonriendo* ("Keep smiling"); *Y este ano, Lorenzo* ("And this year, Lorenzo"); *Adelante con Lorenzo* ("Forward with Lorenzo"). Sawyer—working with the handful of young copeyano politicians staffing the campaign and with the candidate's son, Luis Mariano Fernández—sought to impose some sort of story line on his campaign message. He suggested that they use Lorenzo Fernández's avuncular image, portraying him as a father figure to the nation, a man who could bring people together, a pacifier in restive times. (Venezuela had been dogged by a guerrilla insurgency off and on throughout the 1960s.) Sawyer made a series of long and short biopic films, all around the same theme: *El hombre que esta uniendo al pais* ("The man who is unifying the country"). But Sawyer was the most junior of the American political consultants in a campaign that was already overstaffed by Venezuelan party apparatchiks, all seeking to help a man to victory who did not seem to have the stomach for the election battle. Sawyer's instinct for political narrative was noticed both by his fellow political advisers and by Venezuelans of both parties. But it was not Lorenzo Fernández's story that fired the Venezuelan imagination.

Sawyer, a young man new to presidential campaigning, tried to develop an altogether different kind of persona for Fernández. He and the other advisers made up a new nickname for him—*El Tigre*, the tiger—specifically designed to compensate for the elitist and sleepy persona that Fernández projected. They wanted, instead, to sell the idea that here was a gladiator, a man who ripped his opponents apart, a man-eater in Venezuelan politics. No one bought it. Years later, Sawyer used to love telling the story of how he tried to sell a tabby cat as a tiger—partly as a reminder of how desperate they were to do anything to enliven the Fernández campaign and partly as a cautionary tale about the limits of the political consulting profession: Sawyer was learning firsthand that image-making could not entirely ignore the reality of the candidate.

It was Carlos Andrés Pérez who was, in fact, a force of nature. He began each day with an hour of weight lifting and judo. He had made a name for himself battling the guerrillas when he ran the Interior Ministry in the 1960s. He had populist flair on the stump—for years afterward left-leaning Latin Americans remembered him for describing the cheerleaders of global capitalism in Washington as "genocide workers in the pay of economic totalitarianism."

His campaign was defined as much by what he did as what he said: he walked. He walked all over the country. When he flew into a provincial city, he walked from the airport into the center of town. He walked through city slums and Andean villages. As he walked, he would stop to greet the local elders, pat a baby's bottom, and shake hands with individual voters. Early on in his campaign, as he was walking through a village in the mountains, an Andean woman was heard to cry out, "Ese hombre si camina" (That man really does walk). The phrase was picked up by the Acción Democrática campaign and turned into a song. The campaign poster pictured Pérez smiling and waving as he walked at the head of a happy throng of Venezuelans. The campaign slogan—"Democracia con Energía"—was born of all that walking.

The Pérez campaign was the exact opposite of the Fernández effort. They were only four years apart in age, Pérez at fifty and Fernández at fifty-four, but one captured the Venezuelan imagination as a virile man, the other as an old man. Even their roles in the campaign seemed diametrically opposed: in Pérez's case, the man drove the party; in Fernández's, the party carried the man. Fernández also provided a sitting target for Pérez. He did not renounce any of Caldera's policies, but continued to promise more of the same. Pérez's policy, on the other hand, matched his personality: energetic, decisive, engaging.

Carlos Andrés Pérez used the new media to tackle critics head-on. One of his American consultants, Bob Squier, was an advocate of using television to confront popular suspicions directly. (It was the same attitude that informed Ned Kennan's advice to Kevin White in Boston a few years later, and it was a similar line of thinking that prompted Scott Miller to advise Ted Kennedy to address lingering suspicions about Chappaquiddick when he ran for president in 1980. White listened to this tactic; in Kennedy's case, the advice went unheeded.) The polling showed that people did not like Pérez; some thought he was not Venezuelan but Colombian, that he had killed people. The campaign decided to air the problems on television, putting Pérez before people who would ask him difficult questions. The thinking was that Pérez could handle the punishment and would end up looking even stronger, manlier, and more vigorous, in the public eye. They created a TV program called *Ese hombre da la cara—This man isn't afraid to face you.* Its effect was similar to the Kennedy-Nixon debates in 1960: it brought it all home.

The Pérez campaign was acutely sensitive to the polls, which showed that Venezuelans were preoccupied with local issues. Squier and Napolitan urged the Pérez people to tailor each campaign stop and each walkabout for the local audience. As Diego Arria, a young star on the Pérez team who went on to be one of Venezuela's more distinguished diplomats at the UN, remembers, "We had him talking in his ads about the potholes in the streets of Maracaibo." (This was a clever lift from the U.S. campaign trail: American politicians from Ike to George W. Bush have liked to berate the local mayor for his political ambitions and urge him to get back to fixing the potholes, a laugh line that has the added benefit of suggesting the candidate is in touch with real local concerns.) Squier and Napolitan were entirely preoccupied with the get-out-the-vote operation, "targeting each city, each precinct," Arria said. "Those guys said you have to target their audiences and target them with issues that are local."

David Sawyer's work with Lorenzo Fernández went far less smoothly. He found himself to be a supplicant at court rather than the man behind the curtain. He rarely met the candidate. Many of the suggestions that he and Matt Reese, the political consultant on the campaign, put forward were nixed by the campaign's advertising team or pooh-poohed by the COPEI party officials or agreed to by the campaign team and then ignored by the candidate. It was a lesson Sawyer never forgot: after Venezuela, he always put a premium on direct, personal access to the candidate.

But even where Sawyer was given some room to maneuver, his involvement in the campaign backfired. Sawyer put together a biopic that, as Rafael Salvatierra recalls, was intended "to dilute Lorenzo's weaknesses." It included powerful footage of a rally at the end of 1972 in Caracas, the Plaza O'Leary teeming with people as waves of applause crashed over Lorenzo Fernández. Sawyer had inserted a handful of lines into Fernández's speech so the film would stick to the script, reinforcing his image as the father of the nation. Sawyer's aim, as he explained in a memo to Salvatierra, was to project "the Presidential image of the representative of the entire Nation . . . the sense of collaboration for the good of all." He wanted to pitch Fernández as a "national leader" and Pérez as "a negative partisan politician." In the eyes of Arria and others working for Carlos Andrés Pérez, this was a fundamental blunder: "They made a tremendous mistake. They portrayed Lorenzo Fernández as the pater familias, the grandfather with one hundred grandchildren. On the other side, you had Pérez, who was a tough guy and wanted to put the country in order. Sawyer's campaign was beautiful and ineffective."

The involvement of foreigners in the campaign exploded into a story of its own. On October 27, just over six weeks before the election, the Acción Democrática, Carlos Andrés Pérez's party, held a press conference intended to deal with the proliferation of fanciful, fake polls, so many of which were little more than wishful thinking on letterhead. They presented journalists with George Gaither, the U.S. pollster who was working with AD. He reported that he found Carlos Andrés Pérez was in the lead, with 31 percent of the vote, compared with 27 percent for Fernández, and the rest spread across the also-rans. By the time the story ran in the Sunday papers the next morning, Gaither had cut a series of television commercials and was on a plane out of the country. The AD started running ads showing Gaither announcing Pérez in the lead in Yankee Spanish.

The COPEI retaliated, mocking the poll and attacking the *adecos*—the members of the AD—for allowing foreigners to meddle in Venezuelan politics. (This, of course, despite the fact that they had Sawyer and Reese working on their own payroll.) The use of an American in a campaign advertisement, they charged, was illegal, violating laws governing the participation of foreigners in national elections. AD, they added, was making up the poll to try to get back in the race. In an intemperate moment, Pedro Pablo Aguilar, the COPEI secretary-general and one of Fernández's inner circle of campaign advisers, said, "I want to confess that in elections such as those of 1958 and 1963, when in COPEI we appreciated the electoral perspective was not very favorable to us, we had recourse to that trick of inventing a poll and making it public with the idea that some unwary people could be seduced." This colossal gaffe, as reported by Martz and Baylora in their study of the campaign, drowned out the argument over foreign interference in Venezuela's national politics.

On Election Day, December 9, 1973, Lorenzo Fernández hunkered down at his home, still expecting a decisive victory. The Fernández campaign workers at the Boleíta headquarters were primed to tally the ballots, broadcasting the results as the victory they all expected came rolling in. At midnight on Sunday, it issued its first bulletin: Fernández leading, with 7,499 votes to Perez's 6,722. It was the first and last the Venezuelans heard from the Fernández camp.

Over the hours that followed, it slowly became clear that Carlos Andrés Pérez, the undereducated, energetic Andino, had walked all over the patrician Lorenzo Fernández. Throughout Monday, Fernández stayed at home, unwilling or unable to believe the result. Carlos Andrés Pérez had secured 48.7 percent of the votes to Lorenzo Fernández's 36.7 percent. And still, Fernández refused to concede. By Tuesday, it was getting embarrassing. Fernández was under pressure even from President Caldera to make a statement. A press conference was scheduled for midday Wednesday. Even then, Fernández refused to attend. Instead, he sent a blunt, graceless message: "I declare my recognition of your electoral triumph. Stop. I hope that your conduct of government will be for the benefit of Venezuela. Stop. Lorenzo Fernández."

Venezuela was an unlikely harbinger of things to come. The Caribbean nation in the largely forgotten rump of Latin America is hardly seen these days as a democratic trailblazer. The 1973 election commanded little worldwide attention at the time, less still in the years since. And yet, raking over the ashes of that first foreign election conducted under the influence of American advisers, one finds elements of what became an increasingly common kind of politics: the disintegration of political institutions, the impact of new technologies, and the emerging dominance of personality politics.

Fernández lost partly because he had too much faith in the power of the party. This was not entirely his fault. Modernity—or, in the poetic phrase of the anthropologist Clifford Geertz, "the pervasive raggedness of the world"—has been to blame. James Bryce, whose extraordinary assessment of the American Commonwealth has forever lived in the shadow of Alexis de Tocqueville's *Democracy in America*, wrote, "A majority must be cohesive, gathered into a united and organized body: such a body is a party." The more complex the society, Bryce predicted, the harder to maintain that unity, cohesion, and organization. As societies have become more heterogeneous and more complex, as class systems and community ties have broken down, parties have had to address a wider range of issues and grievances in order to have mass appeal. To do that, their message has been necessarily diluted, and their embrace, while wider, has also become weaker.

Venezuela in 1973 offered David Sawyer a glimpse into the future of politics bereft of powerful party machines, where candidates needed to look beyond the regional bosses and the city grandees and the ward strongmen to new kinds of organizations to marshal public support. "Fernández lost, but we learned some important stuff," remembered Iris Sawyer, who had traipsed reluctantly back and forth from New York to Caracas to work alongside David on the campaign. "The most important thing we learned is . . . that you can only spin so much. People will reject it. They are not stupid. There is a fundamental belief buried in all this that people are very stupid and indifferent. With Fernández, the character that David created in the film was one that people did not recognize."

Sawyer had also learned, to his cost, that the candidate was increasingly becoming the party. In Caracas in the early 1970s, parties already seemed to have lost their singularity of purpose, not to mention their effectiveness. They were changing from being homes for a unifying ideology to being issue-based coalitions brought together in an ever-shifting formula bent on victory. And while Fernández had taught Sawyer a great deal about how not to stand for the presidency, Carlos Andrés Pérez, whose talking did not impress voters nearly as much as his walking, left David Sawyer with the beginnings of a theory about politics in the electronic age that he would hone and develop over the next two decades—"everything communicates."

AT LEAST ONE LOCAL PAPER dubbed Venezuela in 1973 a "Made in USA" election. It was by no means the last.

Venezuela offered a handful of Americans a glimpse of a global market. Soon enough, the men who had worked in Caracas in 1973 were fanning out across the world. And the next Venezuelan election was an

American bonanza. David Garth, who had made his name in New York politics working on the campaigns of Governor Hugh Carey and Mayor Ed Koch, flew down to Caracas to work for Luis Herrera Campins of the Social Christian Party, who proved the surprise winner. Napolitan came back and, once again, worked with Clif White for Luis Piñerúa Ordaz, the AD candidate. Carlos Andrés Pérez, the president barred from running for a consecutive term by the constitution, nevertheless retained his own consultant—Bob Squier—to ensure that his administration's record was effectively advertised. And Diego Arria, who had run Pérez's campaign in 1973 and was standing in his own stead as the candidate of the Common Cause Party in 1978, brought in John Deardourff and Patrick Caddell, a Republican and a Democrat. More than twenty years later Napolitan recalled, "Matt and I have been on campaigns in Venezuela where you could have had a meeting of the American Association of Political Consultants on the patio of the Tamanaco Hotel."

Political beliefs—for the Americans, at least—seemed to get left at home. Napolitan was a liberal Democrat working for Hubert Humphrey back in the United States; Clif White was one of the crusaders for the conservative Republican Barry Goldwater. Yet they merrily worked for the same man in Venezuela. Sawyer and Squier were monogamously Democratic in America but happily made bedfellows with candidates on the left and the right once overseas. Venezuela was where the international political consulting game began—and where it began to get a bad, mercenary name.

For it was the money that had drawn the carpetbaggers of democracy to Venezuela. The election had become what the Venezuelans called the "Dance of the Millions." Caracas was swamped in placards, the airwaves a barrage of ads. The hiring of an American was just another expense in a long list of campaign expenditures, just another pair of shoes in an extravagant shopping spree. There was something grotesque about all this. Most Venezuelans were poor, and yet politics seemed to have become a plaything of the rich. Just a month before the election in 1973, a Venezuelan businessman issued a spectacular wager. Oswaldo Llobet offered one million bolivares ($232,000), certain that Lorenzo Fernández would win, and that no one would take up the bet against him. Three days later, a cattleman named José Coury Torbay accepted. On November 15, he ran a full-page advertisement in a paper depicting himself holding a check and saying, "Here is my million for Carlos Andrés." Just fifteen years after Venezuela had emerged from dictatorship, democracy had become a sport.

The American advisers were just part of the game. Conspiracy theorists and America bashers—and there are plenty of both in the barrios of Caracas—may like to look back and see the United States imposing the worst of its politics on the young, free Venezuela. But there was no grand imperial design to this. The American political consultants came because they were invited, because the money was good, and because, in an off-election year in the States, they didn't have much else going on.

For David Sawyer, though, Venezuela suggested a much bigger opportunity. He had been so well paid in Caracas that he and Iris flew back to New York after Fernández was defeated and went shopping for a new home. On the proceeds of the 1973 Venezuela election, the Sawyers moved out of their cramped rented apartment on the Upper West Side and into a ten-room duplex they bought across the park, on the Upper East Side: a grand residence at 131 East Sixty-sixth Street, one of the finest apartment blocks in New York. And this was on the back of just one election in one relatively small country.

Democracy was spreading across Latin America, Africa, Asia, and Europe, and the ballot box was beginning to look like an untapped gold mine to Sawyer. Soon he was beating back and forth to Puerto Rico to work for Rafael Hernández Colón. The government of Carlos Andrés Pérez became a regular client, not so much for campaign work as for government infomercials. He also picked up work in the 1978 presidential race in Costa Rica. He had begun not only an international adventure but what he thought of as the beginnings of a worldwide business. All he needed was someone to run it.

ON THE NIGHT of the Al Smith dinner, the men of standing in New York gather for one of the great tribal rituals of the American political calendar. Irish and Catholic and proud of it, they squeeze their barrel chests into white tie and tails and file into the vast ballroom of the Waldorf Astoria hotel. They come, officially, to swell the coffers of Catholic charities and honor the memory of Alfred E. Smith, the former governor of New York and the first Roman Catholic to secure his party's nomination for president. In an election year, they really come to see the two presidential candidates perform. In 1980, they saw the beginning of the end of Jimmy Carter.

Joel McCleary stood at the back of the room that night. He was still a kid—just twenty-nine years old—but was bright, handsome, and powerful. He had grown up in North Carolina, where politics is mean and conniving, a perennial Spanish Civil War fought out between ideologues and populists and their partisan followings. He had gone to Harvard, where, among other things, he had been in the habit of bench-pressing 250 pounds, and he remained a big unit, looking more like a bouncer than a White House aide, one of those men whose suits stretch taut across their wide backs. He had come to Washington in his early twenties, and while other men his age were only just finishing their law degrees and rummaging around for internships on Capitol Hill, McCleary was bounding up Washington's pyramid of power. After Carter won in 1976, McCleary was drafted into the White House to help run domestic policy and then was sent over to the Democratic Party headquarters to serve as party treasurer. With a testing election ahead, he had been asked to go up to New York to hold the Empire State for the president in 1980.

The Carter people knew that it was going to be difficult. After all, the 1970s should have been a cakewalk for the Democrats. The decade had been dismal for everyone, but for no one more than the Republicans: Agnew had been indicted; Nixon had resigned; Saigon had fallen; Ford had tripped down the stairs; the stock market had plummeted; oil prices had flared. And still, the Carter people had been up all night in the election of 1976. They had not even carried California. They won with just 50.1 percent of the vote. Despite every advantage, they waited and worried into the early hours of the morning before they knew for certain that they had won the White House. Four years later, it was going to be even tougher.

Their strategy, moreover, was flimsy. Carter's aides hoped that the president would win a second term simply by showing America that Ronald Reagan was a fool. As soon as Carter got in a room with Reagan, the Democrats believed, he would simply blow him away.

But when Ronald Reagan appeared on the dais at the Waldorf that night, he was more than just groomed and rested. It was as if he had come fresh from a blood transfusion and a TV dinner. He stood tall and strong and tanned and Irish. To McCleary, it seemed as if Reagan were channeling John F. Kennedy directly into this roomful of Irishmen; seventeen years after Jack had been taken from them, it was as if Reagan were bringing him back to life.

Reagan thanked the archbishop of New York for bringing the two candidates together in public for the first time. The audience cheered and whistled. Reagan recounted an imagined telephone conversation with Carter before the event: " 'Ronnie,' Carter says, 'how come you look younger every time I see a picture of you riding a horse?' " Reagan replies: " 'It's easy, Jimmy. I just keep riding older horses.' " It was exactly the bonhomie and good, clean humor the Al Smith crowd was looking for.

Carter followed. He looked as if he had had a long day, and he had. He had fielded phone calls and attended meetings and rallies, and had been booed by protesters along the way. He was in no shape to give what was required of him that night: the performance of a stand-up comedian. Instead, his attempts to poke fun sounded sour. "I gave my good friend Mayor Koch some advice earlier today," Carter said. "I told him not to get too close to Governor Reagan. It has nothing to do with politics, but only that [on] the governor's 'I Love New York' button—the paint is still wet." The men in their tuxedoes and the women in their evening gowns booed. Carter said he wanted to put the former governor of California at ease on one point: "I will say publicly and for the record that I am not planning any October surprise"—a reference to the accusation that the White House would stage-manage a foreign policy crisis on the eve of the election—but, Carter continued, "I can predict, however, that one of us is in for a very severe November shock." The tables of New York grandees looked on unamused. And then Carter turned serious, using a platform intended for entertainment to rail against the intolerance of religious conservatives.

McCleary watched with a deepening sense of helplessness. The election, it struck him, was over. The Democrats were going to lose. Carter was lost. And then a White House staffer told him the president wanted him to ride with him back to LaGuardia airport. So, still just a sloppy kid, McCleary found himself sitting beside the president of the United States as they buzzed through New York in a motorcade. He was acutely aware that he had just watched the president fail, and no one felt this more keenly than Carter himself. It seemed to him that the president knew that he was going to have to fight on, but that he had already lost. Until that moment, Carter had seemed to the young aide like a bionic man, somehow able to withstand inhumane pressure, somehow above the average mortal, for some reason smarter, harder, faster than the rest of us.

Yet, there Carter was, in the back of the limo, asking a twenty-nine-year-old know-nothing how to save New York. Carter offered to send McCleary any resources he needed. As McCleary retold it years later: "He starts talking and saying he'll send anything he needs [to]. I am watching the president unwind. That was the moment I realized I had failed this man who had made me, whom I believed in, whom I loved. I realized what I wasn't. He said: 'Tell me what I need to win. Be my campaign manager.' I realized I couldn't help him . . . That was the origin of Sawyer Miller for me. I realized that . . . if you are going to be the consigliere, if you are going to play Machiavelli, you better know what the fuck to do, when they turn to you and say: What do I do now?"

A little over a year later—and a few months after Carter's defeat—Joel McCleary stopped by David Sawyer's office. He was not looking for a job. In fact, he was hoping Sawyer would help on Mario Cuomo's election. Instead, Sawyer invited him to the Knickerbocker for lunch and, out of the blue, asked if McCleary would like to run the firm's international division.

"Do you have an international division?" McCleary asked.

"No," Sawyer replied.

And then Sawyer gave him the "David Sawyer ruggedy buggedy boo: the vision thing, about what Sawyer Miller could do and it was pretty good," McCleary remembers. "He basically said: 'Come run campaigns around the world. Go anywhere you want in the world. Arrive at any government's doorstep you want with the mumbo jumbo that you have something to sell and that you have the magic potion that is going to create power.' And people at that juncture believed that. Now, they always paid the astrologer a little more than they paid you, but you were right up there with the astrologer."

Within a year of Ronald Reagan's becoming president, David Sawyer's accidental foray into political filmmaking had started to look like a proper business. He had hired Mandy Grunwald straight out of college; Joel McCleary, to find new opportunities abroad; and Oren Kramer, another refugee from the Carter White House, to explore political communications work on Wall Street. Scott Miller privately worried that the firm was already in danger of getting too big, that Sawyer wanted to form a big, proper company while he just wanted to keep things small and get on with interesting work. But it barely warranted thinking about. The Sawyer Miller Group was newly formed and hot: Sawyer had earned himself a reputation not only as an inventive visual communicator but increasingly as a shrewd political strategist; Miller was known to have a gift for turning a complicated message into an unforgettable sound bite; and operating out of what was in effect a satellite office in SoHo, Kennan, that randy, foul-mouthed but brilliant pollster, had no qualms about psychoanalyzing any city, state, or country in the world. They had the beginnings of a formidable team: the image-maker, the dumb-down genius, and the shrink.

THREE

"THE REAL THING"

SCOTT MILLER'S most famous commercial featured Mean Joe Greene, a vast, brooding defensive lineman who played for the Pittsburgh Steelers. In the ad, he comes limping off the field sweaty, dirty, and exhausted. A young boy calls to him, "Mr. Greene, you need any help?" He grunts back, but the young boy pushes on, offering him his bottle of Coca-Cola. Mean Joe refuses, and the boy offers it again. The big football player relents, takes the Coke, and drains the bottle in one gulp. He smiles. But the boy doesn't see it, as he has turned away and is walking glumly back up the tunnel. Greene calls back to him, "Hey, kid," and throws him his Steelers football shirt. The kid beams. "Wow! Thanks, Mean Joe!" And the music pipes up. "Coke adds life! Have a Coke and a smile!" The conceit was so simple: a boy and his hero brought together by a single product, a short spot that held out the promise of what a human exchange could be like. It was an extraordinary success, even prompting a made-for-TV movie starring Mean Joe Greene. It also served as a template for Miller as he got more deeply involved in politics.

A year after Miller left the ad agency and had moved into an office down the hall from David Sawyer, both men were asked to come to Washington to work for the Democratic party's most promising challenger to Ronald Reagan: John Glenn, the Ohio senator who had been one of the original group of *Mercury* astronauts and was the first American to orbit the earth, in 1962. Glenn was not a shoo-in for the Democratic Party's nomination, as his rival, Walter "Fritz" Mondale, had the backing of the unions and the party machine. Nor was Glenn a natural wooer of the vote, not an instinctive back-slapping, baby-kissing doorstep operator. To Miller, though, the parallels with Mean Joe Greene, the unapproachable hero, were obvious: "The idea was a kid meets his hero, and what they have in common is Coke," he told Sidney Blumenthal at *The New Republic* at the time. "A product ought to have a leadership quality, make you feel good. Mean Joe and the kid was a moment that had over two hundred million people in tears. In the most crass way, it could have been an astronaut. Coke is a symbol we have in common. It breaks down barriers. Glenn represents without any question some common ground. We can all agree that this man in America's shining moment was the ideal . . . He can bring people together."

Over two days at the end of June 1983, Sawyer and Miller met with Glenn at the Hyatt hotel in Washington to turn the hero's story—the boy born and raised in small-town Ohio who flew combat missions in the war, who led the way into the uncharted frontier of space, and who now looked to lead his nation in uncertain times—into a platform for the presidency. To them, Glenn seemed to embody the high, romantic ideals Middle America held for itself: small-town sincerity, frontier spirit, and, most dramatically, the flinty self-confidence to step into the future. These were the same themes of courage, ambition, and hope, all blind to doubt and the dangers of failure, that were woven through *The Right Stuff*, the movie from Tom Wolfe's book about Glenn and the *Mercury* project, which was being filmed at exactly the time the senator, Sawyer, and Miller were meeting at the Hyatt. Even though they did not know in June how the movie would look in October of that year, they seized on the same idea. At the meeting in Washington, Miller said to Glenn, "The slogan should be 'He'll make us believe in the future again. John Glenn for President.' " Glenn replied, "Why not just say, 'Believe in the future again'?" (A few months later *The Right Stuff* came out; the catchline for the film was "How the future began.")

Over the summer, Sawyer and Miller worked on a strategy with this central idea of pioneering heroism. "Throughout our history, presidential elections have revolved around contrasting definitions of leadership," they wrote in a memo a few weeks after the June 22–23 summit in Washington. "Jimmy Carter did that successfully in 1976: 'A government as honest and decent as the American people' (moral leadership). In 1980, Ronald Reagan said that leadership should limit the role of government (which had failed so often in the past). People accepted his definition." Going into the presidential election of 1984, Sawyer and Miller argued that Glenn had to define leadership in his terms—leadership for the future—in order to control the dynamic of the campaign.

They wanted to position Mondale as the past, Reagan as the present, and Glenn as the future. They argued for a positive campaign, not Carteresque goody-goody stuff but setting the agenda for an America of new horizons. They insisted that Glenn's bid for the White House be "nonpolitical," respectful of the intelligence of the American voter, mindful of his cynicism of things political, and therefore free of grandstanding and rhetorical flourish. Nonetheless, the stump speeches they helped to draw up for Glenn were rich in thematics, light on specifics: "I grew up in the Great Depression, fought in the Second World War, and served in the space program, and each of those experiences told me that we are a strong, determined, creative people, a can-do people."

The Glenn campaign created a new kind of electricity in the offices of Sawyer Miller in the autumn of 1983. After the false starts that were Scoop Jackson's and Ted Kennedy's presidential bids in 1976 and 1980, and after all the mayoral, gubernatorial, and congressional races they had done, Sawyer and Miller had finally found a man they could ride all the way to the White House. They knew that Glenn was not always receptive to their ideas: "That guy takes advice the way Sonny Liston took punches," Greg Schneiders, Glenn's press secretary once said.

Sawyer sometimes sensed that there was a touch of the Lorenzo Fernández about John Glenn, a hint that he felt he deserved the presidency. Glenn was a military man who could give the impression that he had already made the rank of president, that the election process was an insult to his stature and his public service. He was not a fiery or even a passionate campaigner, but he would get incensed at the thought that Ronald Reagan could be considered commander in chief. In October 1983, Glenn attended a Democratic candidates' forum in New York. He was subtly challenged on whether he was smart enough to be president, whether a former marine had the subtlety of mind to command from the Oval Office. *The Right Stuff* had just come out in cinemas, and Glenn was goaded for his celluloid image. Unusually for Glenn, he reddened: "As far as the celluloid charge," he said, turning from his own life in movies to that of the president, "I wasn't doing *Hellcats of the Navy* [a Ronald Reagan film] on a movie lot when I went through a hundred forty-nine missions."

Glenn was seen by many to have won that encounter in New York with his rivals for the Democratic nomination: Walter Mondale, Gary Hart, Jesse Jackson, Ernest "Fritz" Hollings, Alan Cranston, and George McGovern. But as the Iowa caucus and the New Hampshire primary approached at the beginning of 1984, Sawyer and Miller knew that they were still trailing the leaders. Glenn had proved in his life that he had extraordinary reserves of physical strength, but he seemed to have no political stamina. To his media advisers in New York, it seemed as though Mondale would spend the whole day campaigning and gladhanding and then, at midnight, would pour himself a glass of bourbon, fire up a cigar, and begin a round of fund-raising phone calls from some presidential suite in Des Moines or Manchester. Glenn, on the other hand, seemed to fall asleep on his feet at a meet-and-greet at five in the afternoon.

Within weeks, the Glenn campaign had unraveled. Walter Mondale won the Iowa caucus by a hefty margin, leaving Glenn in fifth place with 5 percent; while he did marginally better in the New Hampshire primary, with 12 percent of the vote, he was still far behind Gary Hart, who won, and Mondale, who came in second. Going into Super Tuesday, it seemed that Mondale had the momentum and Glenn was already readying himself for defeat. By late February 1984, it was all over.

By then, Scott Miller had been drawn into another political battle, another argument where he found himself skipping between the lessons of marketing and electioneering, another contest that pitted the red against the blue: Coca-Cola versus Pepsi.

As politics had borrowed from the business of marketing in the 1960s and 1970s, Sawyer Miller saw that the business of marketing—in fact, all businesses—could lift from politics in the years to come. The firm's mantra, it realized, was reversible: every voter, a consumer; every consumer, a voter. And the cola wars of the 1980s proved a signal episode in the politicization of American business, as the battle between Coca-Cola and Pepsi emboldened the men at Sawyer Miller in their belief that politicians and products were much the same.

MILLER, IN PARTICULAR, was intrigued by this idea of consumer democracy and had teamed up to work with Pat Caddell on selling political advice to U.S. corporate clients. In the early 1980s, Caddell was one of the two most famous pollsters in America. He had been the driving force behind Jimmy Carter's victory and then served as the president's chief pollster through the four years of his presidency.

Caddell was a political strategist with a singular fixation on generational change. He had made his mark on Democratic politics—a mark that has endured ever since—with the invention of "Senator Smith," an ideal hypothetical candidate. Not long after he had taken a year off from Harvard to work on George McGovern's polling operation in 1972, Caddell wrote a memo laying out a ready-made candidacy for his imaginary Mr. Smith: it included speeches, advertising campaigns, and the scripts for mock interviews. The idea underlying it all was that the next wave of successful politicians would come from the baby boom generation, challenging the establishment, carrying forward JFK's New Frontier, and imbued with the spirit of the sixties. Senator Smith called for campaign finance reform, he railed against special interests and failed elites. He promised "new-generation leadership." For Caddell, "Senator Smith" would serve as a template for his real-life political masters: Jimmy Carter in 1976, Gary Hart in 1984, and Joe Biden in 1988. Like a battering ram, he made the case again and again that politicians needed to focus on the youth vote. The Democratic Party, Caddell argued, needed to be redefined for a new generation of choice and individualism, institutional distrust, and nonconformism, rebellion and nostalgia.

When Caddell and Miller looked at corporate America, they saw institutions grappling with the same baby boom forces of change. The two men set up a corporate advisory business as an adjunct to Sawyer Miller that they called Flying Fortress, because they spent most of their time on planes. (Caddell, Miller remembers, insisted on setting up a separate outfit because he looked down on Sawyer as a jumped-up poser who had won a few decent mayoral and congressional races but never a presidential contest.)

Flying Fortress started working for Steve Jobs at Apple Computer. Apple was turning in on itself, convulsed by its own internal arguments about management and the growth of the business, when Caddell and Miller were invited to Cupertino, California, in late 1983 for a bite of salad and a conversation about technology, politics, business, and the future of the world. It was a wide-ranging, rambling discussion that, after a few more meetings, led to Flying Fortress's first substantial report on the politics of a big American business. "The Dolphin and the Shark," as they called it, laid out the battleground between Apple and IBM.

Neither Caddell nor Miller knew much about computers, but they knew a lot about the dynamics of a two-horse race. They had been captivated by the ad Apple released in the middle of the Super Bowl in January 1984, which showed a woman breaking through security guards and running into a great hall where workers in rows stood transfixed, looking up at Big Brother on a giant screen. She hurled a sledgehammer at the screen, which exploded and freed the crowd. The tagline to Jay Chiat and Lee Clow's iconic ad was "On January 24, Apple Computer will introduce Macintosh. And you'll see why 1984 won't be *1984*." Without even naming IBM, Apple was positioning itself as the computer for the individual who was standing up to the machine of the bureaucracy, America's Big Brother. Caddell and Miller saw in the competition between Apple and IBM the essential argument in America as it squared up to a rapidly changing future, a choice between an old world (IBM), which wired people into a central machine, forced society to play by its rules, and rewarded them for conformity, versus a new world (Apple), which responded to their creativity, created machines to serve people, and liberated them from the nine-to-five. Caddell and Miller saw Apple and IBM in terms of a much bigger argument about the nature of individual freedom and social conformity in America.

In "The Dolphin versus the Shark," they portrayed IBM as powerful, single-minded, and dark, a menacing presence but one easily surrounded and outmaneuvered by shoals of smart, playful, and quick dolphins. They urged Jobs to see the contest between Apple and IBM not as a battle about computing power but as an argument over how Americans would like to see themselves. For a couple of political operatives who had made their names by backing outsiders, the potential of the insurgent to challenge the incumbent seemed inarguable. To Pat Caddell, the Apple Macintosh seemed to incorporate the values of a new generation of Americans who wanted choice, self-determination, and the right to reinvent themselves again and again.

When they got the call from Coca-Cola, it was to work on the other end of that argument. As Scott Miller knew all too well, Coke had been the embattled incumbent under assault for more than a decade from a challenger that claimed to speak for the "Pepsi Generation."

In the late 1970s, somewhere along the soft drink aisle of some brightly lit American supermarket, a shopper lifted a large bottle of cola into a trolley and a portentous threshold was crossed: Pepsi took the lead over Coca-Cola in store sales of soft drinks. A landmark battle seemed to have been won. Coke was still the most popular drink in America, but as the 1980s dawned, the men who sat on the executive floor at Coke's headquarters in Atlanta sensed that the unthinkable was at hand: Pepsi was poised to unseat Coke as the King of Pop.

"The Pepsi Challenge" was proving to be a hugely successful advertising and marketing drive. In shopping malls up and down America, Pepsi had set up stands and asked passersby to take a taste test. In one mystery cup was Coca-Cola, in another was Pepsi. Time and again, Americans sipped one, then the other, and pronounced that they preferred the "smoother, sweeter" taste of Pepsi.

Pepsi had launched the Pepsi Challenge in the early 1970s in regional markets, where it trailed in fourth or fifth place. The aim was not so much to beat Coke as to make it a two-horse race. Miller was still at McCann and, to his mounting irritation, Coca-Cola did not respond to the challenge for seven years. The executives in Atlanta had a disdain for Pepsi that bordered on the pathological: Roberto Goizueta, the company's chairman, would never refer to Pepsi by name. He was like an Oxford don who speaks of Cambridge only as "the other place"; there was, perhaps, a fear that speaking Pepsi's name would make it real. As Lewis Carroll's Red Queen says: "When you've once said a thing, that fixes it, and you must take the consequences." The Coca-Cola executives justified their failure to engage by arguing that responding to the Pepsi Challenge would just give Pepsi free advertising. Whatever the mixture of arrogance and anxiety, Goizueta and the Coke bosses wanted to ignore the Pepsi Challenge altogether.

Coke's bottlers, however, disagreed, and they grew increasingly frustrated. On one trip down to Atlanta, Miller was buttonholed by one of Coca-Cola's biggest bottlers, Jack Lupton, and invited down to Dallas. He wanted Miller to see the effect that the do-nothing policy was having on morale. He put him on a Coca-Cola delivery truck for an afternoon. Miller remembers the driver laying it out pretty plainly: "I have a lot to do at every store. Argue with the manager. Haul the cases off the truck. Stack the product and check it out. And, if I get a chance, I have to put up a sign that says 'Have a Coke and a smile.' Now, the Pepsi driver has to do all of that, too, but he's got a sign that says, 'We Beat Coke.' And he'll crawl through broken glass to get it up." In those days, the highlight of a sales rally at Pepsi would be the moment that the top delivery men got to take a sledgehammer to a Coca-Cola vending machine and, quite literally, beat the opposition to smithereens.

Miller returned to New York convinced that inaction was absurd. Suddenly every other two-bit cola was running its own taste test: RC Cola, Cott, Double Cola, C&C, and the rest. Pepsi was eating into Coke's market share, turning Coke drinkers into future cohorts of loyal Pepsi fans and making Coke a sitting duck for all other cola companies eyeing a slice of the market. So Miller started to do some work—in secret and without the approval of either Coke or McCann—on some response advertising. He called the comedian Bill Cosby and asked for his help. The ad, he told Cosby, wouldn't necessarily air. He wouldn't necessarily get paid. Cosby, then one of the highest-paid entertainers in America, was happy to help. Coca-Cola had, inadvertently and for the most suspect of reasons, been good to him: Cosby had already done a series of ads for Coke, which were also written and devised by Miller, but McCann top brass had wanted some "balance"—i.e., a white face to go with Cosby's black one. They signed up Bob Hope, the grandest of America's entertainment grandees. To be fair, Cosby had to get paid the same rates as Hope. And that was a lot of money for a little work. Cosby knew that if the ad worked out, he'd be paid plenty later.

The spot was simple. Miller set Cosby up at a table with a bunch of colas on one side and a bottle of Coca-Cola on the other. Cosby pointed at one can of cola after another and his lines went, roughly, like this: "These guys are doing a taste test against Coke. And these guys are doing a taste test. And these guys and these guys and these guys. Everybody's doing a taste test against Coke." Cosby stopped. He pointed at the bottle of Coca-Cola. And he smiled. "Maybe that's why they call this the real thing." Miller had not invented the phrase "The Real Thing" but had exhumed it from Coca-Cola's past. And the men in Atlanta, of course, loved it. They started to go on the offensive against Pepsi. In focus groups, loyal Coke drinkers—not to mention employees—were delighted that Coca-Cola was fighting back. "What took you so long?" they asked. And Cosby did, indeed, end up making a lot of money, at one stage even becoming a bottler himself.

More important, Scott Miller started to see Coca-Cola as a political animal. He thought of the taste tests as a primary, where the lead candidate became the political punching bag for upstart candidates trying to get noticed. Simply by comparing themselves to Coca-Cola, the likes of Safeway Select and Sam's Choice were making a name for themselves.

In 1983, Pepsi signed Michael Jackson to speak to the youth of America. The ads he made were electric. A street of teenagers danced to the Pepsi beat, set to the pulsating rhythm of Jackson's hit "Billie Jean"; one kid moonwalked with a sequined glove in one hand and a can of Pepsi in another. The ads spoke to Coca-Cola's innermost fears. It was the anxiety of an aging institution, the concern that while they remained the drink of Norman Rockwell's America, PepsiCo owned America's future. Twenty years earlier, loyal Coke drinkers had outnumbered loyal Pepsi drinkers nearly five to one; by the early 1980s, Coke-only drinkers outnumbered Pepsi-only drinkers by just one percentage point.

The bigger battle with Pepsi was uncannily similar to a presidential contest. There were two tickets: one incumbent, one challenger. The American public, as it is in every election, was being asked to weigh its conservative instincts against its appetite for change. Coke's unwillingness to get down and fight Pepsi at its own game was a classic example of the arrogance of office. Coca-Cola was the establishment, a nostalgic America wedded to the past, a politician fighting for reelection on a record of achievement. Pepsi was making the most of its underdog status. It promised something different, embodied youth, and held out for the future. It offered change, and as a result it had taken control of the dialogue with the American public. It all looked to Miller like the standoffs he was getting to know on the campaign trail.

The bigger, existential battle—the general election campaign, if you like—was still to come.

ROBERTO GOIZUETA, a refugee from Castro's Cuba, had taken the helm of Coca-Cola in 1980. He had an appetite for innovation. There would be "no sacred cow in the way we manage our business," he said, "including the formulation of any or all of our products." In 1982, he brought out Diet Coke, the first new product with the Coca-Cola name on it since "Doc" Pemberton's invention of the product in 1886. The same year, Coca-Cola bought a Hollywood studio. And a couple of years later, Goizueta introduced Cherry Coke. (The introduction of Cherry Coke converted at least one Pepsi drinker: Warren Buffett. America's most famous investor was a fan of Pepsi, drinking it with a dash of cherry syrup. When Don Keough, then president of Coca-Cola, read about this in an interview with Buffett, he sent along a case of trial Cherry Coke. It became Buffett's favorite drink and the official drink of the hokey annual general meeting of Buffett's company Berkshire Hathaway. The firm bought a $1 billion stake in the Coca-Cola company.) All that time, Goizueta, a chemical engineer, had been in close touch with the scientists in the Coca-Cola laboratories, urging them to explore a new formula for Coke.

It was hard to avoid the conclusion that there was something wrong with the product. Coca-Cola was outspending Pepsi in advertising by more than $100 million a year. Coke had more vending machines. Coke occupied more shelf space. Coke dominated the soda fountain business. Yet Goizueta saw it slipping to second place: Coke had once had a two-to-one lead over Pepsi, but that had been whittled down to 4.9 percent by 1984. The men in Atlanta had to conclude that Americans had possibly outgrown the taste of Coke.

Goizueta knew full well that he was meddling with an American icon. When the company launched Diet Coke, Sergio Zyman, Goizueta's head of marketing and the man who proved to be Miller's chief collaborator at the company, ran a series of focus groups. One day, Goizueta asked him to get the moderators to slip in a question: "I want you to say, 'The last question on the docket today will be a fake story—The Coca-Cola Company is about to launch a brand new cola. As a matter of fact, this new product is already on the shelves in Denver, Colorado. The product is similar to Coca-Cola and, as a matter of fact, it has replaced Coca-Cola. Denver is madly in love with the product. We'd like to get a sense of how you'd react.' " As David Greising reports in his biography of Goizueta, *I'd Like the World to Buy a Coke*, not everyone reacted, but those who did went nuts: "What do you mean you're taking away my fucking Coca-Cola?" one said. When asked about changes to other products, one person was quoted as saying, "We don't give a shit about Budweiser or Hershey, but you can't take Coke away."

Still, the men from Coke's laboratories presented Goizueta with a new formula in 1984 that was sweeter and softer. Goizueta thought it was simply better. And so, it seemed, did everyone else. In blind tests, the original formula lagged behind Pepsi by as much as 18 percentage points. The new formula beat Pepsi by six to eight points. Even Pepsi loyalists, who typically preferred Pepsi 70 percent of the time in blind tests, chose the new Coke formula 50 percent of the time. Goizueta commissioned survey after survey, spending about $4 million dollars and testing out the new product on two hundred thousand people. All the public opinion research seemed to say the same thing: Coke drinkers preferred New Coke; even Pepsi drinkers preferred New Coke. The polls showed that one in ten people—10 to 12 percent of the survey sample—did not like it, but they seemed dwarfed by the vast majority who did.

Goizueta, in furtive consultation with only a few of Coke's most senior executives, decided to push ahead. The New Coke project was shrouded in obsessive secrecy. Zyman, for example, set up his own bunker in an anonymous office in Manhattan and staffed it with a small, handpicked team of marketing men and advertising executives. To minimize the risk of leaks, there were no secretaries or support staff, and a paper shredder was stationed by the door. Coca-Cola was determined that Pepsi not get wind of the change.

In early 1985, Goizueta flew to the home of Robert Woodruff, the ailing patriarch of Coca-Cola, to seek his blessing. Woodruff had created the modern Coca-Cola company, encapsulating the purpose of the company in a single aim: to refresh people. By then, Woodruff was old and deaf, and within a matter of weeks he would be dead. When Goizueta explained his plan to introduce a new, improved Coca-Cola, Woodruff showed him one of his old scrapbooks, showing Goizueta a dog-eared clipping of an article by William Allen White, editor of *The Emporia Gazette*, based in Emporia, Kansas. The clipping read, "Coca Cola is . . . a sublimated essence of all that America stands for, a decent thing honestly made, universally distributed, conscientiously improved with the years." Woodruff pointed to the phrase "conscientiously improved with the years." Goizueta concluded that he had the old man's blessing. In Woodruff's honor, Goizueta gave the launch a new code name: Project Kansas.

A few weeks later, Flying Fortress got the call to come down to Coca-Cola's headquarters in Atlanta to see Sergio Zyman. The chief marketing officer at Coke and the man who held the most coveted job in marketing in America, Zyman had worked closely with Scott Miller for years, having the final say in almost every one of the ads for Coke that Miller worked on during his years at McCann Erickson. Inside and outside the company, Zyman was considered brilliant, unpredictable, and contrary. He wanted to look at the company's biggest marketing challenge in political terms, and presented Flying Fortress with the plans for Project Kansas. Miller assumed it was a reference to *The Wizard of Oz*—as Dorothy put it, "Toto, I've a feeling we're not in Kansas anymore."

When Caddell and Miller looked at Coca-Cola, they saw, of course, a company grappling with generational change. As Miller told *The Wall Street Journal* at the time, "It's ironic that Pat and I have been beating our heads against a brick wall for the last two years with the Democratic Party, to get them to embrace change, and then go to corporate America and it accepts our concepts . . . What we told Coke was simple. Coke is America; America is changing, so Coke can be bold about changing, too." Flying Fortress had a penchant for military analogies and sporting references. Coke, they said, was ceding "change" to Pepsi, allowing what Winston Churchill called "the point of the wedge" to be driven in by their competition. They railed against Coke for adopting Muhammad Ali's "rope-a-dope" technique, taking the punches from Pepsi while hunched on the ropes. They sought to make Coca-Cola executives aware that the launch of New Coke would catapult them into an altogether different kind of conversation with the American public. This was not another piece of consumer goods marketing; it would be public opinion management on a national scale. The target media was not *Beverage Digest* and *Ad Age*; it would be *NBC Nightly News* and the front page of *The New York Times*. They were not in Kansas anymore.

Goizueta knew as much. As well as hiring a couple of Democrats, he also recruited a Republican: Richard Wirthlin, the Reagan pollster who crops up in this story as an unseen adversary to the Sawyer Miller men in Israel and, as we shall see, a predecessor to their work in Britain. In those days, the hiring of political consultants in the corporate boardroom was considered unusual, if not pretentious. Jack Lupton, the bottler who had invited Miller down to Dallas when Miller was the creative director on the Coke account, saw no need to open Coca-Cola's doors to the likes of Caddell and Wirthlin: "Frankly," he told *The Wall Street Journal*, "I can't see the foggiest reason to bring any kind of political animal into the fray." They plainly had no idea how political things were about to become—no one did.

The rollout of New Coke on Tuesday, April 23, 1985, was an extravaganza. The Friday before, Coca-Cola had sent out invitations to the press inviting journalists to "the most significant soft-drink marketing development in the company's nearly 100 year history." (That was enough of a tip-off for Pepsi. On the morning of the press conference in New York,

Roger Enrico, Pepsi's president, took out full-page ads in the papers that read, "The other guy just blinked.") The auditorium in New York was decked out in red. The event opened with a montage of Americana, a cloying reel of fields of golden wheat, sunny city mornings, John F. Kennedy and Dwight D. Eisenhower all smiles, kids playing baseball, men in uniform. Goizueta then took to the mike: "The best has been made even better," he said, reading from his notes. "Some may choose to call this the single boldest marketing move in the history of the packaged goods business. We simply call it the surest move ever made. Simply stated, we have a new formula for Coke."

The press conference started to go awry as soon as Goizueta moved off script and on to the Q&A. The first question was: "Are you 100 percent certain that this won't bomb?" A few minutes later, Goizueta was asked to describe the new taste and he fumbled for the words: "smoother, er, rounder, yet, er, yet bolder . . . a more harmonious flavor." Was this, he was asked, Coke's response to the Pepsi Challenge? He replied sarcastically: "The Pepsi Challenge? When did that happen?" Unfortunately, playing dumb looked dumb. Asked whether Diet Coke might be reformulated, "assuming that this is a success," as one journalist put it, Goizueta snapped back, "No. And I didn't assume that this is a success. It is a success."

For the first day or so, it was. For a short while, New Coke was the most successful product launch in history. By the end of the week, more than 80 percent of Americans had heard about the change. Pretty much every American man, woman, child, and their dog went out to try the new flavor.

Within a matter of days, though, Coca-Cola executives started getting worrying reports from the people manning the 1-800-GETCOKE hotline. The telephone number was principally there to tell Coke loyalists where to go to recycle bottles and to hype Coke promotions. Then, as if a dam had burst, the lines were flooded. Angry callers were demanding to know where they could get Coca-Cola, the Real Thing. By early May, they were getting a thousand calls a day. By June, eight thousand. The hotline operators were buckling under the pressure, turning coat, and bitching about the Coke management.

Coca-Cola executives continued to make stump speeches for New Coke, which, given the influence of Wirthlin as well as Caddell and Miller, echoed loudly with the rhetoric of the 1984 presidential campaign. There

were the overtones of Reagan: "We feel good about ourselves. We're secure in our heritage and who we are." And, as *The Wall Street Journal*
noted at the time, some passages seemed lifted from Gary Hart's bid for
the Democratic Party nomination: "We have chosen to reach out and seek
the promise of our future because the time is right . . . And the time is
right because the mood of America favors change."

The opposition to New Coke, though, was taking off in the way that
only a grassroots movement can. Gay Mullins, a wealthy retiree from
Seattle, formed the Old Coke Drinkers of America and soon claimed to
have the support of tens of thousands of Americans. Nearly forty thousand letters of protest piled up at Coke's offices in Atlanta. The media reveled in the public backlash. *Newsweek* quoted one Coca-Cola drinker
describing the New Coke launch as "like spitting on the flag." Another
said, "When they took Old Coke off the market, they violated my freedom
of choice. It's as basic as the Magna Carta, the Declaration of Independence. We went to war in Japan over that freedom." *Time* magazine had
more people saying much the same: "Changing Coke is like God making
the grass purple or putting toes on our ears or teeth on our knees." Another forlorn Coke drinker said, "There are only two things in my life:
God and Coca-Cola. Now you have taken one of those things away from
me." The editor of *Soda Pop Dreams*, the magazine for soft drink aficiona-
dos, described an encounter in Marietta, Georgia, where a Coca-Cola delivery man was assaulted by a woman with an umbrella while he stocked
a grocery store shelf with New Coke. "You bastard," she yelled, "you
ruined it—it tastes like shit!" When a nearby Pepsi driver chuckled at the
scene, she had a go at him as well. "You stay out of it! This is family business. Yours is worse than shit!"

Americans were voicing more than just an abiding affection for the
flavor of Coke—for what one drinker called that "battery acid tang." New
Coke had touched a raw nerve in America, an acute discomfort at the
seemingly countless little revolutions of modern life. America's military
stood wounded by Vietnam, the presidency smeared by Watergate. The
phone company—AT&T, or Ma Bell—had just been broken up into
twenty-four pieces; IBM was being challenged by the Apple Macintosh, a
new computer for the individual not the institutional American. The
Food and Drug Administration had just approved blood tests for a new
disease called AIDS. Muhammad Ali had retired from boxing, and America was in the thrall of a bleach-blond wrestling showman, Hulk Hogan;

Miss America had just resigned her crown because she had posed nude for photographs published in *Penthouse*. As change seemed to sap the country's strength and nobility, America was developing nostalgia for a past that perhaps had never existed and fear of a future that seemed out of control. New Coke played upon those feelings in the worst possible way; it was a change that seemed to rip away a piece of hallowed Americana all for change's sake.

As such, New Coke exposed a fault line that came to dominate politics in the 1990s and beyond, the divide between the forces of modernization and tradition. In the New Economy, more than ever, the job of the politician would be to shepherd a rattled public through a world of rapid, unrelenting change. The successful politician would have to express both empathy for the public's nauseated bewilderment at the relentless tide of new things and an understanding that government's role was to help people see opportunity in what they tended to perceive as a threat. It was a quality that defined the most successful political communicator of the 1990s, Bill Clinton, who told America on the occasion of his first inaugural address: "Profound and powerful forces are shaking and remaking our world, and the urgent question of our time is whether we can make change our friend and not our enemy."

Back in Atlanta, Coca-Cola needed to be saved from itself. Goizueta and his colleagues realized that things were not going exactly as planned, but they did not appreciate the scale of the problem on their hands. They hoped it could be handled discreetly and over time. One suggestion was to bring back the old formula the following year to mark the company's one hundredth anniversary and brand it Centennial Coke.

Scott Miller, however, thought there wouldn't be much of a Coca-Cola company left in a year's time. He soon recognized that Coke—and, as he puts it now, Coke's "dumb-ass consultants"—had made a giant gaffe. Introducing New Coke may have had its merits; withdrawing the original Coca-Cola was self-assisted suicide. However, Miller saw a way out—and, again, his inspiration was politics. To him, this was equivalent to the moment in a campaign when a candidate is exposed—as a liar, a cheat, an adulterer. His only hope for redemption is confession. In so doing, he shows the people he has listened to them. As result, he empowers them and emerges as *their* candidate. Miller argued that Coke should do just the same.

In the midst of all this, Miller had to go to Europe because Sawyer

Miller was working on an arms-control conference in Geneva for Prince Sadruddin Aga Khan, a philanthropist and diplomat. The top brass of Coca-Cola also happened to be in Europe for a meeting of Coke's advertising agencies. Even in Monte Carlo, Roberto Goizueta and Don Keough were finally coming to terms with the inevitability of a climb-down. The New Coke fiasco followed them to Monaco and to a tiny Italian restaurant in the hills above the Mediterannean, where they were having dinner with their wives. The owner of the place came up to them cradling a wine basket covered with a velvet cloth: he unveiled it to reveal a six-and-a-half-ounce glass bottle of original Coke.

Meanwhile, Zyman and Miller decided to get together. By the pool on the roof of the Loews Hotel overlooking the Monaco bay, Miller and Zyman hammered out what was, in effect, a submission to America for forgiveness: "a strategy of telling the truth and saying we have made a mistake," as Miller remembers it.

On the afternoon of Wednesday, July 11, 1985, the ABC television network interrupted the broadcast of its afternoon soap *General Hospital* to bring its viewers a news flash: Coca-Cola had announced it was bringing back Old Coke. Just seventy-nine days after the launch of New Coke, the American people had been heard, and the company relented. On Capitol Hill, David Pryor, the Democratic senator from Arkansas, described Coke's capitulation as "a very meaningful moment in the history of America. It shows that some national institutions cannot be changed."

Don Keough, Coca-Cola's president, fronted the climb-down. Rushed into a studio in Atlanta to cut a TV spot, he told America that the Coca-Cola Company had been wrong, but it wasn't stupid: he announced the return of Coca-Cola Classic. At a press conference, he said: "There is a twist to this story which will please every humanist and will probably keep Harvard professors puzzled for years. The simple fact is that all the time and money and skill poured into consumer research on the new Coca-Cola could not measure or reveal the deep and abiding emotional attachment to original Coca-Cola felt by so many people. The passion for original Coca-Cola—and that is the word for it, 'passion'—was something that caught us by surprise . . . It is a wonderful American mystery, a lovely American enigma, and you cannot measure it any more than you can measure love, pride, or patriotism."

←——→

EVEN THE MEA CULPA was sugarcoated. Coca-Cola's mistake was neither particularly enigmatic nor exclusively American. In strict political terms, the company paid the price for alienating its "base." And yet, Scott Miller saw the outlines of a sophisticated lesson in the New Coke debacle. He went back to New York and turned the experience into the beginnings of a theory, a creed he dubbed "Move the movable."

In Miller's formulation, any constituency—a market, an electorate, a congregation, an audience—can be sliced into five groups: strong supporters, soft supporters, undecideds, soft opposition, and strong opposition. A candidate (or a product) might as well forget about the strong opposition, as they'll never be persuaded. They hate you and the horse you rode in on. Whatever you do, it won't be good enough. Likewise, your campaign should not spend too much time worrying about the strong supporters. They need to be paid a little attention, of course, enough to ensure they do not feel as though they are being taken for granted. But since they share your beliefs and are vehement critics of your opponents, they have nowhere else to go. The pro-life, tax-cutting, gun-loving Republican is not in a month of Sundays going to vote for a Democrat.

The real action, therefore, lies with the remaining three groups—the soft opposition, the soft supporters, and the undecideds. The soft opposition is willing to hear your case and may even be convinced. Failing that, they might at least be induced to stay away from the polls. Then there are the soft supporters, who need to be ushered into the strong-supporters camp. And, finally, there are the undecideds, the people who really are up for grabs. They are the small sliver of the electorate—or marketplace—who, in a world of increasingly tight races, can hold the key to winning.

In the case of Coke's battle with Pepsi, the political model applied. There were clearly many people in the middle ground—occasional Coca-Cola drinkers, noncola drinkers, and promiscuous drinkers of both Coke and Pepsi. These were the consumers Goizueta was going after with the launch of New Coke. But, like a man on a ladder grasping one rung too far, he reached for the undecideds and soft opponents and lost his footing with his soft and strong supporters. Coca-Cola snubbed the party faithful. The people on the far left or the far right—the Cokeaholics and the Pepsi fanatics—are unlikely to swap horses, but they don't like to be crossed. George H. W. Bush alienated the base of the Republican Party, and it helps explain his defeat in 1992; his son, an assiduous cultivator of the Christian evangelicals, gun owners, and supply-siders, would not make the same mistake. (Karl Rove, George W. Bush's adviser, made a point of taking care of the base first, not last.)

The men at the Coca-Cola Company were, unbeknownst to them, flagging up one of the hardy perennial arguments of modern political strategy—how to balance the needs of the loyal party followers with the need to woo independents. It is the choice that bedevils nearly all campaigns. There are essentially two schools of "alpha dogs," one that believes that elections are won by moving the movable voters in the middle and another that focuses on swelling the numbers of strong supporters who turn out to vote. Scott Miller and James Carville have exemplified the former; Richard Wirthlin and Karl Rove, the latter.

Coca-Cola's humiliation had also provided another, quite separate, lesson about the currents of public opinion. This was, simply, that attitudes are not static. The taste tests and questionnaires conducted on hundreds of thousands of people had found that people liked New Coke. But the focus groups had shown that one particularly enraged Coke loyalist could stir the feelings of the rest of the group. The quantitative numbers were right: seven out of eight people were happy for the company to launch New Coke. But one passionate opponent could change that. The vehemence was infectious. The qualitative research hinted at an important dynamic in American public opinion, the contagion of public anger.

The climb-down from New Coke left Pepsi's Roger Enrico crowing: "This is the Edsel of the eighties," he said, referring to the greatest flop in the history of the American car industry. "This was a terrible mistake. Coke's got a lemon on its hands, and now they're trying to make lemonade." Unfortunately for Pepsi, Coca-Cola did, in a manner of speaking, succeed in making lemonade.

Not only did the return of Coke Classic see all its loyal drinkers flocking back to the "Brown Doctor," but the whole soap opera seemed to have drawn millions more into the Coke fold. By the end of the year, Coke had actually increased its lead over Pepsi by a couple of market share points—equivalent to hundreds of millions of dollars in extra revenue. Coca-Cola's stock soared to an all-time high. Goizueta was rewarded with a $5 million bonus, on top of his $1.7 million package; Keough got an additional $3 million. Keough concluded, "Some critics will say Coca-Cola made a marketing mistake. Some cynics will say we planned the whole thing. The truth is we are not that dumb and we are not that smart."

New Coke was rebranded as Coke II, only to be phased out altogether a few years later. Surprisingly, the threat posed by Pepsi waned. As Malcolm Gladwell pointed out in his book *Blink*, there was a flaw in the taste test: people may have preferred the "smoother, sweeter taste" of Pepsi when they sipped it, but when they drank it in larger volumes—when it came to buying a six-pack—they stuck with Coke. One of the dangers of polling is that the results can be right but they can send you up entirely the wrong path if the questions are wrong.

Roberto Goizueta understood just that in hindsight. When he was asked a few months later if he would have gone ahead with the launch of New Coke if he had known what he then knew, he answered: "Si mi abuela tuviera ruedas sería una bicicleta"—If my grandmother had wheels, she would be a bicycle.

IN A GREAT LITTLE BOOK called *The Selling of the President*, Joe McGinnis told the story of how Richard Nixon was repackaged for the American public in 1968. Eight years after the Nixon-Kennedy debate—the night American politics crossed the threshold into the television age—Nixon was running again. He faced all the old image problems. As Roger Ailes, then a twenty-eight-year-old television producer hired to remake Nixon's image on television, put it, "Let's face it, a lot of people think Nixon is dull. Think he's a bore, a pain in the ass. They look at him as the kind of kid who always carried a bookbag. Who was forty-two years old the day he was born. They figure other kids got footballs for Christmas, Nixon got a briefcase and he loved it." The TV shows Ailes choreographed—he selected the audience, timed the applause, and ensured a mobbing of Nixon at the end of the show—were designed to remake Nixon in the public mind. They were intended to make him look popular. Not smart, not knowledgeable, but well liked. The aim was not to disseminate policy ideas but to project charisma.

Presidential candidates, McGinnis observed, could be rebranded and marketed afresh. Television would not, as some had hoped, expose and demystify the powerful. Instead, "the mystique which should fade grows stronger. We make celebrities not only of the men who cause events but of the men who read reports of them aloud." Television would not serve as a soapbox in America's living room, circumventing the party and bringing the real issues directly to real people. Instead, he wrote, referencing Marshall McLuhan, "on television it matters less that he does not have ideas . . . Style becomes substance. The medium is the massage and the masseur gets the votes." McGinnis peered into America's future, where politicians were packaged and presented to the public like consumer products. The slick artistry of Madison Avenue was being put to work in the supposedly substantive world of politics. Candidates were being managed like cans of Coke.

By the 1980s, the men from Sawyer Miller were coming to see a way of taking this one step further. If slick, savvy marketing techniques could work in politics, why not hardscrabble political lessons in marketing? Coke could be managed like a candidate. David Sawyer made the point in an article for the Yale School of Organization and Management. "Corporations must recognize that it is now in their long-term self-interest to develop much more democratic relationships with all of their constituencies: consumers, employees, shareholders, community members and the public at large," he wrote. "The most important legacy of the information revolution is mass empowerment, not the once-feared Orwellian nightmare."

Sawyer had been peddling the idea of consumer democracy since the early 1980s. His friends at the Knickerbocker Club were not politicians, but financiers and businessmen. And all around him he saw the rules being rewritten for chief executives as much as they were for politicians. The corporation's relationship with its clients and customers, it seemed to Sawyer, was rapidly coming to resemble a politician's relationship with his constituents. It was fundamentally about impressing upon them a sense of shared values. As information channels increased and multiplied, corporations needed to forge an emotional bond. The only way to establish a nontransactional relationship with a customer was based on values. (Over time, this observation became conventional wisdom. It is why Harley-Davidson became about much more than the magnificent chrome of its motorcycles' handlebars or the roar of their double-barreled exhausts, but about an attitude, a way of life.) In the early 1980s, though, Ronald Reagan was transforming the concept of leadership, redefining the role of America's chief executive as more than just the ultimate decision maker on policy but as the explainer of policy to the people, the communicator in chief.

The great corporate patriarchs were a dying breed. They had lost their control of information flow and had found themselves sapped of their authority. They were under assault from all sides: government officials in Washington, eager to be seen getting tough on white-collar crime; business reporters wanting to make their name by exposing greed, avarice, and larceny in the boardroom; restive shareholders looking for a better return and a new executive team to deliver it. Corporations needed to woo their consumers, explain themselves to their regulators, justify themselves to their investors every day. America's bosses needed to communicate more often and much more widely. To David Sawyer, it was clear that they needed to define themselves before their critics did it for them. It was as if they were up for reelection every day.

FOUR

"A DANGEROUS COMBINATION FOR ISRAEL"

"WHERE THE HELL IS MONDALE?" David Sawyer was pacing up and down a small, brown, airless office at an airport just outside Baltimore, waiting for the Democratic Party's presidential candidate, who was an hour late, a week away from the election, and twenty points down in the polls.

Sawyer and Miller had done everything they could to block Mondale from running for president. They had worked for nearly a year on John Glenn's campaign, and then, when that collapsed, they switched to Gary Hart. But Walter "Fritz" Mondale had better understood how to work the party machine and had won the Democratic nomination in 1984. When the Mondale headquarters in Georgetown called over the Labor Day weekend and asked for their help to turn the TV campaign around, Sawyer and Miller heeded their party's call.

Since then, weeks had gone by, and now, as the two men watched the minutes tick away, they seethed at all the wasted time. For months they had pleaded with the Mondale camp to get the candidate in front of the camera, but the staff brushed them off: Mondale, they were told, did not feel comfortable on television; he felt self-conscious; he looked like a halibut. Sawyer and Miller explained that Mondale did not have a prayer of beating Ronald Reagan if he did not master Ronald Reagan's most powerful political tool, television. They sought to convince the Mondale team that Fritz was intelligent, sensitive, charming, even funny—all qualities that would play well on TV.

One evening in mid-October they were sitting in the Sawyer Miller offices on Fifty-fifth Street with the growing sense that the campaign was slipping away when they tuned in to watch Mondale giving an interview to Dan Rather of CBS. Within minutes, they were reenergized: this was the Mondale they had heard about, a man with compelling intelligence and a depth of reasoning, a politician who came across as "presidential." They were on the phone to Georgetown almost immediately, suggesting a half-hour interview of Mondale by Mario Cuomo, the governor of New York who had fired the imagination of the press and the public at the Democratic convention a few months earlier. In the time that it took them to get agreement from Cuomo's office, the Mondale campaign had come back and refused them flat.

Mondale, it seemed to them, was just the last of the old-time, back-slapping, organization-man Democrats. Two decades after television had cost Nixon the election against Kennedy, Mondale was still wedded to the aging party machine, determined to make the rusty old rattletrap work for him one more time. Sitting in what they liked to call their "electronic conference room" in New York, staring at the bank of televisions and watching one Reagan spot after another, the men from Sawyer Miller grew increasingly exasperated at Mondale, furious that he could not see the obvious limitations of the old-party apparatus.

In the first debate, Mondale performed well, making the president look tired and muddled and prompting questions about the health of Reagan's mind. But within a couple of days, the Reagan campaign had a fresh political advertisement out there, showing the president behind the Resolute desk in the Oval Office, looking young, confident, and in command. Sawyer and Miller, meanwhile, had no means of shooting back. There was no available footage of Mondale, no close-ups, no straight-from-the-shoulder shots, no sound bites on the issues. Mondale did not like TV.

Finally, just a fortnight away from the election, Dick Leone, a political hand from New Jersey who had taken charge of running the message for Mondale, called to say that Mondale would stop for an hour at the catering office conference room of the Baltimore airport on his way to Buffalo the following Tuesday. It was hardly ideal, Leone conceded, but Mondale was not enthusiastic even about this. So Sawyer and Miller created a makeshift studio in the backroom office in Baltimore, setting up cameras and lights and preparing a bunch of potential scripts for Mondale to choose from. Then they waited.

After more than an hour had passed, Leone came into the room with an embarrassed look on his face. "He will be another twenty minutes," he said. "The candidate is getting a haircut." Sawyer could barely speak. Not only did this leave them next to no time to film the spots, but it was clear that Mondale was not getting a haircut to look better on TV. He would rather do anything than get in front of the camera.

Mondale eventually arrived. He went through half a dozen scripts and rejected them all. "Why can't we just 'talk it,' " he said, and they agreed to try a few shots of him speaking off the cuff. It did not work. Miller, who by then had worked with Bob Hope and Bill Cosby and Johnny Carson and knew that the most spontaneous comedians never left anything unscripted, tried to point out that "talking it" never works. Mondale reverted to the scripts. He alighted on one that set out the choice Americans had to make for their future: "This isn't too bad," he said. They framed him in the camera and shouted, "Roll tape!"

The technician called a halt: there was a glitch; the machine whirred, but the tape did not run. This was going to be their last chance with Mondale, and after begging for his time for so long, they knew he would be livid. In fact, he was ebullient: "What the hell, happens all the time. Too bad. Great to see you guys," he said, bounced up on his feet, and headed to the plane that was taking him to Buffalo. He was delighted that it was over. A week later, when the full extent of Mondale's overwhelming defeat was clear, he told the press: "I never warmed up to the tube, and to be fair, it never warmed up to me."

Television was in the process of winnowing the Walter Mondales out of modern politics. The election campaign increasingly seemed like a perversion of politics to high-minded men who chose a life of public service because they wanted to govern the people, not to entertain them. The old-style politicians—the awkward intellectuals and the Legion Hall barnstormers—would continue to have a place in parliaments and cabinets, but, unable to play well on television to the vast majority of the general public, they were pushed toward the fringes of public life, often relegated to the cameo role of the beloved political eccentric.

At the same time, the 1984 election underlined for Sawyer and Miller the fact that the campaign itself could only ever count for so much. The election was, as ever, an unparalleled feat of coordination and creativity, the marshaling of ideas, technology, and people, an intellectual and emotional circus, a mixture of show business and shoe leather, heavy advertising expenditure and word-of-mouth endorsements, an infuriating combination of meticulous planning and unexpected events, a strange blend of idealism and scandalmongering, all in the service of Walter

Mondale. But, on November 6, the election distilled the national argument and, in one concerted pull of the lever, captured America's mood. The media message was just one small factor in the final outcome.

To Sawyer and Miller's frustration, they saw all too clearly that the campaign could never be more convincing or more charismatic than the candidate. It was a lesson that was to reassert itself time and time again with a man who proved to be David Sawyer's fondest, longest-running, and most perennially disappointing client.

SHIMON PERES proved to be a towering figure in the modern history of Israel. He led his party, off and on, for thirty years. He served his country several times as foreign minister and three times as prime minister, and he won the Nobel Prize for Peace. And, bound by a mutual fascination with politics, Peres, the Polish Jew, forged a lifelong connection with Sawyer, the Massachusetts preppy: "We had a very close and unusual relationship. I took his advice, without any hesitation," Peres recalled. "He was the most unusual person, a man of great wisdom. Not only wise, but also profound. He had an understanding not only of politics, but also of psychology and, what always impressed me, he was above his profession."

Their long partnership began in 1981, when the elections looked like a foregone conclusion. Menachem Begin, the prime minister, was old and in poor health, and his government was adrift. He had struck a historic peace deal with Egypt, but it was criticized by both hawks and doves. Many Israelis regretted the handover of the Sinai desert. The economy was in worrisome shape: inflation had risen to 130 percent. The polls showed Peres's party, Labor—properly known as Ma'arach, the Labor Alignment—was set to win half the votes; the Likud, which was led by Begin, was set to get just 20 percent. As with Lorenzo Fernández in Venezuela, so with Shimon Peres in Israel: all the public opinion surveys pointed to a thumping win for David Sawyer's client.

Both parties knew, however, that the election would be a contest. Four years earlier, the left had lost for the first time since independence. The same coalition of socialist-minded Zionists had stood atop the Israeli establishment even before the creation of the state. Then, in 1977, came the watershed. The right burst out of perpetual opposition, challenging the left's assumption that it was the natural inheritor of power in Israel. Both parties were, therefore, prepared to have to go to unprecedented lengths to win. The result was an election that was noisier, more competitive, and more bitter than any election that had come before it. And for the first time in Israel's short history, both parties brought in American political consultants.

Menachem Begin hired David Garth. From the late 1950s, when he dropped out of the graduate psychology department at Columbia, Garth had ricocheted from one life to the next and ended up in politics: he started making sports programs; he became the unpaid television adviser to a failed Democratic candidate for the New York City mayor's office. By the late 1970s, he was deemed by *Time* magazine to be America's "most sought-after campaign strategist." He was certainly well on his way to becoming the most influential pollster in the modern history of the Empire State: he had brought the first Democrat in twenty years to the governorship of New York and, with Garth's advice, the underdog Ed Koch had just won the race to become New York's mayor.

Garth was known for his low-key, factual political ads. He shied away from big-charisma politicians, preferring the steadier, unflappable type: not the show ponies but the workhorses. He agreed with Marshall McLuhan that "cool" images are more effective than "hot" ones on television. Menachem Begin, a man who was famously run out of Poland by the Nazis, imprisoned by the Soviets, and hunted by the British, was a natural candidate for Garth. And Mayor Koch was only too happy to recommend Garth to the anxious Likudniks who feared that the old man was trundling toward defeat.

David Sawyer was brought in by the Bronfmans. The Canadian-born heirs to the Seagram's liquor business, Edgar and Charles Bronfman have long used their good fortune for public purposes, particularly Jewish charities and the Zionist cause. On his first visit to Israel in 1958, Charles had met the then deputy assistant minister of defense, Shimon Peres. And when Labor was looking to get back into power in the early 1980s, Bronfman was eager to recruit Sawyer to the campaign. His commission: to present a different image of the Alignment leader—to introduce Israelis to "the new Peres."

The problem was that the people did not much like the Peres they knew. They overwhelmingly preferred Begin. They felt that Labor had been given thirty years to run Israel. Likud had been given just four. People were inclined to give Begin more time. (The polls showed that about

40 percent of people had a favorable opinion of Menachem Begin; about 17 percent had a favorable opinion of Peres. Yitzhak Rabin, who was not even at the top of the Alignment's list of candidates for the Knesset, out-polled Peres.) The Peres campaign team was divided and, worse, compla-cent. They were too willing to believe the polls that showed Labor cruising to victory, even though those same polls showed the Peres lead gradually shrinking.

On their first outing in Israel, American advisers were largely ignored, marginalized, and disdained. Even though the presence of outside advis-ers caused much comment in the Israeli press at the time, the fractured leadership of Labor barely listened to each other let alone lent an ear to a political consultant from New York.

Sawyer and Joel McCleary, who was on his first foreign trip working for the firm, spent days at the King David Hotel in Jerusalem idling by the pool and passing time on the patio looking out over the Old City. When Sawyer did get time with Peres, he returned again and again to the same issue: the changing constituencies within the Israeli electorate. Sawyer saw a demographic revolution sweeping Israel, one that was delivering new electoral blocs to the Likud and, bit by bit, eroding the power base of the traditional party of government, Labor. He was methodical, con-vinced that there was as much science as there was art to campaigning. Technology, he argued, was not just changing the way politicians spoke to voters but the way they understood the electorate. "Electronic democ-racy" did not just mean television but data collection. And, in Israel, the data—"what the numbers are telling us," as he would put it to Peres—pointed to changes in society that could play to the opposition Likud's advantage: the growth of the entrepreneurial, free-market middle classes, the expansion of the voting age population born after 1948, and the in-crease in groups voting on issues not of economy or security but of reli-gious and communal identity. Peres, as McCleary remembers it, did not fully grasp Sawyer's argument that the defining issue for Israeli politics in the next decade would not be ideology as much as demographics. "It was David Sawyer at his best," McCleary remembers. "It was the only time I saw David haunted by the numbers rather than seduced by the dream of what he might project."

Still, Peres's Labor Party colleagues had little time for Sawyer's techni-cal know-how when it came to framing political material on television.

Israel had its own rules for political broadcasts, and the Labor campaign managers insisted that the lessons of the American campaign trail did not apply there.

Garth's sway over Likud was also limited. He tinkered with the campaign, chiefly because, no sooner had he arrived in Israel, than the upcoming election was overshadowed by Israel's tumultuous foreign policy. At the beginning of June, Begin held a historic meeting in Sharm el-Sheikh with Egyptian president Anwar Sadat, underlining his credentials as a statesman and a peacemaker. Three days later, Begin authorized an air strike on the Iraqi nuclear reactor at Osirak, demonstrating an unbending determination to protect Israel from any external threats and a deafness to outside criticism. The events came as the economy, too, was showing signs of life, kick-started by a new finance minister who cut taxes and encouraged a flurry of consumer spending.

On the night of the election it still looked as though Peres might squeak through. His lead in the polls had shriveled over the six months between January, when Begin called the elections, and June 30, 1981, polling day. But he was still a whisker ahead. Indeed, when Israelis stopped voting and switched on their televisions that evening, Hanoch Smith, an Israeli TV analyst, predicted a Labor victory. Peres was referred to as "the next prime minister of Israel."

The exit polls, though, were off. Begin inched out Peres: Likud won forty-eight seats, the Labor Alignment won forty-seven. Begin had done just enough to assert his authority to remain in government, while Peres had not done quite enough to wrest him from it. The Likud clung on. Looking back years later, Peres argued that it was always going to be a much harder election to win than it looked: "The difference between Begin and myself was just one seat. He was considered a great orator, he made peace with Egypt, and he bombed the reactor at Osirak. [Peres had opposed the bombing and, backed by Sawyer, had stuck to that position despite pressure from within his own party.] It was quite surprising that we reached forty-seven."

The irony of Sawyer's entry into Israeli politics was that he did not much affect the outcome of his first election there in 1981. His arrival, however, marked the beginning of a new chapter in Israeli politics. Within a few short years, the Middle East's newest and only democracy was in the thrall of American politics, overrun by campaign consultants who came fresh from Ohio, Pennsylvania, and Florida to work the vote in

Haifa, Tel Aviv, and Be'er Sheva. Unwittingly, Sawyer led the "alpha dogs" into the Promised Land.

THE AMERICANIZATION OF POLITICS has been a highly contentious issue in Israel. Like so much else in that voluble Socratic culture, it has been debated every which way. Some have blamed America's influence for trivializing a national debate that, without exaggeration, encompasses heaven and earth, life and death. Israel has grappled daily with five thousand years of unresolved existential argument—differences over the boundaries of the Holy Land, the observance of God's laws, and the relationship between the people of Canaan and their neighbors. Each and every argument has been drenched in blood. Israel, said the critics of American influence, had trouble enough without sound bites.

Others simply dismissed foreign involvement. Sure, they said, the Israelis have been big buyers of U.S. consumer culture, but Americans have only ever played bit parts in the country's politics. Politics in Israel looks nothing like it does in America. The Israeli parliament, the Knesset, is elected by proportional representation. Dozens of parties compete. The fault lines in Israeli politics are generally not just jobs, health care, and education—they are war and religion. Israeli politics operates on another, higher, level: in 1988, for example, one of the key arguments within the battle for ultra-Orthodox votes was whether one leader was or was not the Messiah.

The fact is, though, the modernization of politics in Israel has had a particularly Yankee flavor to it, for reasons that go beyond the extraordinarily close relationship between Israel and America. If it's a Tuesday, Americans, somewhere, are voting. Americans simply have more elections and ballot initiatives and, as a result, they have more expertise to export courtesy of the multibillion-dollar politics business at home. They know more about polling, direct mail, stump speeches, get-out-the-vote operations, negative advertising, phone banks, and online fund-raising. Americans vote more. And they have the right idea. We all have an appetite for American-style politics; people disparage negative campaigns, but negative advertising moves us; people deride personality politics, but we set great store by "character"; sloganeering is bemoaned, but when polled, we often voice our preferences in precisely the sound bites that have been fed to us. Americans know how to couch politics for the people, how to arrange the music of the high church as a pop melody. The escalation of American involvement in Israel has been only a case in point.

Sawyer and Peres kept working together through the 1980s. "The more we worked, the more he identified himself with our own cause," Peres remembered of Sawyer.

Unfortunately, Peres kept losing. He lost the 1977 election, then lost the 1981 election by a narrower margin. He didn't exactly lose in 1984, but he didn't exactly win, either: he scraped by in a tie. Labor and Likud came to a power-sharing agreement: Peres would serve as prime minister for half the term, then swap with Yitzhak Shamir, who would serve the other half. So, by the time Sawyer returned in 1988, he had developed a rapport with Peres and a relationship with Israel. Peres, for his part, had learned one of Sawyer's favorite lessons about politics: "I learned the effect of the mirror, the difference between glass and a mirror. Glass is open and transparent and you see straightforward. In an election, you have mirrors, which may change the view and change the image. [Sawyer] warned me about this effect. It is not necessary that what you say will be received straightforwardly. You must take into account not only your opinions but the reactions."

Sawyer came accompanied that year by Harris Diamond, one of the stars of the burgeoning Sawyer Miller business in New York. Diamond had been an early member of a group of Greenwich Village liberals pledged to freeing their party from the political machine. The Village Independent Democrats saw it as their mission to hand politics back to the ordinary voter. The point is that Diamond started out an idealist. He has, by his own account, remained one. Idealism, of course, is to politics what peer pressure is to smoking: it gets you started. But one thing common to political consultants is that they almost all start out as idealists, get branded as mercenaries, and swear blind thereafter that they are misunderstood. Diamond is the epitome of the type, a highly talented man who proved to be a pivotal and singularly divisive figure in the history of Sawyer Miller.

The work Sawyer and Diamond did in 1988 had a mostly inadvertent effect: they fired up the opposition. The rumors in Israel that Labor had brought in a couple of Americans who were doing sophisticated public opinion research, targeting undecided constituencies, and marshaling a block-by-block get-out-the-vote operation, all spooked the Likud. (The fact that these rumors were grossly exaggerated was neither here nor there.) "We discovered that Labor had hired American consultants," recalls strategic consultant Eyal Arad, a wiry man with designer stubble and spiky gray hair. "We heard that they had launched phone bank operations. Back then, we were all novices." Arad went on to become an instrumental figure in the triumph of the Israeli right, helping Yitzhak Shamir, Bibi Netanyahu, and Ariel Sharon into the prime minister's office. In the late 1980s, he had just returned from New York, where through the mid-1980s he had worked for Netanyahu, then Israel's ambassador to the UN. "We didn't know what the shit was going on. So we called in Richard Wirthlin." Israel's arms race in American advisers was under way.

Dick Wirthlin was probably the most important pollster in America in the 1980s. If Ned Kennan brought a new emotional empathy to political polling—a sense of soul, libido, and psyche—Wirthlin brought an unprecedented scientific rigor, imposing system and structure on qualitative research. In 1980, he drew up the playbook that brought Ronald Reagan to the White House. Called PINS—political information system—it brought together all the survey research, analysis of the news and media, profiles of the candidate, and campaign plans, state by state, county by county. Through the 1980s, it was a schematic that Wirthlin was happy to export to the Republican Party's ideological cousins in the United Kingdom, Italy, and Israel. To this day, Arad considers himself a student of Wirthlin's. So does Karl Rove.

Wirthlin went to Israel two or three times in 1987. He introduced Arad, Netanyahu, and a handful of the new generation of Likudniks to new technologies in polling—in particular, dial sessions. The process was simple enough. It involved a focus group of above average size, say twenty to forty. As they watched a speech, an advertisement, or a political event, participants were asked to measure their approval by turning a dial hooked up to a computer, twisting it to the right when they approved of something, to the left when they disapproved. The more positively they felt, the more they should turn the dial to the right, the more negatively, the farther to the left. Dial testing sessions took the format of the focus group that Ned Kennan used to run for the big pharmaceutical companies. But they offered more precise and intrusive insights: with this method, pollsters could measure participants' momentary responses to particular words, stories, ideas, and slogans, and also how the candidate's message—word for word, issue for issue—was playing across particular segments of the electorate.

A god-fearing Mormon and the father of eight children, Wirthlin did not want to get directly involved in the campaign while still on the U.S. government payroll. (The involvement of a White House official in a foreign election is, of course, a delicate matter. Wirthlin sought approval from Reagan to go to Israel. The president agreed, on the understanding that the White House would not be seen as endorsing a candidate. And so Wirthlin needed to act discreetly. All parties preferred that American involvement be kept out of the public eye.) So he put the Israelis in touch with a worldwide network of right-wing political professionals. He hooked the Likudniks up with Decima, a Canadian polling company founded by Allan Gregg, who was also a student of Wirthlin's and had become a prominent pollster and a controversial master of the attack ad in Canada. The Israeli team was sent to the United Kingdom to work with the Conservative Party, again amassing technical expertise in the emerging science of polling. Globalization has been facilitated in politics by much the same forces as it has in other businesses: cheap airfares and personal introductions.

Wirthlin left Eyal Arad and his Likud team with three simple lessons: "One. Never let the politicians run the campaign. Two. Never look at the horse race. Look for what drives the vote, not what the outcome will be. Three. Campaigns should be very simple. It should be two, three, four basic messages centered around one theme." (He also left them with a twenty-five-year-old political science graduate named Frank Luntz, who would go on to earn not only an international reputation as a political pollster but also a name for himself in Washington as one of the leading advocates of "reframing"—i.e., casting an old political idea in fresh language or as part of a new story line. Luntz recast the "estate tax," for example, as the altogether more putrid "death tax"; he advised Republicans to embrace "conservation," a word much more likely to conjure images of elks and redwoods and vacations in the national parks than "the environment"; he rebranded the grubby business of "drilling for oil" as the much more appealing "exploring for energy.") For all that, this was an election again overshadowed by the violent realities of life in the Middle East. The import of fancy polls did not impress the likes of Yitzhak Shamir. Born in Poland in 1915, he fought against the British in both the Irgun and the Stern Gang and, as the serving prime minister, was more focused on suppressing the Palestinian intifada than surveying the results of dial sessions.

The results in 1988 were, once again, anticlimactic. The election had been billed as a fork in the road, a critical choice to determine the fate of Israel and the future shape of the territories. It took place in the shadow of the intifada and yet fitted the pattern of the two other elections of the 1980s—the parties drew; the Likud won forty seats; Labor, thirty-nine. It was an example of how nations can behave like people: confronted by an agonizing decision, they can simply end up of two minds. In 1981, 1984, and 1988, the Israeli election was an intense, energetic exercise in ambivalence. The first forty years of Israeli history were remarkable, among other things, for the fact that there was only one decisive transfer of power—in 1977—at the polls.

The 1990s were an altogether different story. The three elections in that busy decade—in 1992, 1996, and 1999—would see power switch from right to left, left to right, and back again.

In the 1990s, Israel reaped what Sawyer had sown in the 1980s. The contests were marked by a new aggressive form of political advertising. Polls determined electoral priorities. The candidates eclipsed their parties. Campaigns dominated by personality encouraged a more intrusive level of personal scrutiny. In turn, the media became altogether more self-referential. Israeli politics seemed undeniably American.

IN 1990, Shimon Peres sought to topple Yitzhak Shamir's precarious government, a frayed, ill-fitting patchwork of the Likud and a collection of smaller parties. The trigger was a vote of no-confidence in Shamir over his stance on a peace initiative backed by both Cairo and Washington. The events that followed were an example of how the politics of the playground can unravel the ambitions of statecraft. Peres was asked by the president to try to form a government. To do so, he got into a set of unseemly negotiations with an improbable cast of characters. He had to pull together the hawks and the doves within his own party, the Israeli Arabs and the ultra-Orthodox Ashkenazim, the hard-line Sephardim, and the disaffected Likudniks. It was shaping up to be something of a predatory Noah's Ark: the animals were coming in two by two; the only problem was that they wanted to eat one another.

Peres had to pay a price for the promise of support from each little party or breakaway faction. And in turn, Shamir counterbid. Peres offered one possible turncoat the transport ministry; Shamir counteroffered with something better—foreign or defense or the treasury. (Shamir, in fact, went further. He promised five members of one breakaway faction seats in the Knesset at the next election and a $10 million security deposit as a guarantee.) Peres's effort to put together a new government crumbled at the last moment. He had been given three weeks to forge a majority in parliament, and on the day he was due to present his government, a couple of wayward ultra-Orthodox members of the Knesset deserted him. He was given another fortnight, but, again, the last few votes eluded him. Shamir was now given his chance. He cut his own series of deals, offering government jobs in return for votes.

The upshot of all this was that Israelis were disgusted. A handful of politicians—ultra-Orthodox extremists and factional egomaniacs—had held the government for ransom. There was overwhelming demand for reforms to mitigate the absurdities of Israel's system of proportional representation. Israelis wanted to reduce the powers of tiny political parties that could hold the prime minister in a headlock. They wanted to enhance the powers of the prime minister and make him answer to the people, not to some freak faction in the Knesset. And so the Knesset voted to overhaul Israel's electoral system and introduce the "direct election" of the prime minister—in effect, a presidential system.

The new rules did not take effect immediately. But the 1992 election was conducted in their spirit. The Labor Party held primaries for the leadership, and Yitzhak Rabin vanquished his old rival Peres. The election was a personal crusade for Rabin, a soldier who had fought to create the state of Israel, served as chief of staff during the Six-Day War, and who now put himself in every way at the center of the campaign: the party officially called itself "Labor headed by Rabin." And he was overwhelmingly rewarded. Labor won forty-four seats, Likud, thirty-two.

An election in Israel tends to fall into one of two categories: an argument over foreign policy or an argument over matters at home. The latter is a luxury in the Middle East. In Israel, domestic policy has only clearly dominated in three elections, those held in 1981, 1984, and 1999. The turnarounds in 1977 and again in 1992 were driven by national security issues. The Yom Kippur War happened just before Israelis went to the polls in 1973, and in the four years that followed, support for the Labor government hollowed, eaten away by Israeli war-weariness, fear, and exasperation.

Likewise in 1992 there was a swing against the Likud, the culmination of slow-burning frustration after four and a half years of Palestinian uprising, the intifada. Neither the Yom Kippur War nor the intifada took its toll immediately. Both caught up with Israeli politics four years later. But, then, politics is an unpredictable interplay between events and moods, one immediate and dramatic, the other often slow and imperceptible.

The 1992 election was the culmination of just such a gradual, gathering change in mood. It was the first swing of the pendulum between those two powerful political forces, hope and fear. In each successive election, those swings would be exaggerated by American influence.

Rabin's victory gave him a mandate, which he used the following year to make a historic breakthrough with the Palestinian Liberation Organization. In 1993, Israel recognized the PLO as the representative of the Palestinian people; the PLO recognized Israel's right to exist. There followed an extraordinary period of optimism, a period pregnant with the possibilities of peace. Israeli entrepreneurs looked to make money out of the high-tech expertise garnered in the military. They boasted of a Silicon Wadi, a Babylon of start-ups to match America's own technology grobag, Silicon Valley. Palestinian investors started work on a beach resort in the Gaza Strip, alive to the extraordinary possibility that the lion and lamb would not only lie down together but also sunbathe. And then Yigal Amir, a Jewish fundamentalist, assassinated Yitzhak Rabin at the end of a peace rally in Tel Aviv on the night of November 4, 1995.

National tragedies are generally good for incumbents. Shimon Peres, Rabin's foreign minister and now the torchbearer for the Oslo peace process, once again inherited the premiership. Jerusalem fell eerily quiet. Israel was a nation united in its grief. Support for Labor, now led by Peres, soared; people deserted Likud and Binyamin Netanyahu's hopes of office seemed to slip away. In the shadow of Rabin's murder, it seemed impossible for Peres to lose.

Wirthlin had been back in Israel in the summer of 1995, a couple of months before the assassination. The Likudniks had brought him back to prepare for an election expected the following year. The old Likud team of 1988—Arad, Netanyahu, and Wirthlin—mapped out a familiar strategy: a simple positive theme for the candidate, an unstinting message of distrust about the opposition. They jotted down a vision of Israel's future on a large white pad set on an artist's easel. Arad still has the plan scribbled down in Magic Marker. Bibi's position on security: "Israelis vs. Arabs." On the economy: "High tech and the future." On personality:

"When you look for a prime minister, don't look to your grandfather, look to your children." And that was it: (1) a tough line on the Arabs, (2) plenty of economic optimism, and (3) the promise of youth rather than the tiredness of age.

The common wisdom after Rabin was assassinated was that everything had changed. The Likud's polling said otherwise. The public opinion research suggested that Israelis still felt much the same about the underlying issues; the Likud just needed time for the sympathy for Labor to dissipate. Their priority, therefore, was to ensure that Peres did not call snap elections soon after the murder. The government of Israel, they argued, is not changed by a bullet. Fortunately for the Likud, they had an accomplice in Shimon Peres. The acting prime minister did not want to trade off Rabin's murder to win office. The reasons for this are still debated in Israel. Some say that Peres was advised that he should not alienate the right wing in the country by exploiting the assassination for electoral gain. Others say he was pigheaded, determined to prove to his now-dead rival that he could win office on his own terms. At the beginning of 1996, the bumpers of Israeli cars were plastered with a simple sticker bidding farewell to Rabin: "Shalom, chaver"—"Good-bye, friend." But Peres chose not to rush into an early election, and Labor's campaign that year made scant reference to their slain leader.

The delay gave Netanyahu valuable time. The only downside was that Wirthlin fell ill. In his stead, the Likud recruited another master Republican strategist, a student of Wirthlin's and a man whose name would become synonymous in Israel with the Americanization of politics: Arthur Finkelstein.

Finkelstein is a secretive, mysterious figure. There is only one published photograph of him, a grainy picture of a plump, forgettable-looking man caught wearing a furtive expression. He travels internationally only on Swiss Air, changing always in Zurich. He checks into hotels under a false name. When working in Israel, he would be squirreled in and out of Likud Party headquarters unannounced and at night. He came and went largely unnoticed, looking like the man who had come to fix the photocopier. Israel is a country, people say, where a secret is something that two people know, one of whom is dead. And yet, on his first engagement in Israel, Finkelstein remained a well-kept secret.

He insists on privacy partly for personal reasons, partly for professional ones. Finkelstein is gay. He is also a conservative Republican who has worked for a number of homophobic politicians. He married his longtime partner in Massachusetts, but he has never had any interest in seeing his love life made public property. He is, he says, also one of the old school who believes advisers should operate from behind the curtain, while the candidates occupy the limelight. (He told me this when he courteously returned my call, the prime purpose of which was to tell me he wouldn't talk to me.)

The cloak-and-dagger mystique, however, is not nearly as interesting as Finkelstein's evident influence. He is often credited with turning "liberal" into a dirty word. Alfonse D'Amato, his client since 1980, saw off a challenge from Robert "hopelessly liberal" Abrams in 1992; George Pataki, with Finkelstein's help, unseated Mario "too liberal for too long" Cuomo from the New York governorship in 1994; Bob Dole, on Finkelstein's advice, attacked Bill "the spend-and-tax liberal" Clinton in 1996. And the list goes on. Liberal bashing—known in some circles as the Finkelstein formula, or Finkel-think—has become a standard Republican play. Finkelstein's career spans from his first work on Richard Nixon's 1972 campaign to "Stop Her Now," an effort to whip up opposition to Hillary Clinton's run for the presidency in 2008.

Finkelstein began in Israel with a review of the polls. The Likud had commissioned reams of research. Arthur Finkelstein took away four volumes of data, each as thick as an *Encyclopaedia Britannica* volume, and studied them for a weekend. He returned, Eyal Arad recalls, with a one-word conclusion: "Jerusalem." Finkelstein went to Bibi Netanyahu and said, "Let's do Jerusalem." And that was the issue with which they hit Peres. The campaign's chief attack on the Labor prime minister was this: "Peres will divide Jerusalem." It was intended to speak to essential angst in Israel, the fear of a compromise too far that would surrender or betray the Zionist cause for a false promise of peace.

The wave of terrorist bombings in the first half of 1996 cast the national argument in a different, darker color. While Labor avoided mention of the Rabin killing, the Likud team rammed home the murder of innocent Israelis. A twenty-five-second spot played over the closing three weeks of the campaign showed again and again the all-too-familiar footage of a smoldering Number 18 bus in Jerusalem, blown up by a suicide bomber who claimed twenty-five lives. The footage was accompanied by a bleak appeal to back Netanyahu: "No security. No peace. No reason to vote for Peres." Israelis had never seen anything like it. Not only did the ad play to Israel's rage and fear, it supplanted an altogether different kind of debate.

Previously, political advertisements on television had been a substantive to-and-fro between the candidates. On the last twenty-one nights of the campaign, a block of TV airtime was given over to the candidates. Each had several minutes to make his case. Israeli politicians had in the past used that time to argue out their differences. They tended to draw up long, literate spots. Each night they generally addressed a fresh issue, keying off the day's events or responding to the previous night's attacks. Television advertising in Israel, therefore, had had something of the quality of a college debate: wordy, cerebral, and long. The Likud, as advised by Finkelstein, ditched verbose articulations of policy and crammed a brutally emotive message into a thirty-second spot—and played it again and again and again.

The personalization of the campaign was both a function of the first direct election of the prime minister—the new voting law came into effect in 1996—and the import of American style. Some of this was lighthearted teasing. Each evening, Israeli TV closed its evening broadcast with the reading of a verse from the Bible; the Likud, instead, started running a nightly parody, a verse from Peres. It was read in a similarly portentous voice that made the great statesman sound silly. This goading was a classic Wirthlin trick, an attempt to get inside the head of the opponent. Karl Rove aimed to do the same thing for George W. Bush, whether it was baiting Ann Richards when the young Republican ran for the Texas governorship or mocking John Kerry when Bush ran for president. "If you get inside their heads," as Rove likes to say, "you've already won." The parody, naturally, drove Peres nuts.

At its core, the Netanyahu campaign was negative, an unrelenting attack on Peres intended to link Israeli insecurity to his weakness and that capitalized on voters' fear. The most memorable spot was short and showed a frosted pane of glass that cracked, splintered, and then shattered to reveal Peres walking slowly up a flight of stairs hand in hand with the Palestinian leader Yasser Arafat. "A dangerous combination for Israel," the announcer said. This was a straight reworking of a device Finkelstein had used for George Pataki: the American ad had shown a series of puzzle pieces put together to reveal an unflattering image of his opponent; the Israelis used shattering glass because it sounded more menacing. The emotional intent was the same—to expose a dangerous hidden agenda.

Even more important in helping Netanyahu to get within reach of Peres was the televised debate, a remarkable American innovation and a successful political export.

In 1996, Netanyahu opened a series of debates looking like a man fresh from his summer holiday. "Good evening," he said. "I am happy to have the occasion to present before you tonight my way for leading the country. In three days you'll have to choose which of two ways can bring Israel true peace with true security. The way offered by Mr. Peres brings no peace and no security. It brings us fear." It was concise, copybook stuff, exactly the formula that is tried, tested, and repeated during weeks of debate prep: Establish self. Offer a choice. Set the terms of the debate. Go negative. Peres, on the other hand, sought to disdain Netanyahu. He barely acknowledged the other man's presence. While Netanyahu addressed Peres thirty-four times, Peres did not address Netanyahu once. The strategy was intended to convey the sense that Peres was a leader and Netanyahu a pretender. Instead, Peres came across as aloof and out of touch. The fact that he spoke so remarkably slowly only added to that impression: in the first ten minutes of the debate, Netanyahu uttered nearly double the number of words (576) that Peres did (301).

As was the case with the people who listened on the radio to the Kennedy-Nixon debate in 1960, those who tuned in to the Netanyahu-Peres debate in 1996 thought it was a tie or that the older man had won. People who watched on television, though, thought differently. Netanyahu, like Kennedy, was a man for television. The Israeli had cut his teeth on the U.S. television circuit during his years based in New York as ambassador to the UN. He had trained diligently for the debate, practicing his responses, and stuck to his allotted time, and knew to sign off an issue with a punchy conclusion. Peres, by contrast, seemed tired. He hated the idea of having to practice for the debate, convinced that his record in politics and government should speak for itself. He rambled on through complex policy issues, several times having to be cut short by the moderator. The following morning, *Yediot*, Israel's best-selling newspaper, judged Netanyahu the winner. Two days later, Israelis went to the polls.

On Election Day, May 29, 1996, it looked as though Peres was going to sneak by after all, and when the polls closed, Israeli television stations reported that he had indeed won. But as the counting continued through the night, his putative lead was whittled away. By the early hours of the morning, it appeared that Netanyahu had, in fact, pipped Peres to the post, winning 50.5 percent of the vote. His victory margin was a slender 14,900 votes. The world was shocked, finding it hard to believe that Israel would vote out the party of Yitzhak Rabin just six months after his assassination. To many, the vote signified Israeli insecurity trumping its willingness to make peace. Netanyahu had railed against the government for putting Israeli lives at risk. He had campaigned on a simple theme, Jews versus Arabs—as discussed with Wirthlin in the summer of 1995—and he had won.

Israelis, meanwhile, were unsettled by the new tenor of their politics. Americans had a long history of "going negative," dating back to the nasty Jefferson-Adams race of 1800. But Israelis felt that they had suddenly caught up with, if not surpassed, a kind of U.S. political discourse that they had once watched with disdain. There was concern, too, about the malign influence of television. Uri Dromi, who handled press and public affairs for Rabin until his assassination and then for Peres during the election campaign of 1996, looked back on it all with regret: "TV makes the discourse shallow. Politics has shifted focus from ideology to appearances to sound bites to simple messages." David Ben-Gurion, the first prime minister of Israel, he said, would not have lasted a second on television. The guy was short. His hair was terrible. His voice was squeaky. Yet look at the things he accomplished.

But in 1996, Israel, a country already riven by religious, ethnic, and sectarian differences, was becoming more polarized—and intentionally so. Netanyahu had followed the advice he had gotten from both Wirthlin and Finkelstein to focus on the Jewish vote, wooing the Orthodox where possible and, more important, striking an anti-Arab pose. This was the application in Israel of an established electoral theory in the United States. "You start with your base and you expand your base," says Wirthlin, recalling from his home in Utah the work he did in Israel in the 1980s and 1990s. "Frequently, people think it is logical to go where you are not strong," but, Wirthlin says, that's wrong: "You start with your base." Apathy is the most virulent enemy of electoral success. If Netanyahu could harness the Orthodox Jewish vote, so Wirthlin and Finkelstein calculated, he would be signing up a bankable constituency—a group of people who not only support him but bother to vote. It was a strategy he followed to full effect. Peres won 90 percent of the Arab Israeli vote, but Netanyahu won 55 percent of the Jewish vote.

The election was another case study in how personality contests clip the wings of the party. The first direct election of the prime minister in Israel in 1996 was a battle between the character of Peres and that of Netanyahu. The party platform was barely heard. And Israeli voters abandoned the two main parties: Labor got 34 seats, Likud got 32—i.e., 66 of the 120 seats in the Knesset; by comparison, the two parties controlled 76 seats four years earlier and 79 four years before that. This was largely the result of split-ticket voting: when it came to electing members of the Knesset, people checked the box for Netanyahu for prime minister but not for his Likud Party. Across the Israeli commentariat there was disbelief at Peres's loss and displeasure at the nature of the election: Israel represented an experiment with Americanization, having embraced not just political techniques but also the format of the election. Israelis feared that the caliber of their national debate was worse for it.

That said, the next election was so infused with American input that it made 1996 look organic. When Ehud Barak took over the reins of his party and readied Labor to challenge Netanyahu in 1999, he had no qualms about looking abroad for help.

Barak originally wanted to get the British in. He asked Tony Blair, then flush from winning the 1997 general election in the United Kingdom, to send over Peter Mandelson, the prime minister's confidant, hailed as the architect of the New Labour revolution. But Blair preferred to keep Mandelson, for the time being, in his cabinet. Instead, he put Barak in touch with Philip Gould, who had been instrumental in killing the "Loony Left" fringe, pushing the Labour Party into the center, and reassuring British voters that a Blair government would not jeopardize their economic future. Gould's involvement in Israel, though, did not last long. He did not feel comfortable there, nor was he entirely confident in the candidate. Instead, he hooked Barak and the Israeli Labor party up with the Three Musketeers who had been so useful to Blair and Labour in Britain: James Carville, Bob Shrum, and Stan Greenberg. They were, in every way, an equal and opposite match for Finkelstein. They were showboats, as visible as Finkelstein was hidden. They were as devoutly Democratic as Finkelstein was unwaveringly Republican. And, like him, they were the hardy perennials of American campaigning.

Carville was a late starter in politics, already in his forties when he began advising candidates. He had not been that long out of a Baton Rouge, Louisiana, law firm when, in 1987, he got hired alongside Sawyer Miller to work on Wallace G. Wilkinson's seemingly pointless run for the

Kentucky governorship. That summer, he spent much of his time up at the firm's offices on East Sixtieth Street, working with Mandy Grunwald. Wilkinson won. It was one of the political upsets of the year, one that made Carville's name and burnished the reputation of Sawyer Miller.

Bob Shrum's dealings with David Sawyer had been brief. They had first worked together when Ted Kennedy ran for president in 1980. Sawyer was brought in to offer media advice; Shrum was Kennedy's press secretary and, more important, his speechwriter, one of the Democratic Party's most elegant and powerful modern writers. That's how he started in politics, writing for McGovern in 1972. And that was how he made his name, penning the rousing last lines of Kennedy's withdrawal from the presidential race in 1980. In the quarter of a century that followed, Shrum became a curious fixture in the back room of the Democratic Party. A political consultant with an enviable knack for getting Democrats elected to the Senate, he is also an inside-the-Beltway joke when it comes to *presidential* contests: he retired from political consultancy after John Kerry's defeat in 2004 with a win-loss record of zero for eight. However, his undimmed talent as a writer has meant that he still crafts and rewrites critical speeches for political friends, such as Britain's Gordon Brown. And it was his skills as a wordsmith that first took Shrum into international work: Sawyer called Shrum in 1981 and asked him to help write a few speeches for Shimon Peres.

Stan Greenberg, too, started out as a political professional working alongside David Sawyer. After a decade in academia, Greenberg set up his own political research firm in 1980, the year both he and Sawyer went to Connecticut to work on Christopher Dodd's campaign for the Senate. For Sawyer, the Dodd campaign was to prove deeply rewarding; the senator and the political consultant became friends, and Dodd, seen as an up-and-coming man in the 1980s, hooked Sawyer up with a number of other politicians campaigning for seats on Capitol Hill. For Greenberg, the Dodd campaign proved even more meaningful; he met his wife there: Rosa DeLauro, now the congresswoman representing the Third District in Connecticut, who was, at the time, Dodd's campaign manager. And on the back of Dodd's victory, Greenberg quickly became the pet pollster of the progressive left. In the mid-1980s he produced a seminal piece of research examining the attitudes of Reagan Democrats in Macomb County, Michigan, making the case that if they wanted power, Democrats needed to eschew the doctrinaire left and embrace populism. This became a credo for Bill Clinton and the Democrat modernizers, a shibboleth adopted by Tony Blair's New Labour, and a foundation stone for Third Way progressives around the world. Greenberg served as Clinton's pollster in 1992, and, stationed in the "war room" with Carville, he made his name—a reputation he has since traded on internationally, advancing the progressive cause and expanding his political research firm. In the decade following Bill Clinton's election, Greenberg helped steer center-left candidates in the Clinton mold to power, all the way from South Africa to the United Kingdom, Germany to Bolivia: Mandela and Blair, Schroeder and Gonzalo Sánchez de Lozada have been his clients. Greenberg's reach has been extraordinary. Polling is generally a fragmented, parochial business. Greenberg is a one-man multinational; like a cormorant, he pops up everywhere.

While Finkelstein slipped surreptitiously in and out of Israel, the Labor trio of Carville, Greenberg, and Shrum were as discreet as a fireworks display. They held a seminar on how to run a campaign. They gave interviews to Israeli TV. They hosted dinners for the Israeli press at their Tel Aviv hotel. The Barak campaign brought in a photographer to take a picture of Stan Greenberg eating falafel. When Barak appeared with his celebrity consulting trio in front of the cameras, he was sometimes upstaged.

Carville, Greenberg, and Shrum hosted their own press conference six months out from the election. Adam Nagourney, a political correspondent for *The New York Times,* reported on what seemed to him a "journalistic ambush" in Israel. The Israeli press went to work on the three visitors, men who intended to steer Israeli politics with barely any knowledge of the affairs of state. What did Carville think of Aryeh Deri? Well, he plainly didn't know who the man was. (At the time, Deri was the leader of an ultrareligious party, the third largest in Israel.) Bob Shrum intervened. "I don't think we pretend that we're somehow or other experts on Israel," he said. "We're here to help General Barak." Even that comment earned Shrum a put-down. Americans like to drape their candidates in titles, reminding voters of their man's record of public service. In Barak's case, the use of "General" was merely intended to reinforce recognition of his distinguished military record. But in Israel, a country where everyone does military service and which prides itself on its informality, they call their politicians by their first names—Ehud and Bibi. At the end of the TV interview, Haim Hecht, an Israeli journalist, turned to

Carville, Greenberg, and Shrum: "I'll take the chutzpah to give you advice, and I won't charge you for it: Drop the 'General' bit. It won't fly here."

A few years later, when he was working for John Kerry and traipsing between town-hall meetings in snowy New Hampshire, Bob Shrum explained what they had been trying to do for Labor in Israel. The chief priority was to blunt Netanyahu's criticism that Barak would be soft on terrorism. So they focused on Barak's military record, his reputation as an outstanding chief of staff of the Israeli Defense Forces, and his citations for valor. The stories of Barak's bravery on the field of battle personalized the argument about national security. Instead of being between a gun-shy left and a hawkish right, the contest was between a decorated general (Barak) and an ambitious politician (Netanyahu). The "soft on security" attack was neutralized and Labor was freed up to attack Netanyahu's government for failing the Israeli people where they were feeling it most, namely in their pockets. Unemployment, the cost of living, and the price of health care were up. These were issues that James Carville didn't need an interpreter to understand.

Shrum made sure that the election in 1999 was exactly what every challenger wants an election to be: a referendum on the incumbent. Sure enough, there was a fierce exchange of nasty slogans. Netanyahu, Labor charged, was "stuck in the Lebanon mud"—stuck on the economy, stuck on the peace process, stuck in the Knesset. Barak, as Netanyahu said again and again, was "weak." A carefully tailored campaign was launched to target the Israeli electorate voting bloc by voting bloc. Both sides ran elaborate get-out-the-vote operations. And yet, Barak's thumping victory was ultimately just a statement of Israeli frustration with Netanyahu. Both the economy and the peace process had stagnated, and Bibi was being held responsible.

The issues in Israeli politics are existential: borders, settlements, bombings. A fundamental debate in Israel between consolidationists and expansionists will determine the future of the state. In the meantime, it is a country where Harold Macmillan's view of what matters in politics—"Events, dear boy, events"—holds true. In 1996, Peres might have been carried into office by the murder of Rabin, but the bus bombings turned public opinion against him and made possible Netanyahu's win. In 1999, Netanyahu lost support on the right by giving back part of the historic

Land of Israel under the terms of the Hebron Accords and stoked the resurgence of Labor by failing to make any progress with the Palestinians.

Nonetheless, the increasingly American style of politics practiced in the 1990s did have an impact. The professionalization of the campaign seemed to detract from the importance of the election. Israelis became intrigued by the tactics—the short advertisements, the poll findings, the hiring of consultants, the television debate. Everyone started playing pundit. As a result, the whole election was demeaned. The press began treating it as a horse race, a piece of sporting entertainment. Politics, it was felt, had become a victim to the modern media.

It didn't help that Netanyahu and Barak were such profound disappointments. Yaron Ezrahi, a political scientist in Jerusalem, gave voice through the 1990s to the growing disgust with the new style of politics: "The question is whether by making the images that made the candidates win, they have also invested in their own destruction. The images are short-lived because of the uncontrollable 'facts' which negate them." Netanyahu, he points out, was brought down by the qualities that made him a candidate: he came to be seen as a skilled communicator but also a man bereft of substance. Likewise with Barak. So much was invested in his personality that the failures of his administration—to make peace, to revitalize the economy—came to be seen as fundamental flaws in the person of the prime minister.

The American presidential system—the direct election of the prime minister—lasted just three elections: 1996, 1999, and 2001. A month after he won a decisive victory over Barak in 2001, Ariel Sharon returned Israel to its old habit of voting for the party, not the prime minister, with the overwhelming support of the public. Israelis wanted less personality in their politics.

In 1999, James Carville was eating pasta on the Tel Aviv oceanfront when Stan Greenberg's polling numbers came in. They showed that Barak was set to clinch a first-round victory. Carville finished his plate and announced that he was "outta here." He would be back in his Virginia farmhouse in time to see Barak's victory count on TV. One thing that is true for all American political consultants, Democrat or Republican: they go home after the polls close.

Israel was one of the few places where American consultants brought back more than just a check and a tan. Certainly, they returned to the

United States well paid: the estimate was that the Carville, Greenberg, and Shrum trio got four hundred thousand dollars for their work in Israel. Wirthlin says he got considerably less, working more for ideological reasons than commercial ones. Finkelstein, too, is said not to have made much money. But Sawyer—and the political consultants who followed in his footsteps—launched a trade in political tactics and ideas that was by no means one-way. Israel's boisterous young democracy served as a hothouse for political ideas and techniques, a place where consultants learned lessons about wedge campaigning, religious sensibilities, and moral-values voters that could all be applied back in the United States.

They also reimported the occasional strategy. Just over five years after Ehud Barak won in Israel, John Kerry bounded through a thronging Fleet Center in Boston to address the Democratic National Convention. It was the evening of July 29, 2004. He clasped and hugged his way through the crowd, skipped up the steps, and addressed the frenzied party faithful as well as the millions watching at home on TV. "I'm John Kerry and I'm reporting for duty," he said, snapping out a crisp salute. He spoke of the American flag that "flew from the gun turret behind my head," when he was fighting in Vietnam. In the aftermath of September 11 and in the midst of the war on terrorism, he presented himself as a man who could fight for his country. It was a speech written by Bob Shrum, and a strategy that obviously echoed that of Shrum's previous client, Ehud Barak, in his bid for power in May 1999. Just as the Shrum team had sought to reassure Israelis that a Labor leader could be trusted with national security in Israel in 1999, the aim in 2004 was to neutralize the Democrats' image as the Mommy party, good at rocking the cradle but frightened of a fight. The method used with Barak was the same as the one with Kerry, namely to trumpet the military heroism of the party's candidate. Of course, it did not work: Kerry served four months on the battlefield in Vietnam; Barak was the most decorated soldier in the history of the state of Israel. It was one of the few occasions when Americans got a chance to see for themselves that politics doesn't always translate.

American political consultants also learned a little more in Israel about one of the most slippery questions hovering over their profession—when election campaigns matter and when they don't. They saw elections that were turning points in history, where there was an obvious gulf between the ideologies of the parties or the charisma of the candidates, and the campaign did not count for a lot. And they worked on elections where there was not much at stake in terms of ideas or much to distinguish the candidates, and the campaign really made a difference.

Years later, Philip Gould captured this distinction when he addressed the simple question: Do campaigns matter? Gould, the political adviser to Tony Blair who styled New Labour and who, years later, worked as an occasional collaborator with Scott Miller, came to see a distinction between substantive elections and contingent ones. Over a twenty-year period, he worked on five United Kingdom national elections and sat in on five presidential contests in the United States. A substantive election, Gould judged, is "one in which all the elements come together in what is effectively an unstoppable force. The flow of events; the tide of opinion; the stature of leadership; the modernity of the policies; the quality of campaigning, all fuse into one inexorable victory." Substantive victories happened in the United Kingdom in 1979, when Margaret Thatcher dispelled the left; in the United States in 1984, when Ronald Reagan won a conservative mandate; in the United States again in 1992, when Americans voted in a new generation of leadership in the form of Bill Clinton; and in Britain in 1997, when Tony Blair took a modernized Labour Party to power. The paradox of these elections was that the campaigning may have been brilliant but it was not decisive. Gould concluded: "When history is on the turn, campaigns embellish but do not normally decide the ultimate result." Contingent elections, on the other hand, have hinged on the campaigning. In 1988 in the United States, George H. W. Bush was not riding a historic tide, but his campaign destroyed Dukakis; in 1992 in Britain, the Conservatives might have lost but they sneaked through by ruthlessly exploiting public doubts about the dangers of a tax-and-spend Labour Party; both of George W. Bush's election victories were contingent on the campaigns—in 2000 and 2004, America did not coalesce around one man and his ideas. Good campaigning (and a Supreme Court ruling), rather than overwhelming ideas, were critical in propelling Bush to power.

In Israel, Sawyer Miller watched the substantive and the contingent unfold before their eyes: they saw foreign policy trump a good campaign in 1981, and the failure of an effective campaign—and the shortcomings of their candidate—costing them victory in 1984 and 1988. In the United States, this lesson was even more hard-won. Within days of the 1984 election, Sawyer and Miller looked back on their work for Mondale and knew it had been pointless. No campaign, however smart and slick, could have saved him. In 1988, on the other hand, when they worked for Michael Dukakis, their frustration was much more intense: it would prove to be an election that was winnable but was squandered by a mismanaged campaign.

IN ONE OTHER SENSE, David Sawyer's involvement in Israel marked another transition: the unraveling of his impossible marriage with Iris.

His wife had been instrumental in Sawyer's personal transformation from failed actor to successful political consultant. She reinforced his drive and, in the early days, added political judgment to his filmmaking instinct. But their relationship had operated like the subplot to a sitcom, a story line of screaming fits and mutual fascination and sulphuric mistrust and heady reconciliations that all played largely offscreen. On occasion, the relentless drama at home had burst violently into public view.

Joel McCleary remembers one evening coming back from the Café des Artistes as David Sawyer was holding forth on the injustices of trickle-down. It was 1982 and David and Scott had just cut an ad for the Democratic National Committee that showed champagne being poured into a pyramid of glasses, with barely a drop reaching the bottom—the tagline: "It's not fair, it's Republican." Sawyer was looking out of the window of their Lincoln Town Car on the way back uptown and, as they slowed in front of his apartment on East Sixty-sixth Street, he muttered sadly about the poverty in New York City, the people sleeping on the streets, and pointed to one man picking a jacket to wear out of the trash. McCleary recalls Sawyer's double take: "That's my jacket," Sawyer yelled. Not for the first time, Iris had tossed his clothes out of the apartment window and down onto Lexington Avenue. On another occasion, Scott Miller woke with a start at two in the morning at his weekend home in Amagansett to the sound of the phone ringing and then a tirade from an angry Iris, desperate to know where David had disappeared to. Even John Glenn once got the hair-dryer treatment when he inadvertently picked up the phone in David Sawyer's hotel suite and was treated to a hot, high-volume rant from Iris.

Sawyer had always been impatient. He would fly into a meeting in Colorado and, even before he went in to meet the prospective client, would stop at the secretary's desk and ask her to book him an early-evening flight back to New York. When he was in the city, he traveled everywhere by bike rather than taxi, because he could not bear being caught in a standstill in traffic. His restlessness applied to women, too. He was handsome and athletic, a man who loved sailing, skiing, and tennis. He appreciated serious music, was particularly fond of Beethoven and Bach, and his friends were cultivated, keen chess players, connoisseurs of fine wines and important figures in the New York art world. Throughout the 1970s, he had had a number of short-lived and discreet affairs. As he traveled back and forth to Israel in the early 1980s, the assumption in the New York office was that there was more to this than just his yearning for perpetual motion, but that he was avoiding his increasingly estranged wife and had struck up a relationship in Israel. This was true, but their final separation was prompted not because David strayed, but because Iris did.

On the night of February 22, 1981, David was in Israel and Iris was taking the evening flight from New York to Los Angeles. They had recently bought a house there, expensed through the company, to serve as the West Coast headquarters of what was still, in those days, D. H. Sawyer and Associates. Sitting next to her in first class on the American Airlines flight that night was Tom Kempner, an investment banker more widely known for being the husband of one of New York's most famous society hostesses and collectors of haute couture, Nan Kempner. (The Kempners owned a vast duplex apartment on the corner of Seventy-seventh Street and Fifth Avenue, where she became famous for hosting Sunday-night dinner parties with friends such as Nancy Reagan and Princess Diana.) Iris Sawyer and Tommy Kempner talked all night on the plane, and when they arrived in Los Angeles, he offered to drive her home. It was the beginning of an eight-year love affair. To begin with, it was a romance that, Iris Sawyer recalled years later, was so gloriously jet-set that "most of the relationship was conducted in the air."

As Iris began to spend more and more time with Tom Kempner, David Sawyer started taking a more serious interest in other women, in particular Nell Michel McFarland. In the intertwined world of the Upper East Side social set, she was the daughter of Clifford Michel, the multimillionaire investment banker who happened to be a partner of Tommy Kempner. She was also an acquaintance of Iris Sawyer's, which was how David got to meet her. And she was, like David, very unhappily married. Over a long courtship, Sawyer found himself falling more and more deeply in love with her. They would meet for lunch at the Hotel Meridien, and Sawyer would book a room upstairs for the rest of the day but felt too awkward to make his intentions known. For months, the room went unused.

In December 1984, David and Iris Sawyer divorced. By then, Iris Sawyer and Tom Kempner were becoming one of Park Avenue's best-known secrets. They were already three years into the relationship, which they marked on February 22 of each year by taking a special anniversary flight from New York to Los Angeles. Meanwhile Nell McFarland had found happiness in her affair with David Sawyer, a clandestine relationship that was common knowledge in the offices of Sawyer Miller—the two East Coast WASPs traveled together and booked into hotels under the improbable name of Mr. and Mrs. Rafael Hernandez.

The Israel election of 1981 marked, among other things, the beginning of the end of David and Iris Sawyer's marriage, but also the start of two relationships—Iris and Tommy's, and David and Nell's. Theirs were two extraordinary love stories that began with such glamour, relief, and joy. They were to become pathetic and cruel.

PART TWO

Lastly, see that your whole canvass [election campaign] is a fine show, brilliant, resplendent, and popular, with the utmost display and prestige; and also, if it can be managed at all, that there should be scandalous talk, in character, about the crimes, lusts and briberies of your competitors.

—Quintus Cicero,
Handbook for Electioneering, 63 B.C.

FIVE

"STAND UP AND FIGHT LIKE A WOMAN"

IN EARLY 1985, a few months after Sawyer Miller's exasperating stint with Walter Mondale ended in defeat, one of the firm's more successful clients stopped by the office on Fifty-fifth Street.

Daniel Patrick Moynihan, the New York senator, was probably Scott Miller's favorite politician, not least because he always wanted to talk about anything but his own political campaigns. Moynihan, who worked for three administrations and as U.S. ambassador to the United Nations, had started out as a sociologist. His early work had explored the idea of the American melting pot and ethnicity, then, later, the government's failure to deal with the African-American community and the breakdown of the family in America. Sawyer and Miller had worked for Moynihan on the fringes of his successful run for the Senate in 1976 and again in 1982, but they always felt as though they got more from him than he had from them.

On that spring evening, Moynihan was talking about what a remarkable job the Soviets had done in making Israel look like a pariah state, but, he said as an afterthought, "Russia is over."

It was the height of the cold war, and Leonid Brezhnev was in power. Scott had recently cut a TV spot for the the Democrats parodying Ronald Reagan, after he had caused brief alarm and no small embarrassment by joking about launching a nuclear strike on the Soviet Union. (Just before he began to give his weekly radio address in 1984, Reagan was asked to do a sound check and, for the fun of it, he said, "My fellow Americans, I'm pleased to tell you today that I've signed legislation that will outlaw Russia forever. We begin bombing in five minutes." He did not realize that the tape was rolling.) Miller's political ad had shown a pair of big, hairy hands holding a microphone, a glass of vodka on one side and a cigarette smoldering away on the other; a voice was heard in Russian counting down, then bursting into a deep, throaty laugh: "You can tell the Americans we've just let loose the nuclear warheads . . ."

Moynihan's conviction that Russia was on the brink of collapse was completely out of step with the conventional wisdom, and certainly the national apprehension, of the time. But Miller remembers Moynihan's point: "The world economy is going to be based on information. They can let information in and face political chaos. Or they can keep it out and face economic chaos. Russia is over."

This was not only a view of the world that Sawyer and Miller shared, but a vision that seemed to sum up their growing business.

David Sawyer and Scott Miller had earned a name for themselves as irrepressible advocates of a coming revolution, a world order transformed by modern communications. They chided fellow Democrats who liked to think of Ronald Reagan as a mummified matinee idol; they held the Gipper up as the herald of the new age, the whiz kid of the coming electronic democracy. They forecast that the media, which was already revolutionizing politics and business in the United States, would change the world. Television, they told anyone who would listen, would spread democracy, educate audiences, and determine the form and idiom of politics. In their pitches to potential clients, they used the same lines again and again: "It won't be the threat of Star Wars or the Peacekeeper missile that brings down the Soviet Union's despotism, it will be Ted Turner and J. R. Ewing. Electronic communications democratize like nothing before in history. Give us choices; we want more. Give us information; we want more. Give us dialogue; we want more." At a time of great uncertainty, as multichannel TV sapped official authority and accelerated the pace of politics, Sawyer and Miller offered something that was both revolutionary and reassuring: clarity of political understanding and skill at image-making.

Soon they were hauling in business. In the 1984 election cycle, they had worked on more than a dozen Senate, congressional, and gubernatorial races across the United States as well as the presidential race. There was regular work coming in from Costa Rica, the Dominican Republic, Puerto Rico, and Israel, and a growing roster of clients in Greece, Spain, Argentina, and Brazil. Sawyer redesigned the Midtown offices to look like a cross between an editing suite and the headquarters of a Hollywood talent agency, with banks of television screens, glass-walled meeting rooms, and consultants positioned behind big black desks. And he and Miller sat there, promising that the modern media would be the handmaiden to a democratic revolution in a far-off land. They just didn't know where.

ON NOVEMBER 3, 1985, David Sawyer was at home watching political talk shows as he did every Sunday.

Ferdinand Marcos, by then an unsteady and puffy version of the charismatic, handsome president that the people of the Philippines had elected twenty years earlier, was appearing before a panel of journalists on *This Week with David Brinkley*:

"President Marcos, there is a perception here that your problems derive from the fact that your mandate is gone, whatever it once was . . ." George Will, the young conservative columnist, began. "And there are some people here who wonder if it is not possible and if you would not be willing to move up the election date, the better to renew your mandate soon, say, within the next eight months or so. Is that possible, that you could have an election earlier than scheduled?"

Marcos answered: "Well, I understand the opposition has been asking for an election. In answer to their request I announce that I am ready to call a snap election perhaps earlier than eight months, perhaps in three months or less than that . . ."

Sam Donaldson, ABC's White House correspondent, seemed to be taken by surprise:

"Are there any catches, Mr. President?"

"I'm ready. I'm ready. I'm ready," said Marcos.

"Mr. President, are there any catches?" Donaldson asked again. "Can anyone run in this election? If Corazon Aquino wants to run, if Senator Laurel wants to run? Everyone can run?"

"Oh yes," Marcos said. "Anyone."

After the commercial break, Donaldson, pumped up as only a journalist can be when news breaks around him, resumed: "Okay. My question is, since the allegation against you is that you have conducted massive voting fraud in the past, if you hold elections in sixty days or so, will you allow outside observers into the Philippines to oversee the elections to make certain they're fair?"

"You are all invited to come," said Marcos, "and we will invite members of the American Congress to please come and just see what is happening here."

None of it was as impromptu as it looked. Marcos had been primed to call a snap election. In fact, he had been advised to do it on Brinkley's show on a Sunday morning by Paul Laxalt, a Republican senator and the Reagan White House's informal go-between with Manila. Laxalt had suggested to Marcos that such a dramatic flourish of his democratic credentials on political TV would go down well with Americans. As Raymond Bonner notes in *Waltzing with a Dictator*, his chronicle of America's long, tawdry relationship with Marcos, the fact that the Filipino president took up the suggestion says much about Marcos's intentions: "It was not an election for Filipinos; it was an election for Americans, specifically for the American critics of his regime." It was also the beginning of the People Power revolution—the peaceful uprising of millions in Manila who swept Marcos and his extravagant wife, Imelda, from power and became the model for a wave of democratic revolutions in Eastern Europe, Latin America, and Asia—and it began, fittingly enough, on an American television show.

For the better part of twenty years, Ferdinand and Imelda had charmed, seduced, and wooed Washington—the words used in the press reports and diplomatic communiqués to describe the Marcoses' relationship with the White House tend to be faintly sexual because there was something extremely intimate, sometimes coquettish, about the way they conducted foreign policy. Imelda Marcos redecorated the Malacañang Palace in Manila to host the Nixons, and insisted on a special dessert to honor the president's wife—Délice Patricia. When she came to Washington, Imelda demanded some private time with Nixon and, despite the protests of the State Department and the presidential schedulers, she got it. The Marcoses were the Fred and Ginger of U.S. foreign policy, binding a bilateral relationship on the dance floor: Ferdinand and Imelda two-stepped Lady Bird and Lyndon, Pat and Richard, Nancy and Ronnie. In order for there to be cordial relations between the United States and the Philippines, Imelda Marcos seemed to demand effusive compliments on her beauty, and from a succession of Americans—Lyndon B. Johnson, Richard M. Nixon, Ronald Reagan, and even that recalcitrant flirt Henry Kissinger—and she got them.

Even after Marcos declared martial law in 1972, the friendships he so assiduously forged with America's presidents helped ensure U.S. support for the Filipino regime. It helped, too, that the United States had other reasons for supporting the Marcos leadership. America was embroiled in Vietnam, and it wanted Asian allies. (The "if you can't be with the one you love, love the one you're with" rule to U.S. foreign policy applied here: China was "lost," Southeast Asia, in the thrall of left-leaning nationalist dictators, Korea broken in two, and Japan entirely self-involved.) There was also a fear of Communists taking control of the islands of the Philippines, an archipelago that was home to U.S. military bases. Marcos was seen as a bulwark against the Filipino Communists, the New People's Army. The United States also had historical reasons for overlooking Marcos's creeping authoritarianism: the Philippines was a former U.S. colony, a country America liked to consider a showcase of democracy in Asia. It required an unpalatable piece of revisionism for Americans to consider that they, like so many other colonists, had bequeathed to their subjects a weak, infant democracy susceptible to overthrow by a canny dictator.

By the 1980s, though, Marcos had strained even the most forgiving of his friendships in Washington. On the back of his martial powers, he had ushered in what he promised would be a "New Society." It proved to be a case study in crony capitalism and constitutional dictatorship. He stripped businessmen and landowners of their assets and handed them out to his family and the friends of his regime. He suffocated press freedoms, outlawing all media outlets other than the state press. He sought a democratic veneer for his rule, holding elections in 1978 that were riddled with reports of fraud and cheating. In the next national elections, in 1981, the opposition simply refused to run. His chief opponent, Benigno "Ninoy" Aquino, was imprisoned for eight years and then ushered into exile.

For the Filipinos, a devout people who see the hand of the Virgin Mary in their history, there was something providential about the life of Ninoy Aquino. He was born into a wealthy, well-heeled family and then broke all the records for political precociousness: he was the country's youngest-ever municipal mayor at twenty-two, the youngest-ever vice-governor at twenty-seven, the youngest-ever senator at thirty-four. He was, in many ways, much the same breed as Marcos, an exceptional man who seemed predestined from youth to lead his country. He was also a vicious critic of Mr. and Mrs. Marcos. In a speech savaging the "Pantheon to Imelda," Ninoy dubbed the Cultural Center Imelda had lavished

$8 million upon and used to entertain then-Governor Ronald Reagan as a "monument to shame." Marcos responded by calling Aquino a "congenital liar." When martial law was declared in 1972, Aquino was locked up on charges of murder and subversion. He was given a furlough in 1980 to be treated for heart disease.

Aquino knew that a return to Manila could be dangerous. At a speech before the Asia Society in New York in 1980, he said, "I have asked myself many times: Is the Filipino worth suffering or even dying for? Is he not a coward who would readily yield to any colonizer, be he foreign or home-grown? Is a Filipino more comfortable under an authoritarian leader because he does not want to be burdened with the freedom of choice? Is he unprepared or, worse, ill-suited for presidential or parliamentary democracy? I carefully weighed the virtues and the faults of the Filipino and I have come to the conclusion that he is worth dying for." Aquino received several warnings that he would be killed on arrival if he stepped back on Filipino soil. Nonetheless, in 1983, he decided to go back to Manila. On his journey back to the Philippines, he stopped in Los Angeles and stayed at the Ambassador Hotel, and went down to where Bobby Kennedy had been assassinated to examine the shape of his murdered body, etched where it had fallen on the floor of the hotel kitchen.

Minutes after landing at Manila International Airport, Benigno "Ninoy" Aquino was shot in the head. His body was splayed on the tarmac in full view of the world press. It was as if he had foreseen his assassination, framing his death as the ultimate validation of his case against the regime in Manila, his murder the killer point in his argument with Marcos.

He became an instant martyr; his murder seemed a brazen statement of defiance by the Marcos government. The Filipino president himself denied any personal or government involvement in the killing and set up an investigation. But the assassination lit a fire under the Filipino protest movement, prompting an estimated two million people to come out onto the streets. Corazon Aquino would later tell a joint session of the U.S. Congress: "His death was my country's resurrection." It also shamed Marcos's dwindling band of supporters in Washington. The Filipino president had lost the support of powerful Republicans in Congress, senior diplomats at the State Department, and most of the top brass at the Pentagon; he was barely hanging on to his most precious remaining backers, namely President Ronald Reagan and his national security team.

By the time Marcos appeared on the Brinkley show at the end of

1985, he had a PR problem in America, not to mention at home, and he knew it.

At the suggestion of a sympathetic Republican in Washington, he hired Black, Manafort and Stone, a political consulting group closely tied to the Reagan White House. Paul Manafort, who managed the account, checked with Reagan's staff to ensure that the Marcos job would not compromise the firm's relationship with the president. He got the White House's approval to get involved. Imelda Marcos personally delivered the first check of $60,000 for a contract reported to be worth $950,000 for a year's services. And then Manafort set out to enlist sympathetic conservative journalists—Bob Novak, John McLaughlin, and Fred Barnes—to come out to the Philippines to help foster Marcos's image as a bulwark against the Communists.

In the years to come, Black, Manafort—and its offspring—would come to represent the Republican equivalent of Sawyer Miller. They were central to a right-wing lineage of American political consultants who worked overseas. Indeed, the two-party dynamic that is the overlay for all political arguments in the United States quickly began to cast its shadow over American political work abroad. In the Philippines, a bunch of pretty incorruptible Republicans at Black, Manafort were soon squaring off against the gang of staunch Democrats at Sawyer Miller, playing out partisan rivalries on foreign fields: Black, Manafort in the fight against communism; Sawyer Miller in the struggle for freedom.

The Filipinos still remembered a recent experience of meddlesome Americans—specifically, men from the Central Intelligence Agency playing God. In the 1950s and the early 1960s, the CIA pulled the strings in Filipino politics. The United States was fearful that corrupt politicians and presidents might allow the Huks, the burgeoning rebel movement, to gather momentum. They preferred to have their own people in place to keep the Huks in check. In 1953, Col. Ed Lansdale, a CIA officer, more or less stage-managed Ramon Magsaysay's victory. Lansdale took a suitcase full of $1 million in cash to fund the campaign and then squeezed the big American corporations in Manila for more. He directed Magsaysay's spending, scripted his speeches, and, when that wasn't enough, allegedly drugged President Elpidio Quirino's drink just before he was about to give a speech. (Lansdale went on to Vietnam and became the inspiration for Graham Greene's "quiet American," Alden Pyle.)

In 1958, the CIA sent out another man, Joseph B. Smith, to scout for a reliable Filipino president after the United States lost confidence in Magsaysay's successor. Smith funneled money into the campaign of Diosdado Macapagal and paid a rising challenger to quit the race. When Macapagal came back after one campaign stop, where he had delivered a speech that had been neither written nor vetted by Smith, the American is alleged to have punched the Filipino candidate in fury. Years later, Smith explained CIA involvement to Stanley Karnow, whose book *In Our Image* is one of the lasting works on U.S. policy in the Philippines: "It was the American century, and we Americans had been chosen to do good in the world. We had a unique relationship with the Filipinos, special obligations toward them. The CIA was on the side of the angels, there's no doubt about it. We hoped to bring a political, economic, and social revolution to the Philippines, break up the old oligarchy and promote genuine democracy."

Then, in 1969, came Joe Napolitan, fresh from his historic near-miss on Hubert Humphrey's presidential campaign and a few years from running into a young David Sawyer on the campaign trail in Venezuela. After the chaotic Democratic convention of 1968, Napolitan and his team of scriptwriters, media buyers, and producers had almost pulled off one of the great election upsets of the twentieth century. Humphrey scraped back from twelve points behind to come within seven tenths of winning the White House. Nixon, of course, moved into the Oval Office, but Napolitan had made his name. In early 1969, Imelda's brother Benjamin Romualdez got in touch. Over lunch at the Metropolitan Club in New York, he signed up to help Marcos become the first Filipino president to be reelected to a second term. Napolitan developed some quality TV spots and walked away handsomely paid—according to industry lore, Bob Squier, Napolitan's collaborator in the Philippines, was paid in briefcases of cash. (Squier has since died; Napolitan would neither confirm nor deny.) At any rate, Napolitan says, "Marcos was always a bullshit campaign. There was no way he was going to lose that election." That, certainly, is true. Encouraged by the Americans, Marcos fought dirty. He cast aspersions on his opponent's contacts with the Japanese during the war, bought votes wholesale, outspent his challenger four thousand to one, and trounced the opposition: when the fraudulently skewed tally came in, Marcos had won nearly 62 percent of the vote, Sergio Osmeña, Jr., 38 percent.

In the years since Napolitan went to Manila and became, by his own account, the first American professional political consultant to work an election abroad, the Americans who got involved in Filipino politics tended to arrive from Manhattan rather than Langley. They came not as operatives of the U.S. government but as consultants from American political firms. The fact that these businesses trod in the footsteps of the Agency always aroused suspicion. Sawyer Miller, in particular, operated in places where Washington had strategic stakes: Panama, South Korea, Greece, Colombia. While the original founders of the business—a cinema verité filmmaker, a Coca-Cola account executive from Madison Avenue, and an Israeli psychologist who knew a lot about American attitudes toward oral hygiene—were not hooked into the Washington intelligence community, there would be suspicions, as the firm grew, that some of the staff working on international accounts did, at the very least, have friends at the Agency. In their lives before and after Sawyer Miller, at least two people have done jobs for the U.S. intelligence services. And on one occasion, the firm discovered after the fact that it had worked on a CIA project: Scott Miller went to assist Napolitan on a polling project in Sudan; Joel McCleary discovered years later that the project was funded by U.S. intelligence.

For all that, Sawyer Miller was not a front for the CIA. David Sawyer's business was built in the shadow of Wall Street, not the Capitol; it was set up to serve Mammon, not Uncle Sam; it consisted of antiestablishment egotists who thought of themselves as their own masters, not the types to take instructions; its staff was drawn to the international campaign trail by the romantic adventure of it, not because of some surreptitious patriotic purpose; and it boasted only one person who spoke any language other than English. More to the point, if the CIA wanted to get a steer on what the men from Sawyer Miller were up to, they didn't need to put them on the payroll; they just had to give them a call. As the firm spread internationally, it increasingly traded on its relationships in Washington, and the men from Sawyer Miller were eager to be on first-name terms with people inside the National Security Council, the Pentagon, and the Agency. If Sawyer Miller men met staff from the intelligence services, they did not meet in underground parking lots, but over porterhouse steaks in the restaurants off Pennsylvania Avenue.

In the 1980s, American involvement in Filipino politics changed. It was no longer just diplomats and agents pulling the strings, but Black, Manafort, and Stone and Sawyer Miller: American professionals driven by ideology, opportunity, and the hope that they could make an international business out of foreign politics.

THE MAN who brought Sawyer Miller into the Philippines was Robert Trent Jones, Jr., an unlikely stagehand to a revolution. His father was one of the greatest golfers and, without rival, the greatest golf course designer of the twentieth century. And Jones had gone into the family business. A world-class golfer in his own right, he inherited his father's mantle as the most celebrated course designer of his generation. He has been in the vanguard of golf's conquest of the world, building courses from Japan to Australia, California to Malaysia. He was sent to Russia in the early 1970s to discuss with Leonid Brezhnev building a Moscow country club; it took twenty years to complete, but at its opening he declared the cold war over. "The reds," he said, "are on the greens." If one man can, Jones has personified the successful side of globalization. Carried by the triumph of free markets and free men, he has built new coastal links and country clubs around the world. In the 1960s, he had gone to the Philippines to build a course for the Cojuangco family—Aquino's father. He had met Ninoy, who reminded him of the young Kennedys. They had been friends ever since. After the Aquinos came to the United States so Ninoy could have heart surgery, Jones helped settle him into a berth at Harvard and a home in the well-heeled Boston suburb of Chestnut Hill. In 1983, when Aquino decided to go back to the Philippines, Jones warned him against it—he had been passed word that Marcos's assassins were waiting. After the murder of Aquino, Jones pledged to Cory and her brother Jose "Peping" Cojuangco to help overthrow Marcos. So Robert Trent Jones, Jr., joined the People Power revolution for personal reasons. "I was pissed that they killed my friend; it was that simple. Every once in a while, like a Quaker, you get called." Jones was well placed to sway policy: powerful men play golf.

When Marcos called the snap election, Jones and Peping realized they would need some professional help. Jones called Jimmy Carter, who in turn suggested that he get in touch with David Sawyer. The former president had relied heavily on Joel McCleary in his dealings with Panama, and he recommended Sawyer Miller as one of the very few firms he considered both politically effective at home and savvy overseas.

Jones remembers going up to New York with Peping Cojuangco to meet Sawyer. They were impressed by him but shocked by his proposed fee. "We can't afford that," said Peping, who explained that the Aquino campaign had very little money. "We have to recycle the confetti." Sawyer agreed to waive his fee; Jones offered to cover expenses, which came to about five thousand dollars. It was just before Christmas 1985. Jones was happy to pay the money.

For, by then, the anti-Marcos campaign led by Corazon Aquino had a PR problem of its own.

Cory, as she was known, was the ideal candidate in all respects but one. She had endured her husband's eight-year imprisonment and then become his noble widow, the embodiment of stoic suffering at the hands of the Marcos regime. She was a convent-educated girl, a devout Catholic in a God-fearing country. She was, apparently, without personal ambition. Vicente Paterno, a Filipino businessman, told a senior opposition figure in 1984 that it had to be Mrs. Aquino. As he put it years later in *People Power*, an eyewitness history of the revolution, "If somebody else other than Cory had been the candidate, if it had been an old politician, I'm not sure if I would have been as enthusiastic . . . the president we needed was someone who did not want to be president. We needed a person who would not have reelection in his mind."

For a firm like Sawyer Miller, she was almost too good to be true, for she was the ultimate anti-politician in a country entirely disgusted with its politics. The Sawyer Miller men had noticed in U.S. campaigns that Americans tended to pigeonhole politicians as either men of moral principle or people with political savvy. And, time after time, they looked to their candidates to be moral and despised them for being political. Cory Aquino did not initially seem interested in the election, knowing full well from her husband how dirty politics can be. She sensed that Marcos's successor was doomed to disappoint. But she came under enormous pressure to run from her mother-in-law, the opposition leadership, and the Church. As remembered in *People Power*, Cardinal Sin, the Archbishop of Manila, and one of the most influential men in the Philippines, later recalled that Mrs. Aquino came to him and said:

"Cardinal, Ninoy is inspiring me. It seems that he is talking to me, telling me that I should run."

"When did you have that inspiration?" I asked.

"When I was praying at the Pink Sisters' Convent in Hemady."

"All right," I said. "Pray more. It is not a joke to go against Marcos."

One day, she came here and said: "All right, I will run. I have decided. My decision was made on December 8." That was the closing day of the Marian Year. She was on a retreat at the Pink Sisters' Convent. "I am now sure to run. It is God's will," she said.

"All right, kneel down," I said. "I will bless you. You are going to be president. You are the Joan of Arc." At that moment I thought God answered the prayers of our people. He chooses weaklings. And why weaklings? Why a weak woman? . . . That is how the Lord confounds the strong.

A spiritual people and a popular revolution make for purple memories, and it is impossible to know how accurate such recollections are. But Cory fit the bill. She was the image of the Christian liberator, a Filipino Joan.

The only problem was that she had no experience in the real world of politics. She was, by her own description, "just a housewife," with no understanding of how to run a country. Marcos asked of Cory, "What qualifications does she have except that her husband was killed?" When *The New York Times* paid her a visit, she told them, in effect, that she had none.

"What on earth do I know about being president?" she told the newspaper in what was arguably the most humiliating, self-denying interview ever given to them by a presidential hopeful. She said she didn't have a government program in mind; there were two issues still dividing the opposition she now led, but she couldn't remember one of them; she said she wanted to remove the U.S. military bases; she said she wanted to start negotiations with the NPA, the communist rebels. "Marcos is probably thinking, 'Oh gosh, what is this crazy woman talking about?' " she said. In fact, that's what *The New York Times* and America's foreign policy establishment thought. The newspaper had sent its most senior delegation to meet her: Abe Rosenthal, the newspaper's executive editor; Warren Hoge, the foreign editor; and Seth Mydans, the correspondent covering the Philippines. Hoge still remembers being "appalled" at Aquino's unpreparedness for government. Rosenthal, too, was flabbergasted. He made a point of having Aquino's comments run at length on the front page of the paper. Marcos had the story reprinted and plastered across the cities of the Philippines. Suddenly, the elections—just ten weeks away—looked set to turn not on Marcos's record of authoritarianism but on Aquino's apparent incompetence.

The men from Sawyer Miller were drafted in the days after *The New York Times* fiasco. The senior partners—David Sawyer, Scott Miller, and Joel McCleary—all became involved in the Cory Aquino campaign. But they kept their distance, working from New York. Mrs. Aquino was suspicious of the Americans. The Aquino campaign wanted to maintain its image as a spontaneous popular uprising. They had told their supporters that there were no Americans involved. McCleary, who by then had nearly five years' experience working international campaigns, was the obvious man to send to Manila. But the broad-shouldered, foghorn-voiced American was hardly the inconspicuous puppeteer the friends of Cory Aquino were looking for. More to the point, McCleary had been told by Republican friends in intelligence circles in Washington that Marcos would have him killed if he came to the Philippines. (" 'You know, Joel, they might not want to do it on the tarmac, but . . .' " McCleary recalled the tipoff with one of his dark laughs.) So it was decided that the man they put on the ground should be Mark Malloch Brown, a journalist who stood at a towering six feet and four inches and spoke with a velvety English accent.

Unbeknownst either to them or to him at the time, Malloch Brown would become the driving force behind Sawyer Miller's global expansion for the next five years. His work in the Philippines would give the firm a worldwide reputation for helping Davids aim their slingshots at Goliaths. And it would propel Malloch Brown into a career as "consigliere" to some of the most powerful men in world affairs: George Soros, the busy billionaire philanthropist; James Wolfensohn, the president of the World Bank; and Kofi Annan, the secretary-general of the United Nations.

Back in 1985, though, Malloch Brown was still an unkempt reporter with next to no experience of the campaign trail. He had worked for the United Nations and was now working for *The Economist,* having established a small offshoot of the magazine that focused on poverty, *The Economist Development Report.* He had been an unsuccessful candidate for a seat in the House of Commons, an attempt at a political career that stalled even before it began: he was working in Geneva at the time for Sadruddin Aga Khan, and the SDP, a new center-left party, did not want to allow a commuter from Switzerland to stand in their name. But it was through his work for the Aga Khan, who was organizing a meeting on nuclear disarmament, that Malloch Brown came into contact with the men from Sawyer Miller.

The firm had gotten involved with the nuclear disarmament issue through Maria Becket, a friend of David Sawyer's and one of those people who, over the years, served as a matchmaker for the firm, looking out for political clients and potential recruits. She had put some election work Sawyer's way in Greece in the early 1980s. And during the preparation for the nuclear disarmament meeting in Geneva in 1985, she held a dinner in London where she introduced Mark Malloch Brown to the men from Sawyer Miller. To him, Sawyer, Miller, and McCleary did a magnificent line in global positioning and issue management, even though it seemed that they did not actually know many journalists. To them, Malloch Brown obviously had brilliant tactical instincts and a similar set of liberal values, even if he was not quite as polished as the New York consultants. On again and off again throughout 1985, Sawyer and McCleary tried to draft Malloch Brown into the firm. When the Philippines job came along and it was clear the Aquino campaign did not want an American, Malloch Brown seemed to them the ideal man to put on the ground, and an election campaign against a corrupt dictator was a project he could not refuse. Robert Trent Jones, Jr., discreetly checked Malloch Brown out, calling the editor of *The Economist*, Andrew Knight. "He's very intelligent, but a little more liberal than us," Knight told him. This as good as sealed it for Jones, a liberal Democrat who had made his home in the beautiful hills around San Francisco.

Sawyer Miller did not immediately offer Malloch Brown a job: he was not sure he wanted one, and they did not want someone on their staff in the Philippines. But they gave him a brown paper envelope with five hundred dollars in it and told him to get himself a proper wardrobe. He went to a tailor in London's Burlington Arcade, and bought himself his first made-to-measure worsted woolen suit: "I was transformed overnight, from disheveled journalist to smooth consultant." The suit was, of course, entirely unsuitable for the thick heat of Manila.

THE PHILIPPINES was a dangerous place for the foreign friends of Cory Aquino in the weeks before the 1986 election. When Robert Trent Jones, Jr., stepped off the plane at Manila International Airport and into a waiting car, he found a bodyguard's AK-47 slung on the seat of the limousine. Jones had been warned that Marcos wanted him dead, but he remembers that he declined the gun. "You got a seven-iron back here?" he said, jokingly, to Peping. "I'd be much better with a seven-iron."

Jones had come from California, via Honolulu, to present Mark Malloch Brown to Aquino. She was speaking at a huge rally in Iloilo, a flat corner of Panay Island that sits right in the middle of the Philippine archipelago. After the chaos of Cory's speech to the vast crowd and the jostling in tiny vans through the streets of Iloilo, they went for dinner at the home of a local grandee. Standing in the kitchen, Jones introduced the man from Sawyer Miller; Aquino politely reminded him that she would have no Americans on her campaign. "That's why I've brought you a Brit," Jones said, smiling. Cory and her supporters wanted a campaign by the people for the people, not one stage-managed by U.S. professionals. Malloch Brown's credentials allowed them, more or less, to maintain that truth. He came to the Philippines as a "journalist," still officially registered as such for *The Economist.* (With a worldly smile, Malloch Brown looked back years later and said, "I was probably a little guilty of not complete clarity.") Aquino made clear that Sawyer Miller's job was to manage the American PR end of the Filipino election campaign following the *New York Times* debacle. It just so happened that the question those pesky hacks from *The New York Times* were asking—namely, does Cory Aquino have what it takes to run the Philippines?—was exactly the one that tens of millions of Filipinos were asking themselves.

To this day, the Aquino camp generally belittles the role of Sawyer Miller. The good reason for this is that Filipinos are proud of the 1986 revolution and, understandably, resentful of suggestions that Marcos was swept from power by anything other than the undiluted will of the Filipino people. More than that, there is often something religious in the Filipino telling of Marcos's downfall. In his historical account, Francisco S. Tatad, a devout Christian who became a member of the Filipino senate, wrote: "Ranged against this [Aquino-Laurel] ticket was Marcos's well-oiled machine. It counted on men, money, the media, a historic vote, and 20 years of presidential experience. Aquino had nothing. No campaign organization worth its name, no campaign manager to the very end, no spokesman until a couple of days before the elections, no personal contact with most of the local leaders, none of Marcos's unlimited resources, no experience." The force that swept Marcos from power was, undoubt-edly, the Filipino people. But behind the scenes there was political art to it as well.

Malloch Brown first went to work on redressing the damage Cory Aquino had inflicted upon herself in her interview with *The New York Times*. The candidate quickly made clear that she would not negotiate with Communists. She reversed her position on the removal of the U.S. military bases. In mid-December, she may have described herself as a "housewife" and a "crazy woman," but by the beginning of January she had changed her tone: "Some who support my candidacy say that if I am elected, my role will be that of Mother of the Nation. I am honored by that title, but I am campaigning to be president of our country. It is in that capacity that I shall serve. And as president, I assure you, I shall lead. If elected, I will remain a mother to my children, but I intend to be a chief executive of this nation. And for the male chauvinists in the audience, I intend as well to be the commander in chief of the Armed Forces of the Philippines."

Malloch Brown was living on the fringes of the press corps, picking up the scuttlebutt. He came to see the campaign in simple binary terms, knocking Marcos down and building Cory up. That meant going after Marcos on his corruption, his health, his war record, and his management of the economy; it meant neutralizing the question of Cory's competence. Twenty years later, Malloch Brown sat in his office on the thirty-eighth floor of the United Nations building and said that Cory had to be pushed to go negative, but that the decision to get more aggressive, dirtier, had been quite deliberate: "We set out to make it about Marcos. It was a very negative campaign. Marcos didn't really deserve his war medals. Marcos said Cory is weak, she'll let in the Communists. We'd say Marcos is cor-rupt, he will let in the Communists."

Just after Marcos made his sudden call for elections, Alfred W. McCoy, then a professor at the University of New South Wales, chose to release a story he had been sitting on for years. McCoy, a student of Southeast Asian history, had lived in the Philippines for many years. He had inter-viewed a number of priests who claimed to have been imprisoned and deported by the Marcos family during the war. As part of his research, he had gone to the States, where he discovered evidence that the Filipino president's claims to an array of war medals were fabricated. Marcos, who had built his early political career on claims of wartime heroism, was held up as a fraud.

Malloch Brown played the fake medals furor for all it was worth. He knew that *The New York Times* was poised to run the piece, but understood they would be held off over the weekend while they checked facts. In the meantime, he wrote Cory a speech in which she railed against Marcos for refusing to debate, for declining to come down to the Luneta Park and make his case against her before the people. She taunted him, saying that he had been honored by the Filipino and U.S. military, that he had so many medals, that he was supposed to be a man of courage, and yet, "why don't you debate me, why don't you stand up like a woman and debate me." It was incendiary enough, but the following morning it really caught fire: *The New York Times* claimed Marcos was a phony, a man who had faked his medals and falsified tales of derring-do on the battlefield. With his bravery under scrutiny, it suddenly seemed to make sense why Marcos would not debate Cory Aquino, why he would not "stand up and fight like a woman": he didn't have the courage he claimed to have.

Conveniently enough for Malloch Brown and the Aquino campaign, the allegations against Marcos were piling up in the American press. The *San Jose Mercury News* had run a series of articles in the summer of 1985 detailing Marcos's rogue use of state funds, his "hidden wealth." The TV networks got onto the story. Then *The Village Voice* started investigating Marcos's property investments in New York City. Imelda Marcos had paid $51 million for the Crown Building on Fifth Avenue in September 1981; she bought the Herald Center on Thirty-fourth Street and Broadway for $60 million in 1982. Not bad for the wife of a man on an official salary of $7,500 a year. Stephen Solarz, then a young congressman from New York and an energetic Marcos critic on Capitol Hill, decided to hold hearings, ensuring that the stories of the Marcoses' boundless corruption would run. "I held these hearings about his holdings in the United States, primarily with a view to contributing to his delegitimization in the Philippines," Solarz told me. "This would be played back over a megaphone in Manila." People like Mark Malloch Brown saw that it was.

The Philippines campaign was fought out in the American media. The U.S. press gave acres of space to the Philippines because it was a former colony, because a large number of Vietnam veterans had settled there, and because it was home to U.S. military bases. Marcos had his reasons for wanting U.S. airtime, namely to demonstrate his democratic credentials to his critics in Washington. Aquino simply had no choice. The Filipino press was state-controlled and under orders to ignore her. Malloch Brown stumbled upon—and then systemized—a simple but clever way of getting the Marcos press to run the Aquino message. Malloch Brown and his associates at Sawyer Miller called it "the backboard shot" and it worked like this: American journalism requires that when you run a negative story, you give the aggrieved side a chance to rebut the allegations. So they would feed a critical story on Marcos to a U.S. journalist. The reporter or the TV crew would then go to Marcos or his spokesman or one of his ministers. Once they had responded, the Filipino press would feel honor-bound to pick up on the comments made by the Marcos government. In order to put those comments in context, they would have to report the original allegations made against him by the Aquino campaign. It was a long round-trip, but it worked, time and again. "Our one access to daylight was the U.S. media and its knock on to the Filipino media," says Malloch Brown. For example, Marcos refused to debate Aquino, but when Ted Koppel interviewed her on ABC's *Nightline*, the Filipino president agreed to equal allotted time to make a counterargument. "It was," remembers Malloch Brown, "a huge, huge stitch-up."

Still, Aquino faced the same public perception threshold test any challenger to an incumbent has to cross—namely, convincing the public that she has the competence to handle the pressures of high office. It is what Bob Shrum, Sawyer's onetime colleague and longtime competitor, calls "the viable alternative threshold." For Cory, crossing it was not going to be easy. Rafael Salas, an old Marcos aide who had turned against the dictator and who was a friend of Malloch Brown's from his UN days, told him that his job in Manila would be, simply, "saving Cory from herself." This was a little unfair. Malloch Brown remembers being impressed by Aquino's subtle political savvy. He remembers going to a town in the south one day and sitting on the floor of a minibus. (She often asked him to sit on the floor of the van because, at six-four, he was awfully conspicuous sitting alongside his Filipino colleagues on the campaign. She wanted to make sure that, by Filipino standards, "a normal amount of me" could be seen through the window.) Thousands of people had come out to greet her. Still, she wasn't happy. She noticed the Chinese merchants' shops were all shuttered and barred, proof, as she saw it, that the moneyed class was not behind her. She was, says Malloch Brown, "an instinctively smart candidate": it was Aquino who saw the simple power of always dressing in yellow, and as more and more crowds came to her rallies dressed in yellow, too, the color became the national symbol of freedom: the Yellow Revolution.

Still, she also delivered her speeches in a monotone and bungled her answers in interviews. After sitting on the sidelines and watching her fall into one trap after another set by Bob Novak, Malloch Brown stepped in. He explained what an interview is for a politician: not an obligation to answer the question but an opportunity to get your message across. (As Henry Kissinger once put it to a group of journalists when he walked into a press conference: "Now, which of my answers do you have questions for?") Simple stuff, but "getting her to deliver this message was part of the job. Speaking succinctly and tightly did not come naturally to her." At the family's business headquarters in downtown Manila and at the old family estate Hacienda Luisita, Malloch Brown would coach Aquino, he, the badgering interviewer; she, sticking doggedly to a simple script. As with all Sawyer Miller campaigns, the message was distilled into something with bumper-sticker simplicity: This is a fight for democracy. Marcos is corrupt. It's time for a change.

The next step was encouraging a reluctant Mrs. Aquino to attack Marcos personally. She was, after all, a convent girl. Her family, the Cojuangcos, were part of the same elite political class as the Marcos family. She was not naturally inclined toward character assassination. Nevertheless, after Marcos said she was only "worth one bullet," Aquino found it easier to go negative. She attacked him on his medals, on his corruption, and on his efforts to disguise his age and frailty. The campaign discovered that he was sick and had only ever appeared in public for thirty minutes at a time because he needed to get back on the dialysis machine. She pressed him to get off the platform and show that he could walk. The line of attack was claiming that he was not just a crook but a dying one.

Aquino had a team of Jesuits writing her speeches, too. Malloch Brown and Teddy Boy Locsin, a young Filipino man who had been an aide to Ninoy Aquino and who had his own long political future before him, were the factory wordsmiths. The effect was that it was an ambidextrous campaign, dirty on the one hand, holy on the other. When she addressed her final crowd on the eve of the election, Aquino spoke in biblical language of a moment of destiny: "We have nothing to lose but the chains that have bound us for so long. We must be able to tell our children when we grow old, when we talk about these historic times, that we did what we had to do, we responded to the call of the times, we faced the challenge to fight for our future. We staked our lives for a noble cause—a free tomorrow." The following day, Filipinos went to vote. The election campaign ended that day; the battle to remove Marcos began in earnest.

Teddy Boy Locsin remembers a conversation between Cory Aquino and Mark Malloch Brown late in the afternoon on Election Day. During Malloch Brown's time in the Philippines, Locsin was more often than not by the Englishman's side. On that afternoon, Aquino and Malloch Brown decided to start work on Cory's victory speech. "We knew Marcos was going to claim victory," Malloch Brown explained. "We were going to pre-empt him." She said she wanted to go out for some sushi and tempura. When she got back, she hoped her victory statement would be written. It was. She recorded it at home, just as the polls were closing. And it was released just before midnight.

There would be nothing extraordinary about this, but for the fact that the counting of the Filipino ballot was expected to continue for three days. Malloch Brown says: "We were jumping the gun very deliberately on midnight that night." Marcos, according to his aides, had gone to bed when Aquino declared victory. He and his team were caught by surprise. His plan had been to wait for a day or two before announcing that he had won, in order to give his victory greater credibility. Now the presidential palace scrambled to get the Marcos team together to hold a press conference countering Aquino's announcement. By the time Marcos declared that it was he who had won the election, it was three in the morning. Too late for the Filipino deadlines, even if he could make the New York papers.

Malloch Brown had provided the statistics for the presumptive victory statement in addition to writing it. He had put together a rudimentary exit poll, which he still insists offered an accurate snap assessment of the Filipino vote. (Peter Jennings was always unconvinced of Malloch Brown's exit polls, claiming they were "a little ahead of the science on this.") The effect of the victory statement and the exit poll news reports was that the momentum coming out of Election Day was with Aquino. And it was at this stage that the Sawyer Miller team, both on the ground in Manila and back in New York, went to work. As Joel McCleary remembers it, "Our real campaign wasn't to win voters in the Philippines . . . Our campaign was to convince Ronald Reagan and Mrs. Reagan that Marcos was a goner."

There were two battlefronts, one in Manila and the other in Washington, in a campaign that seemed to have many different moving parts, for both Filipino and American hearts and minds. Hundreds of foreign correspondents were in the Philippines in 1986. There was an election monitoring team from the United States led by Senator Dick Lugar, a pivotal figure in making the final determination on election fraud and Marcos's fate. Two rival Filipino election monitors were making contradictory statements about the outcome of the election: one, which had been resurrected by the opposition to police the elections, counted Cory ahead; the other, the official state overseer of the elections, put Marcos in the lead. And two bodies of authority were at odds over the results: the parliament said Marcos had won; the Church, crucially, came out against him.

Just a week after the elections, the Catholic Bishops Conference of the Philippines declared that the government had no moral basis: "The people have spoken. Or tried to . . . In our considered judgment, the polls were unparalleled in the fraudulence of their conduct."

Reagan initially seemed unwilling to accept that fact. He made a statement that there appeared to have been fraud on both sides. This was far less equitable than it sounded. It effectively sought to discount the claims of vote-rigging by the government and served as an endorsement of Marcos. It was a huge setback for Aquino.

The Sawyer Miller team sought to turn a problem into a crisis. They hinted at a frothing revolution. Teddy Boy Locsin remembers Mark Malloch Brown rolling him out before the American cameras: " 'You're perfect. You forgot to shave. You look like a mess. You look like an Iranian terrorist. We'll put you on TV.' " And, as Locsin remembers it, Malloch Brown composed a militant threat for the young Filipino, exhausted and disheveled after weeks of ceaseless campaigning. Locsin delivered it to the network news cameras. "If this is how you are going to treat the people who fight for freedom, then we will treat you all as enemies."

As the drama continued, Malloch Brown did his level best to make sure that the moments were made for television. Two days after the election, thirty-five computer engineers at COMELEC, the government's ballot-counting center, got up and walked out. They had found discrepancies between the numbers they were counting and the numbers being reported. Initially, they had assumed it was a bug in their computer system. When it became clear that the numbers were being altered deliberately, they refused to cooperate. They had planned to leave the building, get some supper, and go home. But the press demanded a statement, and the five men and thirty women were ferried to the Baclaran Church, where they set up a press conference, each sitting beneath the high altar in the white blazers that were their official uniforms. Malloch Brown helped set it up and made sure that the U.S. television network reporters were there to see these apostles of truth, dressed in white, and exposing the Filipino Herod in the House of the Lord.

After the election, Aquino had called Filipinos out onto the streets for a People Power victory rally. She had called for a boycott of "crony establishments," which put the banks aligned with the Marcos regime under enormous strain. It was into this increasingly febrile situation that President Reagan sent another go-between, Philip Habib, to try to mediate a compromise, a sharing of power between Marcos and Aquino. Locsin remembers one particular interchange: Aquino had refused to form a government with Marcos, demanding his exit from the presidential palace. Habib asked her how long she was prepared to continue stirring up mass protests on the streets of metropolitan Manila. "Maybe one week, maybe one month, maybe six months, maybe one year, maybe two years," she said. As he left, Locsin was sure he could hear Habib mutter under his breath, "She will win." In the States, Joel McCleary was trying to convince the Reagan White House of just that.

While the Philippines drama was playing out on the streets of Manila in front of the world's television cameras, a seismic shift was under way, unseen, in Washington, D.C. And while Mark Malloch Brown was assigned to work on the script and the stage directions in the Philippines, the more subtle and precarious job of nurturing the opinion within America's power elites and directing the story line within the policy-making circles in Washington fell to Joel McCleary. Through his work in Panama, he had a host of contacts in the Central Intelligence Agency. In particular, he had become close to Stuart Spencer—Stu-ball, as he was known—then the dean of political consultants, the man who had steered Ronald Reagan to the California governorship and then the White House and who was now one of the president's closest advisers.

So it fell to McCleary to work the interagency team—the State Department, CIA, Pentagon officials—focused on the Philippines. He also kept in close contact with Spencer. Scott Miller remembers watching it unfold: "Mark and Joel managed a brilliant PR campaign in Washington." They had the exit polls that Mark had conducted, as well as the CIA's own secret assessment of the election, which was that Marcos had committed massive electoral fraud and that Cory Aquino had won. They leaked those findings on Capitol Hill. They then bought themselves some time, interpreting Reagan's statement that there had been fraud on both sides as evidence that the White House was taking stock. "Not to say Reagan is wrong; Reagan is supporting an autocrat. They said Reagan is thinking about it, Reagan is considering these results."

Malloch Brown was coaching Aquino to speak in terms that chimed with Reagan's vision of the world. Echoing the phrase that Reagan had used for Nicaraguan freedom fighters, Aquino declared that she and the Filipino people "stand tall for freedom." (Aquino, educated in the Catholic schools of the United States, initially refused to use the phrase. It was, she said, grammatically incorrect: you can't stand tall *for* freedom.) Meanwhile, McCleary was forever on the line to Stu Spencer, seeking to coax from the White House some public show of support for Aquino. Ten days after the election and a week after Reagan's initial, equivocal judgment on the outcome, Malloch Brown got a call from Stu Spencer in the wee hours of the night in Manila. "What does my guy have to say to get your girl through?" Malloch Brown remembers Spencer asking him. (Spencer, for his part, only faintly recalls the conversation—it was higher up the list of other people's priorities, he says, than his.) Malloch Brown fed him a line. The next morning Reagan was picked up on the Catholic Radio Veritas delivering the message in California that a sleepy Malloch Brown had garbled into the phone in the middle of the night. "It showed me the power of this stuff," Malloch Brown, a self-described "novice" at the time, says. "Rather than working through diplomatic channels, you could deliver [through a few key advisers]."

Bobby Trent Jones, too, was back in the United States, working on what was known as "the second campaign." He saw it as his task to make sure that if Cory Aquino won, the United States would honor her victory. He had previously made his case on the Philippines before Congress, urging an end to America's mollycoddling of Marcos. He counted as friends, golfing buddies even, some powerful people on Capitol Hill: Bill Bradley, the senator from his native New Jersey; Sam Nunn, then the ranking Democrat on the Senate Armed Services Committee; and Alan Cranston, the senator from his adopted home, California. As soon as the results came through, he called Sam Nunn, then in Geneva. Nunn came back and made a declaration in Aquino's favor, saying that the United States and the U.S. military based in the Philippines could not stand by an illegitimate Marcos government.

Malloch Brown was not privy to all the intense, tortuous discussions going on in Washington. (More than twenty years later, his version of events still clashes with McCleary's. Joel had originally hired Mark, but he came to marvel both at his protégé's strategic intelligence and his main foible, self-aggrandizement: "The American that had the greatest impact on that outcome was Stu Spencer . . . Of course, in the storytelling [Mark] became the grand chess master but in reality much of what happened was because of the effort of so many in and out of government. In reality, Mark was more pawn than master of that campaign.") Marcos would not go without a clear signal from Reagan that his time was up. But the president simply did not want to dump his old friend. Nancy Reagan was regularly on the phone to Imelda. Don Regan, the White House chief of staff, also stood squarely against pressure to force Marcos out, and Caspar Weinberger, the defense secretary, was reluctant, too. Still, even within his own administration and his party, Ronald Reagan was increasingly isolated: George Shultz and his staff were pressing for Marcos's exit; Dick Lugar had returned from Manila and was adamant in private with the president and, unusual for a loyal Republican, in public, too, that Marcos's claims of victory were fraudulent and that his time was up; Philip Habib had returned from the Philippines convinced that there was nothing for it but to offer Marcos asylum in the United States; the U.S. ambassador in Manila, Stephen Bosworth, was busy arranging Marcos's getaway.

And yet, it was not the back-channel discussions between Malloch Brown and Stu Spencer in the middle of the night, nor the conversations between Reagan's national security team over blueberry muffins at Shultz's home on a Sunday morning, nor the statement issued by the bishops that ultimately forced Marcos out. In the end, it was millions of Filipinos who forced Marcos to flee. "Victory has a thousand fathers. Clearly, the primary credit goes to Cory and the Filipino people," Solarz told me. "At the end of the day, it was a million people in the Philippines. Ordinary people stopping the tanks with nothing but their prayers and their presence."

On the Saturday afternoon of February 22, the usual playing of "Onward Christian Soldiers" on Radio Veritas was interrupted by an emergency news conference called by Defense Minister Juan Ponce Enrile and Armed Forces Vice Chief of Staff Lt. Gen. Fidel Ramos. They announced that they had withdrawn their allegiance from Marcos and said that Cory Aquino was the winner of the election. To underline the point about fraud, Enrile revealed that he himself had faked nearly four hundred thousand votes for Marcos. Accompanied by just fifty guards, they then holed up in two military compounds on either side of Epifanio de los Santos Avenue, the main highway running through metropolitan Manila. Marcos held a press conference of his own, urging Enrile and Ramos to stop their "stupidity." But the call went out from Cardinal Sin and others to swarm the streets around the military camps and provide support— with food, prayer, and numbers. Within twenty-four hours, there were estimated to be more than one million people cramming the EDSA boulevard. A helicopter division sent to attack the rebel soldiers defected, landing peacefully among the cheering crowds. The numbers continued to swell, and Marcos, in his own shining moment, appeared on television that Monday and ordered his chief of the armed forces not to fire on the crowds. Whether this was an instinctive act of statesmanship or a ploy to recover flagging popular support, it came too late. Cory Aquino was returning to Manila to be sworn in as president the following morning. Ferdinand Marcos, still insistent that he had won the election, scheduled his own inauguration for that afternoon.

In Washington, Reagan was coming to terms with the reality that Marcos had to go. Shultz had come to the conclusion that the compromises Marcos kept grasping for were unworkable. On Monday afternoon in D.C.—the middle of the night in Manila—Reagan put out a statement signaling his shift: "Attempts to prolong the life of the present regime by violence are futile. A solution to this crisis can only be achieved through a peaceful transition to a new government." Marcos wanted to know if this was just another State Department initiative to ease him out or if it came from the president himself. He called Paul Laxalt, the Republican senator with whom he'd discussed the snap election before he went on the Brinkley show just four months earlier. Stanley Karnow recounts these final hours as if reporting on a death row convict's last hopes of a reprieve. Marcos asked Laxalt if Reagan really wanted a "transition" or if he could stay on until 1987—after all, he'd been elected in 1981 and had only called the snap election to assuage critics in the United States. He could, perhaps, serve as Cory's senior adviser while retaining the honorary title of president. At a meeting with Reagan in the White House, Laxalt raised these suggestions. Shultz dismissed them as impractical. Reagan nodded. The meeting lasted just thirteen minutes. Laxalt retired to an office down the corridor and called Marcos, who wanted to know if Reagan wanted him to resign. Laxalt dodged the question. "Senator," Marcos asked, "what do you think? Should I step down?"

Laxalt responded immediately: "I think you should cut and cut cleanly. I think the time has come."

There was a silence so long that Laxalt wondered if they'd been disconnected. "Mr. President, are you there?"

"Yes," responded Marcos. "I am so very, very disappointed."

Late that afternoon in Manila, Marcos and his family left the palace as they had arrived—in style. They went out onto the palace balcony and, over the throng of people below, sang a final, farewell duet: "Because of You."

AMERICA'S POLITICAL CONSULTANTS have been propelled by three irrepressible American forces: idealism, capitalism, and adventurism. They carry with them, inevitably, the values Americans hold dear: a commitment to faith, wealth, and liberty. So, their motivations, as with America's, can be hard to pin down. David Sawyer and his colleagues went to Venezuela in the 1970s chiefly for the money. They worked in Israel in the 1980s and 1990s because the opportunity presented itself—they did not go for the money or to answer a Zionist calling, but the opportunity was just too fascinating to turn down. In the Philippines, they waived their fee and worked for what they considered to be the higher purpose of spreading democracy. (One Sawyer Miller man remembers being taunted afterward by Matthew Friedman, who had worked with Paul Manafort for Marcos: "We lost, but we got paid." Indeed, they finally terminated their contract with Marcos the day before he fled the country.) It is the nature of the alpha dogs that they do not fit neatly into a moral category: the people who make a business out of politics tend to have a certain ambivalence, being idealistic and hopeful believers in the mundane miracle of democracy as well as canny and cynical operators who seek to manipulate the public mind. They can have one eye on breaking the establishment mold, while the other is on getting into bed with corporate power. They were not just freedom's carpetbaggers or political thrill-seekers or ideological warriors, but a bit of all three.

Back in New York, McCleary was a case in point. Even as Sawyer Miller triumphed in the Philippines, he was falling out of love with the firm. He was drawn to the Tibetan cause while, at the same time, increasingly disillusioned by the commercial ambitions of Sawyer Miller. He chose to take a year off and head to the Himalayas. Bob Perkins remembered hearing this with a laugh. When Perkins himself left the firm—he was David Sawyer's first Republican recruit, one in a series of vain attempts to make the firm bipartisan, and he soon went back to Washington to fund-raise for Senate candidates—he went to the Carlyle Hotel with Joel to interview his replacement, Harry Clark.

Joel settled into a chair across from Harry and began the conversation like this: "The goal of the firm is to be very rich." Harry smiled, not averse to riches. They talked on for a few minutes. And Joel, who is prone to interrupt, interrupted. "I just want to be clear. What we want to do, what I want to do is to make a shitpot full of money." Harry said he was on board with that. They talked on. What seemed like three minutes later, Joel had a point to make: "I want you to understand the objective here is to make a lot of money. To get rich." So Harry asked him how much money qualified as rich. Joel said they each wanted to make $5 million. And what, asked Harry, would Joel do with it if he made that much money. Joel said he would live and work among the exiled Tibetan Buddhists in Dharamsala, India. He was a Buddhist. Harry made the obvious point. "But if you're going to an ashram in India, you don't need five million dollars." "True," said Joel, "but if I don't like it and come back, I want to be able to have dinner at the Carlyle."

The men from Sawyer Miller liked the idea of advancing the cause of liberty, but they also enjoyed eating at the Carlyle. Over lunch years later—funnily enough, at the Carlyle—Joel offered a different interpretation of that meeting with Harry Clark. He was heading off to work for the Dalai Lama and, as he remembers it, the point he was making to Clark was that he wished he had the money to be free of financial concerns and to work on the campaigns he wanted to work on. He felt a real conflict working for large fees and doing campaigns, because "good causes and good pay were usually miles apart."

Ever since Scott Miller started applying the political model to American companies, it had been clear to both him and David Sawyer that there was far more money to be made from U.S. corporate clients than from foreign political candidates. The partners and consultants providing political advice to American executives liked to point out that their work was not only fascinating but also economically rational: the corporate practice was soon paying the rent. The men who loved the foreign campaign trail, on the other hand, claimed that the soul and unique selling point of the firm lay in politics: what made Sawyer Miller's advice to American companies worth buying was the latest experience garnered in the political arena. Over time, two discernible factions emerged within the firm—crudely put, the "business" faction and the "politics" faction, each side revisiting and rehashing a recurrent argument about Sawyer Miller's priorities. For years, David Sawyer was able to square the circle, arguing that politics fed into business and vice versa. He would point to the example of the Philippines.

For the firm may have worked on Cory's campaign pro bono, but it made up for its selflessness in the months after she took office, picking up a contract with the Philippines Ministry of Information, which agreed to pay Sawyer Miller $180,000 a year plus expenses for general advice and help ushering President Aquino on what proved to be an exuberant victory lap through the United States in September of 1986; Sawyer Miller also got a $360,000 annual general contract to advise the government of the Philippines, brokered through the Filipino embassy in Washington, D.C.; the firm also agreed with the Philippines Central Bank that for a fee of $180,000 a year, it would help to get U.S. support for Filipino debt restructuring; the company picked up another $180,000-a-year contract to represent the Philippines Sugar Administration; there was a six-month contract for $272,000 (including expenses) to promote the Philippines Coconut Authority in the United States; and, after the dust settled, the Filipino opposition parties repaid Sawyer Miller for the expenses incurred during the election campaign. So, in the end, they did, in fact, pay for American advice. Malloch Brown spent the next five years going nearly once a month to the Philippines, which, for a while, wasn't so bad: he was going out with a girl named Giselle, Cory Aquino's niece.

Over the years, then, Sawyer Miller was very well paid by the Philippines—so much so that it came to see the real commercial value of election campaigns not so much as the fees charged in the run-up to the vote, but as the business that would later flow from advising the government in office, lobbying on behalf of foreign governments in Washington and making infomercials for ministries around the world. Political communication, it concluded, was even more of a business when it came to governing the people than canvassing their votes.

The Aquino victory in the Philippines served as a beacon to people struggling for freedom around the world. Sawyer Miller, a firm that had a head start in the international elections business, looked out from New York and saw a burgeoning marketplace for modern competitive politics. After the Philippines, they had credentials as the underdog's champion, the professional adviser to the popular insurgent. "We knew the magic of jujitsu leverage," says Malloch Brown, who officially joined Sawyer Miller after the Philippines campaign and took up McCleary's job as head of the international division. "The right message in the right media could take out political giants."

The Philippines promised to open up a world of business, opportunities both to do good and make money. The expectation was that international elections would not only produce a handy income in the off years in the United States but also put Sawyer Miller on first-name terms with the political and business elites in countries around the world. A steady stream of retainers would flow from victory. The firm now set about selling its wares with unprecedented ambition. They swept across Latin America—politicians, governments, and state businesses in Ecuador, Colombia, Bolivia, and Peru were all soon clients. They started doing more work in Europe, finding opportunities in Spain, Portugal, and Greece. There were also big opportunities closer to home: Canada, the Dominican Republic, and Panama were soon all buying Sawyer Miller's services. As the Soviet Union creaked, Eastern Europe started to look promising, and as soon as the regimes toppled, Sawyer Miller's people were in Russia, Poland, and Hungary. In the two to three years after the Philippines, the firm mushroomed from a business of a dozen people to one that employed more than fifty.

Turning politics into a bankable proposition proved endlessly frustrating. The corporate world always seemed to pay better. In fact, the corporate world paid—business clients honored their bills, which was not always the case with politicians. But the Grail was always out there. David Sawyer, Scott Miller, and the small cadre of consultants they had recruited into the offices at East Sixtieth Street now wanted to repeat the rewards of the Philippines and get the kudos, the glory of victory, the contracts that followed, the satisfaction of advancing freedom, and that irreplaceable sense of mattering in the world.

The Aquino campaign held out the possibility that democracy, already a business in the United States, could be a money-spinner worldwide. As Malloch Brown put it, "We had established through the Philippines this franchise." Democracy campaigners from Asia, Eastern Europe, and Latin America started seeking out the firm. Former congressman Stephen Solarz looks back and says, "The triumph of People Power in 1986 sent a powerful message elsewhere: tyrants who had been tolerated for a long period of time need not be tolerated in perpetuity. It was not altogether unrelated, what happened in South Korea the next year." Indeed, it was not.

SIX

"NO"

IN MARCH 1986, just a few weeks after the People Power revolution inspired democrats everywhere and Sawyer Miller became the toast of the
political consulting world, the firm got a telephone call from Seoul, South
Korea. "We have a Cory Aquino of our own," said the voice on the other
end of the line, and he inquired if some of the stardust Sawyer Miller had
sprinkled on Aquino could work on their man. "Do you think he should
wear a yellow suit? How about a yellow tie?"

The man who took the call was David Morey, still a pretty junior guy
in the firm. Pushy and overconfident, as they all were, Morey was a young
man from Doylestown, Pennsylvania, who had fallen into politics as a
victim of history. He had been a decathlete at the University of Pennsylvania who had dreamed of competing in the 1980 Olympics. Whether he
was just deluding himself or whether he had a real crack at a medal,
he would never know. His sporting fantasy was crushed by the cold war
when the United States boycotted the 1980 Moscow Olympics. The event
stirred an interest in international relations, so he went to study politics at
the London School of Economics. When he got back, he touted his newfound worldliness around Washington and got signed up by John Glenn's
presidential campaign to work on foreign policy issues, which was how he
met Scott Miller. Within a matter of months, Glenn had lost and Morey
was working at the firm, where he was dispatched to assist Mark Malloch
Brown in the Philippines. (It was Morey who coined the term "backboard
shot" for bouncing the Aquino message off the American media into the
Manila press.) He was the man Sawyer suggested to help the Bronfmans
with their worldwide work in the Jewish community.

After he got the call from Korea, Morey walked into David Sawyer's office hoping that this would be his chance to run a presidential candidate of his own. Little did he know he was signing away ten years of his life to a man who for much of the time would seem like a heroic waste of hope.

Kim Dae-Jung had already become a symbol of democratic struggle in South Korea, standing against the military dictatorship that modernized the country but suffocated political freedom. By the time Morey flew out to meet him in a safe house in Seoul in August 1986, Kim had already survived several attempts on his life: the Korean intelligence services had strapped him to a boat, intent on drowning him in the Sea of Japan; a few years later, he was sentenced to death for alleged sedition. (Both times, U.S. intervention saved his life.) Morey was inspired by Kim and, buoyed by his experience in the Philippines, convinced he could usher another Asian country into the fold of competitive democracies.

He knew nothing about Korea. As he recalled years later, he spent "the first week and a half learning the country. Driving around looking at Korean bars and Korean girls and Buddhist temples." But Morey was convinced that Sawyer Miller had gone a long way toward cracking the code of democratic success anywhere. The dynamics of democratic politics seemed to them to transcend language, history, and culture. In one of the very first memos he sent to Kim, Morey wrote, "We must position all speeches, statements and communiations on the correct side of the axes detailed below . . . The first axis is: Moral vs. Political." In the TV age, candidates came across as one of two things: principled or opportunistic, driven by conviction or motivated by personal advantage. "We have found around the world—whether it is Israel's Begin vs. Peres in 1981, Britain's Thatcher vs. Foot in 1983 or America's Reagan vs. Mondale in 1984—the individual perceived as the moral, rather than the political, leader wins."

Kim Dae-Jung was steered away from the mistakes that some of the old Sawyer Miller candidates had made in the United States. Chief among them was failing to answer what came to be known as the "Mudd question." When Ted Kennedy sought the Democratic nomination in 1980, he was asked by CBS reporter Roger Mudd why he wanted to be president. He had no clear answer. Time and again, Morey sought to reinforce Kim's need to project a sense of mission and purpose, a claim to be the moral unifier of Korea. The medium for that, of course, was television. "Television's modern power is awesome," he wrote. "It is a trusted friend to Americans. They've watched history through it. The Philippines was an election called and won on American TV. Images made the difference: Marcos squirming, Aquino tough and confident, nuns standing before tanks as Americans ate brunch ... TV shaped views. It moved Americans. This power and phenomenon must be managed again."

Morey worked with Joel McCleary on the Kim Dae-Jung account, a project that would bring them face-to-face with a different kind of political testosterone: at one demonstration, a man screamed at them that he did not simply support Kim Dae-Jung, but loved him, then cut off his own finger and wrote, "I support Kim Dae-Jung" in blood. For McCleary, who had been dispatched to Bogotá and São Paolo, France and Nigeria, to sit in on focus groups that measured levels of support for the candidate in marks out of ten, this was an eleven. And yet, for all the apparent frenzy of the Korean rallies, Morey and McCleary were always attuned to public discontent with politics. "Voters are tired," Morey told Kim. "They view politicians through a prism of cynicism." The most powerful force in politics, they felt, was antipolitical sentiment, and they sought to harness it to win power. That there was something topsy-turvy, even disingenuous about this, was not the point.

Kim was drip-fed what were quickly becoming Sawyer Miller's stock-in-trade essentials of winning politics in America. "The key is this: Find fear and offer hope ... Political campaigns are won this way. Ronald Reagan scared people in 1980 that big government was killing the economy. He made voters afraid in 1984 of a Walter Mondale presidency ... Fear is at the heart of voting motivation ... Make people afraid, then provide the alternative." Their memos provided instructions on how to spin, they emphasized the necessity of coordinated message discipline across the top ranks of Kim's party, they urged him (for years in vain) to stop bothering to define the party and focus instead on defining himself personally. They referred him back, again and again, to the public opinion research. They drafted stump speeches and scripted sassy replies for him to use in media interviews and in the TV debates. They suggested he invent a story about an encounter with an undecided voter who had joined the Kim Dae-Jung camp because he had "the courage to change." It became a leitmotif to the work of the firm in the late 1980s and early 1990s.

The real breakthrough for Kim Dae-Jung came years after the first call to Sawyer Miller. Following his defeat in the 1992 election, he resigned from politics. He issued a farewell statement, announcing his plan to become a "plain citizen." The following day Morey sent him a note: "Your concession was magnificent and courageous and classic. It was correct, too, strategically. It has opened up many more doors than it closed." The Americans quickly started positioning Kim as a democratic campaigner and statesman in the cause of peace. Kim's retirement was genuine, but his advisers saw it as a colossal opportunity to rebrand him. Having been involved in politics since 1954, suddenly Kim was standing outside it. To his advisers, a phoenixlike resurrection in the election of 1997 suddenly seemed possible. They helped establish a Kim Dae-Jung foundation. They lobbied the great and the good to submit Kim Dae-Jung's name for the Nobel Peace Prize. And, by 1995, they started putting in place a campaign plan for if and when Kim should choose to return to politics. This time, they said, he needed to have an actionable plan. "Newt Gingrich's 'Contract with America' is the most successful midterm post-election strategy in decades because it chose what it could achieve . . . We need to develop a 'Contract with Korea,' " Morey suggested. Kim Dae-Jung finally won the presidency on December 18, 1997. The following day, Morey sent him a note: "Congratulations on a magnificent victory," it said. Morey also pitched his services as an adviser on Kim Dae-Jung's first hundred days in office.

The Kim account was the first to flow from the Aquino victory, and it took the longest to come to frution. But it was by no means the only piece of new business to flow into Sawyer Miller. In the late 1980s, it seemed as though there was no corner of the world that did not need them, no kind of project where their skills did not apply.

The Sawyer Miller Group was in its heyday.

SCOTT HAD ALWAYS TRIED to rein in David's urge to hire more people, because he liked the idea of working in an office of four or five guys (and Mandy, a woman), who had full freedom to roam and none of the office politics or corporate bureaucracy that he had found so tedious at McCann. Sawyer, though, believed they were building the undiscovered hub of a rapidly interconnecting world, a little hothouse of unrecognized power and influence, operating at the heart of a new, unfolding world order. He thought that Sawyer Miller saw connections in world politics before others did, that they understood the key ingredients in the people's mood and that they were able to devise and implement strategies that really could steer public opinion. He was convinced that they were forging a new kind of communications consultancy, poised to create a new breed of business that would be worth hundreds of millions of dollars, reach from New York around the world, and dominate media and marketing in a way that McKinsey had made its mark on management. And even if Scott did not entirely share David's dream, it was hard to argue with the simple fact that they needed more staff.

When Pat Klecanda joined as David Sawyer's executive assistant in 1986, it seemed her boss was forever on a plane: he was working with the governor of Kentucky and the prime minister of Israel; he had just started doing some work with Colombia, trying to help them turn around their international image as a narco-state; and he was making inroads on Wall Street with Goldman Sachs, the investment bank, and KKR, the private equity firm. Trish Cronan had also just joined the firm, to sit on the other side of the glass wall of Mandy Grunwald's and Mark Malloch Brown's offices. Trish was twenty-four, blond, very good looking, and straight out of Denison, a liberal arts college in Ohio. Mandy had interviewed her and liked her, while Mark thought she was a little too innocent for Sawyer Miller but would get tougher and cannier on the job. Anyway, Grunwald and Malloch Brown were even more absent than David Sawyer: Mandy was on the road across the United States, doing gubernatorial races from Kentucky to Arizona, and Mark was building up the international practice, picking up work from the top to the bottom of Latin America.

By then, the firm also had a president, Jack Leslie. He had worked in Ted Kennedy's office in the Senate in Washington and got to know Sawyer when they had worked briefly on Kennedy's 1980 presidential bid. In 1983, after Kennedy discussed and then discarded the idea of making another run for the White House, Leslie had asked Sawyer to keep his ear open for any jobs in New York. Sawyer promptly offered him one, where he would be doing a bit of everything. He got involved with international work in Colombia; he was the firm's point man on the Helms-Hunt race in 1984, a contest that involved more political commercials and a greater ad spend than any other Senate election in U.S. history; and he took charge of the day-to-day running of the firm, because Scott wanted nothing less and David was too frenetic to take responsibility for workflow and billings. Very soon, Jack Leslie became what was in effect the chief operating officer of the firm. He was the businessman—likable, reliable, and numerate.

David Sawyer was also recruiting a second generation of younger consultants, men in their twenties who had shown promise in Washington or on the U.S. campaign circuit and who were eager to spread the political gospel in the corporate world and across the international scene. He hired Peter Schechter, a young staffer on the international finance committee on Capitol Hill. He hired Mark McKinnon, a young Democrat from Texas. He hired Rob Shepardson and Lenny Stern, a couple of friends who had gotten into politics on the Pennsylvania campaign circuit. And he signed up Don Campbell, who produced political spots.

The unspoken arrangement between David Sawyer and Ned Kennan was in the very long and slow process of becoming a formal partnership. The two firms—the Sawyer Miller Group and Kennan Research and Consulting—were only a couple of miles apart on the island of Manhattan, but culturally, they were on different continents. The Sawyer Miller men in Midtown liked fat cigars and fine wine and good French food. They were all energetic practicing heterosexuals, men who struck up a series of relationships with people they worked with. Jack Leslie started dating a woman he met in the editing suite. Harris Diamond was seeing someone who worked with Sawyer Miller on media buying. One of the young hires, Robert Mead, was seeing a woman named Katia, who had worked at the Moscow Circus before joining the firm. There was an attractive assistant who was involved in a number of office flings—some real, more imagined. And there was always the joke that the sofas in David Sawyer's office—the only place at Sawyer Miller where the walls weren't made of glass, where the door locked, and where there was room to lie down—had been used for more than entertaining clients. (David Sawyer's sofas were also the only place where people pulling all-nighters could lie down to sleep. One of the greatest sleepers was Trish, Mark Malloch Brown's assistant. One night, Mark took Peter Schechter into David's office to show him Trish, fast asleep. "Have you ever seen such serenity?" Mark asked Peter, covering her with his leather jacket. Peter Schechter thought at the time that such tenderness was strange within the offices of Sawyer Miller. It did not cross his mind that something might be going on between them.)

As Ed Reilly saw it when he arrived down at the KRC offices in 1986, the guys at Sawyer Miller were a bunch of towel-snapping frat boys by comparison with the group of Bolshevik nonconformists at KRC. Reilly had just agreed to move from Boston to New York to try to marshal Kennan's comrades into a profitable business. KRC was brilliant, but veering toward bankruptcy. It was operating out of offices at 80 East Eleventh Street in what was known as the "pink building," as most of the other tenants were unions or groups with strong left leanings. Kennan prided himself on often hiring gay men and women, because he thought they were original, creative thinkers who looked at the world from the outside in. He had a lot of part-timers, particularly academics finishing their Ph.D.s. There was a pretty tolerant attitude toward sex in the office and an understanding that it was the 1980s and people were going to do drugs. The place was anticorporate, an office that worked for big businesses but where it was perfectly common to roll up a joint in the early evening and spend the night stoned, poring over the polling numbers. Nonetheless, David and Ned were good friends, and KRC, while not officially part of the Sawyer Miller Group until 1989, was the firm's preferred vendor of polling through the late 1980s.

To house all the new people and capture the buzz of an office in the electronic age, Sawyer Miller moved from the cramped space on West Fifty-fifth Street to new offices on the eighth floor of 14 East Sixtieth Street. The new place was unlike the beige-walled, boxy offices with faux mahogany desks of its competitors. There were no green desk lamps, no shelves of leather-bound books. Enough political consultants out there were working in places that looked like they had been designed by a prim firm of lawyers. Clients who came to East Sixtieth Street were being invited to step into the future, as envisaged by David Sawyer. The foyer had a bank of six television screens, always on and tuned to CNN and C-SPAN and the networks. The ticker tape of world news ran across the screen, a constant stream of information and fragmented opinion. The conference rooms had glass walls so that people outside could see what was going on inside and vice versa. The deep purple walls and the vast matte-black desks were closer in spirit to Hollywood than Washington. The shelves were crammed with strategy notebooks and VHS videotapes, the firm's two products: ideas and images.

Scott Miller sat at the far end of the corridor, down to the right, his Apple Macintosh blinking on his desk, the TV blaring away, and his dog, Spike, sitting under the desk. When he was in full campaign mode, he would don an old army helmet. (When asked why, he said he did it for the same reason Andy Warhol wore a wig: magical thinking.) At the other end of the office, David Sawyer had his office, furnished with sofas and big TV screens and a bar. In between, there were editing suites, meeting rooms, glass-walled offices for Joel, Mark, Mandy, and Jack, as well as cubicles for the assistants and the new hires. Corporate hierarchies may have been unraveling in the new media world they described, but they were alive and well inside the offices of Sawyer Miller.

The pay for most of the junior staff members was not terrific, but the sense of possibility was intoxicating. Not only did the most powerful people in the Democratic Party trip through the offices at East Sixtieth Street, but so did presidents and presidential aides from the Philippines, Colombia, Greece, Portugal, Spain, Argentina, and Chile. Sawyer Miller was like a miniature United Nations, stripped of the layers upon layers of suffocating bureaucracy but giddy at the thought that the world could be improved by a handful of clever people in New York. (The office also seemed alive to another kind of possibility: Robert Mead, who had earned his spurs doing state politics in Texas, working, among other things, for a young Texan politician named George W. Bush, joined Sawyer Miller in the late 1980s and remembers the scene at 14 East Sixtieth Street: "I was twenty-nine and single, the women were beautiful and smart and single, and we all worked until ten or eleven or twelve, so everyone in the office was having sex with everyone else in the office." He ended up dating and then marrying Katia, who worked at the firm.) And with the power came the glitter: Richard Gere was popping in and out of the office because he was working on a film about a political consultant and fashioning his character, Pete St. John, after David Sawyer; Sean Connery would stop by because he was doing some public service announcements about the Kurds in Iraq; David Bowie made an occasional appearance.

Not surprisingly, Sawyer Miller was one of the first political firms alive to celebrity power. The Ethiopian famine had had a seminal impact on David Sawyer and Scott Miller: after two years of newspaper reports that had resulted in little more than a global shrug, they had watched in 1984 as TV footage of the famine galvanized the world into action. First British pop stars recorded "Do They Know It's Christmas?" then U.S. musicians recorded "We Are the World," both in aid of famine relief. In 1985, Ken Kragen had gotten in touch with Scott Miller and Mandy Grunwald in an attempt to revive the Live Aid spirit and harness it once again in the service of a homegrown problem: hunger and homelessness.

The result was Hands Across America, an attempt to create a human chain that stretched 4,125 miles from the Atlantic to the Pacific. Kragen, the Hollywood promoter who had been instrumental to the USA for

Africa effort and the "We Are the World" celebrity sing-along, enlisted Sawyer Miller for what was a mass mobilization akin to a general election. Miller and Grunwald worked on the logistics, as well as the music video that drummed up public enthusiasm for the event. And on May 25, 1986, roughly five million Americans lined up to hold hands from one ocean to another. The country had never seen stars—film stars, pop stars, the great and the good—come out for a cause in such numbers: Jane Fonda, Rev. Billy Graham, Oprah Winfrey, Speaker of the House Tip O'Neill, C-3PO, Kenny Rogers, Robin Williams—the list went on and on; in Washington, D.C., Ronald Reagan and his staff on the White House lawn were joined by the Olympic gymnast Mary Lou Retton and Coretta Scott King; in Iowa, Rev. Jesse Jackson stood between a Motel 6 manager and Mr. Goodwrench; on the West Coast, Mickey Mouse and Goofy hooked up with the televangelist Robert H. Schuller. The event was, ultimately, deemed a failure. The joke was that there were hundreds of miles where the chain was broken, huge stretches of desert where no one was holding hands, only the occasional truck driver honking his horn in a symbolic effort to fill the gap. More to the point, it had cost $17 million to put on and raised only $50 million.

As far as Sawyer Miller was concerned, though, it was another example of how the firm's vision of the world could be put to work everywhere. Ken Kragen said years later, "We hired campaign organizers, and it was very much like a political campaign. Instead of 'get out the vote' it was 'get out and hold hands.'" The firm was selling its combination of skills—strategic political thinking and creative media production—to politicians in Washington, to the entertainment industry in Los Angeles, to financiers in New York, and to people aspiring to power all over the world.

The men and women at Sawyer Miller felt as though they were reinventing the world—that they were not getting the credit for it didn't matter. They, at least, were aware of their greatness. As Mark Malloch Brown put it to the magazine *Manhattan Inc.*, "[Ad agencies] are the easiest of any of our rivals to displace. I mean, they are just so second-rate. As soon as they get to be any size, this sort of corporatism takes over. We take pleasure in kicking the butts of advertising agencies around the world." Likewise, State Department diplomats, administration officials, and Capitol Hill staffers: "We just go sort of more wired than the dreary guy from Washington who shows up at the presidencia in South America and tells some poor guy struggling with a peasantry mired in debt and poverty, 'Can't you get this place into shape? You know, those congressmen in Washington are really worried about the narco problem. And frankly, I mean, you know, your government isn't going to be worth shit until, you know . . .' " Scott Miller broke in: "Their principal communications tool is the cocktail party." Sawyer Miller was not a household name, but that was not the point. It was a nexus of power. And it was a thrill to be a part of it.

Questions, of course, hovered over the place: What did they think this power was for? What was their purpose? What was the political agenda not of its clients, but of Sawyer Miller itself? When asked, the firm's answer was democracy: choice and change. "What we believe," Miller told *Manhattan Inc.,*

> and it always sounds stupid to say so, but our experience has taught us in domestic politics, international politics, working for governments or corporations, or selling beer or soda pop, that democracy's a good thing. And democracy is basically dialogue. And more democracy is better. And a more fluid dialogue is better and fluid democracy is the best thing of all, whether it's in a country or whether it's for a politician in a campaign or whether it's in a company between management and labor.

As succinct and sharp as Sawyer Miller's messages were for its clients, its own manifesto was woolly, vacuous, and self-serving. The company liked to tout its credentials as Democrats, but around the world it championed free-market reformers with privatization agendas who would emulate Reagan and Thatcher. Sawyer Miller liked to say that its clients were "progressives"—it didn't matter whether they were right or left. Rather than have an ideological position of its own, Sawyer Miller saw itself as part of the process of sweeping away ideology. Mark Malloch Brown said he tried to convince candidates to see voters as consumers: "The concept of class and class antagonism [has been replaced] with the concept of the political consumer. An election isn't always some inevitable play of historical forces. We reject Marxism. Our way is much more pragmatic. It lacks the grand sweep." Marshall McLuhan had observed that "the medium is the massage"; Sawyer Miller seemed to say that "politics is the campaign."

Even in these salad days for Sawyer Miller, some people began to fear for the values of the firm. They worried that it was falling into the thrall of its own communications work, that it was becoming more excited about the process of politics than about the outcome of government, that it thrilled at being clever as much as it liked being right. It seemed to worry less and less about being on the side of the angels. It didn't even mind if it didn't back the winner. It just loved being in the game. But if that bothered the partners of Sawyer Miller in the wee hours of the night, they rarely let it show. For a start, there was too much work to do: suddenly it seemed that everyone—Democrats from across the United States, politicians from all over the world, chief executives all over America—was on the campaign trail.

IT WAS AROUND THIS TIME that Sawyer Miller set off on another giant-slaying expedition, a venture to topple a dictator in the Marcos mold.

Augusto Pinochet had ruled Chile since a violent coup in September 1973, which left President Salvador Allende dead and the government in the hands of a military junta. Pinochet, the commander in chief of the army and the man who had led the coup, proclaimed himself supreme chief of the nation, then president and, later, captain general. His dictatorship had two distinguishing features: on the one hand, the liberalism of its economic policy, borrowed in large part from the economic teachings of Milton Friedman and the other free-marketers at the University of Chicago who became known as the Chicago Boys; on the other, the meticulously thorough suppression of its opponents, who were all tarred as dangerous Communists, tortured, imprisoned, and murdered as part of a regime that not only sought to silence its critics inside the country but also pursued them around the world as part of Operation Condor, a coordinated crackdown on dissent conducted by Chile alongside other dictatorships in Latin America. The Chilean opposition parties were fragmented and bickering, despising one another nearly as much as they were distrusted by the general public.

Almost as soon as Aquino took office, the men at Sawyer Miller started pitching for work in Chile. Through the summer of 1986, Mark Malloch Brown was in discussions with George Soros, the hedge fund manager who was just getting known for his support of insurgent democracy movements around the world, and Juan Gabriel Valdes, the son of a Chilean senator and the convener of an opposition think tank in Santiago. (Sawyer Miller's services were not cheap—one of the first estimates of their costs was $190,000, which was a lot for a bankrupt coalition of squabbling opposition parties—and they were looking to Soros to foot the bill.) At the same time, Peter Schechter, who as minority staff director for a congressional foreign-assistance subcommittee had worked on human rights issues relating to U.S. financial aid to Chile, was also repeatedly making the case to Juan Gabriel Valdes's father, Don Gabriel Valdes, the Christian Democratic leader, that the Chilean opposition badly needed political help.

Schechter, newly plucked out of Washington, was the only person at the firm who seemed predestined for international political work. His father had been a Viennese lawyer who escaped Austria after the Anschluss, arrived in the United States, and was promptly sent back to Europe to work on radio propaganda for the Allies following the invasion. He had met Peter's mother at a speech given by Abba Eban at the United Nations in the early 1950s, when he joined the U.S. diplomatic service and headed abroad: the young boy grew up on foreign postings in Rome, then La Paz, and then Caracas. His first language was Italian, and he spent his childhood known as Pietro. He then learned English alongside his Spanish. Portuguese, German, and French came afterward, in quick succession. While working as a staffer on the international finance committee in Congress, he was introduced to Mark Malloch Brown.

Within weeks, Sawyer Miller was flying Schechter up to New York, hungry to recruit him into their international business. He went for lunch at the Knickerbocker Club with David Sawyer, who peppered him with all kinds of questions, barely giving him room to answer before firing off the next one: Do you have friends? How do you make friends? Who do you count as friends? How do you choose who is going to be a good friend and who is not? Why? Do you like working? Are you a workaholic? Sawyer badly needed someone with the energy to bulk up the burgeoning international business, not to mention a consultant who actually spoke languages other than English. "I am trying to build a firm of brilliant, eclectic people who come from different walks of life: journalists, advertising people, and government people, political people, academics," Sawyer told him. "We are only united by one thing and that is a love of politics and the political process. The firm that I want to build will have more influence than any other place in the world."

No sooner had Schechter settled in at East Sixtieth Street than he was selling that same vision to the Chilean opposition: "Our deep involvement with Corazon Aquino in the Philippines elections brings to the table a large body of experience in maximizing political opportunities for an opposition group under 'difficult' circumstances," Schechter wrote to the Chileans in the early summer of 1987. He suggested they needed Sawyer Miller's assistance on three fronts; first, the practicalities of the campaign, ranging from media to securing polling stations against fraud; second, strategic planning for not just the voter registration effort but also the prospect of a plebiscite to oust Pinochet and, ultimately, an election to replace him; and, third, public opinion management back in the United States, where political and popular sentiment would be critical to any effort to unseat the junta.

The opportunity to remove Pinochet was bizarre: a chance to challenge the authority of the president, but on terms and conditions set by Pinochet himself. If the opposition wanted to remove Pinochet, they were going to have to participate in a plebiscite that Pinochet himself would control.

In 1980, Chile's Constitutional Tribunal had concentrated legislative power in the hands of the president of the republic, General Pinochet, for an eight-year term. In the years that followed, the Chilean opposition challenged his authority in vain. In the early 1980s, mass protests and labor demonstrations prompted Pinochet to declare a state of siege and suppress his opponents in the name of saving Chile from the specter of communist tyranny. In 1985, the moderate parties came together to produce a national accord that set out a transition to democracy, but Pinochet so successfully sowed rancor between the parties and stoked public fears of economic instability that the movement lost its momentum. In September 1986, the commandos of the far left staged an attack on Pinochet on a hillside road outside Santiago that failed to assassinate the president but left five of his bodyguards dead.

By early 1987, then, the fractured and despondent Chilean opposition's unlikely hope of removing Pinochet came down to the upcoming vote on his next eight-year term: a national plebiscite that offered the Chileans the choice of voting yes for Pinochet or no for someone else and an uncertain future. Many opposition figures thought they should boycott a plebiscite that had no credibility, particularly after the suspicions of widespread voter fraud in 1980. They feared that participating would only give legitimacy to Pinochet's dictatorship. Others were convinced that the referendum was unwinnable but that it should be used as a chance to voice criticism of the dictator that might stir up public anger and spark a popular uprising that would sweep Pinochet from office. In other words, Mark Malloch Brown and Peter Schechter were pitching into a muddle.

Their first and most consequential decision was to start with grass-roots public opinion research. Since 1973, the opposition parties in Chile had figured out their strategies on a top-down basis. As Don Gabriel Valdes of the Christian Democratic Party told them, opposition politicians made their choices based, essentially, on the "well-educated guess." Malloch Brown and Schechter started with a fundamental dilemma. What was this campaign really about: should it be a passionate anti-Pinochet campaign or a campaign for free elections? Taking the battle to the president might fire the imagination of disgruntled working-class voters, but it could scare middle-class Chileans who had been willing to sell off a bit of their political freedom for economic success. On the other hand, an appeal to Chileans to support free elections and register for the vote had the benefit of being positive and unthreatening to a cowed Chilean public, but it also carried the danger of boosting turnout for Pinochet's rubber-stamp vote in 1988. The Sawyer Miller men turned to Kennan Research to do the first piece of motivational research in Chile.

Ed Reilly was heading home from Chicago in 1987 when he got a call from Mark Malloch Brown, asking if he would like to come down to Santiago to figure out how to unseat Pinochet. Reilly was a steak-eating American, with no international experience but a political education learned street by street, precinct by precinct in the counties of New Jersey. He was training to become a priest when, as a young man, he abandoned the seminary for politics and made his start in Essex County, getting out the black, Italian, and Irish working-class vote under the flight path of planes coming into the Newark airport. In short order, he was hired to work for the New Jersey governor, then poached to help the Democrats in Massachusetts. In 1984, he made his name as a pollster when he went against the grain and predicted that Walter Mondale would lose New Hampshire in the primary. He was right, and he was soon drafted into the Mondale campaign to research the reactions to Democratic messaging, which was how he first met Sawyer and Miller, who were working on the candidate's TV spots. Reilly had heard about a zany but brilliant Israeli based in New York and contracted out some work to him. That was how he got to know Ned Kennan. Both men were fascinated by not simply the nature of the public's opinions, but what made them move.

In Chile, their findings were startling. For example, 82 percent of people interviewed indicated that they believed it was better to keep one's beliefs to oneself rather than express political opinions freely. When Chileans were asked about the future (i.e., "Do you believe that the political future of this country is a serious problem or do you think that things will work out quite well?") nearly half the people either said "don't know" or refused to answer. In sum, their questioning told them that the Chilean electorate was proud but scared. It would need to be coaxed to register for the vote and would back the process of easing out Pinochet if, paradoxically enough, it could be done in a nonconfrontational way, cast as an apolitical celebration and seen as an act of national "self-affirmation." Ned Kennan, who was reviewing the polling numbers back at the KRC offices in New York, concluded flatly: "They have lost their dicks."

The political class was, indeed, emasculated. The quantitative research survey conducted in December 1987 and January 1988 showed that the public had no confidence in the political leadership within the opposition. Name recognition was "low and mushy." A plebiscite cast as a campaign to remove Pinochet was frightening; a referendum pitched as the first step in a process to elect a new president was seen as highly political and therefore pointless. As Reilly commented in notes accompanying the polling figures: "Images of internal political struggles among opposition figures would most likely reinforce the people's sense of futility: that nothing can be done and nothing can be changed."

Pinochet headed into 1988 confidently preparing for victory in the presidential plebiscite. The vast resources of the regime were mobilized to ensure his triumph and another eight-year term. Provincial governors and city mayors, all of whom had been appointed by Pinochet himself, served as his local campaign bosses. Lucia Hiriart, Pinochet's wife, headed a national network of women's groups, which were marshaled into a grassroots operation to get out the "yes" vote. Pinochet controlled the state media, which started showing a series of spots that boasted of the government's many accomplishments, not least the sudden spending spree on low-income housing.

When the heads of the dozen or so opposition parties gathered in a low outbuilding behind the home of Don Gabriel Valdes in an upmarket suburb of Santiago in early 1988, it fell to the team from Sawyer Miller to lay out a strategy that steered around the public's fears and defeatism. The consultants from New York—Joel McCleary, Mark Malloch Brown, Peter Schechter, Ed Reilly, and Joe Glick, Ned Kennan's KRC partner—were almost as unlikely a bunch of misfits as the fragile coalition of fratricidal politicians they were advising. And their task was a simple paradox: they had to craft a "No" campaign that wasn't negative. So, for a project designed to get rid of the president, they settled on a counterintuitive strategy.

They began by laying out the poll findings. Schechter was translating into Spanish each of his colleagues' individual presentations. He was not particularly concerned when the normally soft-spoken Joe Glick took the microphone to go through the focus group results, but Glick soon warmed to his theme as he painted the picture of what had occurred over the last decade in Chile. "Chilean men exchanged their freedom and liberty for economic prosperity. And in this devil's pact, Chilean men lost their penises." Schechter's translation skidded to a stop. He paused and, in the style championed by Ned Kennan years earlier, he told the truth with wicked relish: "En este pacto con el Diablo, los hombres chilenos perdieron sus organos sexuales."

Then, they told Don Gabriel Valdes and the dozen other opposition politicians that the 1988 campaign would not be about either Augusto Pinochet or, for that matter, the alternative, but it would be about the righteousness of democracy, the joy of having a choice, the time for renewed optimism in the future. It would be an emotional campaign, one that steered clear of all the issues and presented an unrelentingly positive outlook for Chile.

Sawyer Miller started drafting speeches for the bishops of Santiago. "As Chilenos we have a unique opportunity this season, this year, to rise up from a winter where our dignity as God's children as been ignored," they wrote, in a briefing note to be translated and distributed to the clergy. "For many years we have been unable to vote; we have been unable to express our views. We have been unable to fully speak the voice of a Christian." The political leaders who had gathered at Don Gabriel Valdes's house had helped create a coalition of fourteen parties dedicated to bringing out the "no" vote. An all-volunteer force backed by the Socialists and the Christian Democrats then collected signatures needed to legalize the parties and registered voters: by the cut-off date, 92 percent of Chileans had signed up to vote.

Then Malloch Brown's team started working on a message for the TV ad campaign. Again, they returned to the idea of a nation that seemed to have lost its manhood, but where the women made the decisions and carried the hopes of the future. They crafted a spot that made no reference to Pinochet: there were just beautiful images of Chilean kids playing, singing, and running with kites in a park; as the music reached its final rousing chorus, two kites drifted together, one had an N on it, the other an O. The two kites came together to spell, simply, "No." It was a campaign devoid of fact, laden with feel-good sentiment, but the upbeat ads stunned people, drawing them into the promise of a reunited Chile and a return to the democratic traditions they were proud of. The government responded with a wave of negative ads that warned of a return to the chaos and instability of the early 1970s. Not only was the tactic tired but it only reinforced the "No" campaign's image as hopeful and forward-looking, its own as retrospective, fearful, and grim.

As the plebiscite approached, the Chilean opposition grew in confidence, but Mark Malloch Brown became more apprehensive. He found it hard to believe that the military would honor its promise to hold a free and fair election, and he advised the "No" campaign to put in place many of the same safeguards that had worked in the Philippines. He advised that they set up their own quick count, which could be used with the Chilean press and the public on election night to preempt any skewed poll by the Pinochet regime. He told them not to worry about the fact that Pinochet had ruled out foreign observers, which were, anyway, a "mixed blessing," but pressed the Chilean opposition to brief the press and point them in the right direction: "They are covering a computer story, not a riot story." Finally, he told them to start fund-raising. The real cost of an election to oust a dictator would come in the rallies after the vote, not before it. He signed off: "You are part of a historic moment; and all over the world your friends are holding their breath for Chile."

On October 5, 1988, the voting proceeded quietly and without incident. When the polls closed at 9:00 P.M., the opposition's tallies seemed to suggest that they had won. The government, however, kept suspiciously silent. Rather than releasing the numbers on their computers, the state television station switched to a comedy series from the United States. Behind the scenes, some government officials were trying to foment violence on the streets that could have resulted in an army crackdown and an excuse to nullify the vote. But just before three in the morning, government television announced that with 71 percent of the vote counted, the "no" vote was in the lead. The military establishment had pledged to guarantee the outcome of the vote and, it seemed, Pinochet was unable to overrule their determination to adhere to the rules they had all agreed upon. The following night, a morbid-looking Pinochet appeared on television and acknowledged his defeat: 54.5 percent for the "no" vote, 43 percent for the "yes."

Tim Bell, the British advertising executive who had made his name helping Margaret Thatcher to power in 1979, worked for Pinochet and the parties of the right in Chile in the late 1980s. Nevertheless, he watched the men from Sawyer Miller with professional admiration for their artful work: "It was one of the greatest campaigns of all time," he said with a laugh, years later, "because it didn't have anything in it except saying happy people vote 'no.' It was the most brilliant proposition in the world—want to be happy? Vote 'no.' "

On the back of the success in Chile and the Philippines, Sawyer Miller spread across the South American continent: Mark Malloch Brown and Peter Schechter expanded the client roster from Venezuela, Costa Rica, and Panama—the most "gringo" countries in the hemisphere—to every single democratic country in South America except Brazil. From Argentina to Bolivia to Paraguay, they did not lose a pitch. They worked for four Colombian presidents, three Ecuadorean ones. They were an unlikely combination: the Cartesian, artful strategist and the multilingual, passionate wannabe Latino. (Schechter was not actually born Latin American, but he spoke like one, dressed like one, looked like one, and, it seemed to everyone in the office, really wanted to be one.) They became a regular double act south of the Rio Grande. Schechter remembers Malloch Brown turning to him as he settled into another first-class seat on an airplane heading southbound out of John F. Kennedy airport and saying, "Here are the Lone Ranger and Tonto off again to vanquish evil."

THE CHILE CAMPAIGN WAS, though, the last time Mark Malloch Brown and Joel McCleary would work together. Even as the firm was brimming with its own success and swelling with new recruits, there were glimpses of tension in the offices at East Sixtieth Street—and the first farewells.

McCleary had, by his own admission, a little bit of the Heart of Darkness in him, a desire to get a little closer, "to go a little farther up river." He had taken an unusual route into politics: he had left Harvard in 1971 and headed to Washington, New Jersey, where he sought out Tibetan teacher Geshe Wangyal, from whom he hoped to understand the secrets of Zen asceticism, to travel the path beyond the corruptions of real life and into the white light of enlightenment, to start to become a Buddhist monk. But, as McCleary recalled years later in an article entitled "Confessions of a Buddhist Political Junkie," Wangyal shaved McCleary's beard, not his head. He fed McCleary boiled lamb, and they played countless games of chess, and after a few months, he tossed him "back into the twentieth century, insisting that the door to englightenment was to be found in the very stuff of ordinary reality. His [Wangyal's] mantra was not just to say 'om mani padme hum,' but to do something useful. Over our games of chess, he coaxed me into politics."

When McCleary was working in the Carter White House, he used to escape now and again to go back up to Wangyal's New Jersey retreat for meditation and long games of chess with the monk. And during his years with Sawyer Miller, working in Shagari's Nigeria or Marcos's Philippines or Noriega's Panama, McCleary clung to the wisdom he had garnered over the chess board, the belief that Buddhism was not about self-absorption, detached meditation, or an otherworldly intoxication in Eastern philosophy but a conviction that Buddhists should strive to alleviate suffering in the here-and-now, that they should be politically involved. This idealism was sometimes hard to discern in McCleary, a bombastic bon viveur who talked fourteen to the dozen, traded international conspiracy theories and Washington lore, and seemed to love politics the way some people love opera—namely, paying little attention to the words but being carried away by the music. Even McCleary himself would acknowledge that the outcomes of the political chess he played, both in the White House and as the head of the international division of the Sawyer Miller Group, did not always match the purity of his motivation: "More often than not, I lost track of which were the white and black pieces. I often found the game with the darker players, the black pieces, to be more engaging, seductive, and even more honest than that with the sometimes pious, precious, and self-proclaimed forces of good."

By the late 1980s, McCleary found himself drifting away from the firm—in part because it had become a more professional and disciplined place. He had taken some time off in 1986 to travel to Dharamsala, the home of the Tibetan government in exile, and by the time he got back to New York, Mark Malloch Brown was settled in running the international division of Sawyer Miller and making a big success of it. The firm was getting bigger, staffed by younger, more energetic, and more disciplined consultants. Sawyer "had hired all these gladiators," McCleary remembered, "and they were not staying down in the arena." In part, there were real ideological tensions between McCleary and Malloch Brown. While Joel liked working with the "darker pieces," particularly in Manuel Noriega's Panama, Mark thought that his work in Central America would tarnish the reputation of the firm and prove the undoing of Sawyer Miller. In part, McCleary left because he was finding it harder and harder to see in the offices of East Sixtieth Street the adventure and romanticism that had first drawn him to the idea of working for David Sawyer.

Not long after the trip to Santiago, Joel McCleary resigned to work pro bono for the Tibetans. He canvassed opinion in Washington, Moscow, New York, Hong Kong, Dharamsala, and Delhi to draw up a strategy to deal with the Tibetans' struggle with the communist government in China, which had invaded Tibet after the 1949 revolution and then seized control of the country in 1959. Ever since, the Tibetans had operated a government-in-exile in the foothills of the Himalayas, and the Chinese had insisted that Tibet was an integral part of the People's Republic.

McCleary produced a 164-page campaign document for the Dalai Lama that applied the principles of international public diplomacy as conceived by Sawyer Miller on an unprecedented scale: it proposed the appointment of a prime minister and a foreign minister as part of a restructuring of the government-in-exile in order to confer greater legitimacy on the Tibetans; it laid out succession plans in the event of the Dalai Lama's death; it identified the key figures in Washington to advance a policy agenda that would put pressure on China; it suggested the introduction of monthly national radio addresses by the Dalai Lama to be taped and distributed clandestinely inside Tibet; it laid out plans to create a pan-Buddhist organization to align religious believers with the plight of Tibet; and it planned a media program for the Dalai Lama and a public relations drive that would harden American public opinion against Beijing. This was, he concluded, an "imposing-looking list. But, as with every campaign, if you work hard to get yourselves through the organizational stage, you will find the rest of the process much easier." The real challenge, he advised the Tibetans, was in "raising the adrenalin level. Once that is done and your troops are committed, the campaign will begin to have a momentum of its own." It was vintage Sawyer Miller: the most ambitious campaign on behalf of the most enfeebled underdog against the most improbably powerful incumbent, the People's Republic of China.

It is a campaign that is still a long way from being won, but McCleary maintains to this day that it was the best work he ever did. "We won, in an odd way," he says. "The Dalai Lama, not Mao, is the talk of universities today. His Holiness is more popular than any other religious leader in the world. The campaign we launched in 1986 helped the world see who he was. In my view, Buddhism will one day reestablish itself in China, and His Holiness will have done what the Polish Pope did in eastern Europe."

Just as McCleary took up the Tibetan cause, the Sawyer Miller Group was delving deeper into corporate work and, as far as McCleary was concerned, losing its heart and soul. He could not have done the Dalai Lama campaign with a firm that was becoming ever more commercially minded: "Good fees never come with good causes," McCleary says, but, he adds: "What I did for the Tibetans came from what David and Scott taught me . . . It was done in the spirit of the old firm at its best."

James Carville was also parting ways with Sawyer Miller at this time. Though not formally on the Sawyer Miller staff, Carville spent a fair amount of 1987 in the firm's offices working with Mandy Grunwald on Wallace Wilkinson's campaign for the Kentucky governorship. In those days, Carville was still a relative unknown: it was a few years before he had done his turn as the P. T. Barnum of the Clinton circus in Little Rock; a decade before he parlayed his Cajun patter into cable television celebrity. He was just a young talent from Louisiana, a breeding ground for political hacks who can both quote Walt Whitman at length and list the storied brothels on the outskirts of Baton Rouge, who grasp both the dark, anxious side to America's optimistic character and who can sniff out the human frailty in a squared-away, all-American candidate for Congress.

But Carville's work on the Wilkinson campaign had gotten him noticed. Wilkinson, a Democrat businessman born and raised deep in the Republican heart of Kentucky, was running against a couple of former governors and an incumbent lieutenant governor. He trailed for a long while at 1 percent in the polls. As in Chile, so in Kentucky: Sawyer Miller put its faith in focus groups and in-depth interviews. It found that Kentucky voters were appalled by the higher-tax proposals of the two main Democratic candidates. Sawyer Miller tested the idea of introducing a state lottery. On the back of apparent public support, the idea became the central proposal of Wilkinson's campaign. At the same time, they produced a series of political ads that cast Wilkinson as a political outsider with a track record of getting things done in business: the man from Casey County was filmed walking up the dirt roads of rural Kentucky in his shirtsleeves, then getting off a private jet to tour one of his warehouses, then seated at a computer, and then on a construction site. It was a formidable combination of poll-driven policy making and finely pitched messaging. Wilkinson was catapulted to a snowball's-chance-in-hell victory. The race forged a lasting political friendship between Carville and Grunwald. Ever since, she says, they talk to each other almost every day.

David Sawyer began an arduous courtship of Carville. He hoped to woo and cajole the obviously talented Cajun into running the domestic political business for the firm. He failed. Jack Leslie remembers having Carville into his office: "We want you to build the political business," he told him. Carville replied, "Build? Build? Fuck build. I don't want to build a fucking business for you guys. I want to find a candidate to run for president and help him to the White House." Which was what he did. In 1992, Carville was Bill Clinton's chief strategist. He ran the "war room" and he ran his mouth—both were lively operations.

There were just a couple of quiet departures and a couple of largely contained discontents in an otherwise blooming enterprise. To be sure, it was an office of shouters—David Sawyer shouted regularly; so did Joel McCleary; Harris Diamond was an inveterate shouter; Mandy Grunwald did not shout, but she did not need to, as she could be so dismissive and full of spleen that she could reduce her secretary to tears a couple of times a week without even raising her voice. But when the doors really slammed and the screaming hit an unbearable pitch, it was usually because Iris Sawyer had stopped by East Sixtieth Street.

After their divorce, David had quickly married Nell McFarland, but Iris had continued to conduct her not-so-secret affair with Tom Kempner. The two of them enjoyed a luxurious and clandestine romance, spending weekends up in South Hampton or in Los Angeles or Aspen. In the mid-1980s, Tom Kempner encouraged Iris to go into business with him renovating houses on the Upper East Side. They built two giant properties, 157 and 167 on East Sixty-third Street. To invest her share, Iris borrowed $1.2 million. This barely seemed like a financial gamble: she was dating one of the most successful financiers in New York; she had had a decent financial settlement from David; and she was plowing money into real estate in one of the most sought-after neighborhoods in Manhattan.

After eight years, though, Nan Kempner, the wiry socialite married to Tom, called time on Tommy's affair. The secret had become so public that it was slipping into the New York gossip columns and becoming an embarrassment. Tommy was told he had to cut Iris off. And in the summer of 1988, he did. "I love you," Iris remembers him telling her, "but the price is too high." Worse, he also liquidated the investments they had together in the property venture. Iris begged him not to, but Nan insisted that he sever all ties with Iris. Suddenly, she was plunged into debt. She lost money on 157 East Sixty-third Street and, for a while, rented out 167, but she could not cover the mortgage payments, and the banks foreclosed. She moved into a rental apartment ten blocks up and started to sell off the things she owned. She also started making more regular visits to the Sawyer Miller offices at East Sixtieth Street, desperate to pursue David for money. Infuriated that he was hiding (and she knew he was hiding), she would curse him for short-changing her in the divorce settlement. She grew increasingly convinced, too, that Nan Kempner and her circle of friends were trying to destroy her. They cut her out of the Hamptons social set, which ensured that none of their friends from the old days who sat on the board of the Metropolitan Museum of Art would lend her money, and pretty soon none would see her at all. Once, when the brake fluid seemed to have been drained from her car, Iris became convinced that Nan wanted her dead.

Nearly eight years after Tom Kempner dumped her and set in train her downfall from New York society life, Iris successfully sued David Sawyer for $200,000 arrears in pension payments. It was enough to get her a flight to London and an apartment on Pond Street, where, for the seventh time, she assumed a new name. This time, it was Susan Lennox, not so much in memory of the Greta Garbo movie *The Second Life of Susan Lennox*, but because she lived around the corner from Lennox Gardens in London. She started making and designing her own jewelery. It was picked up by the society magazines: *Tatler, Harper's, Queen, Country Life.* Within three years, she had made just enough money to go back and rent a place in New York. She chose East Sixty-third Street and a single-room apartment, across the street from the house that had almost destroyed her.

PART THREE

I am not an old experienced hand at politics. But I am seasoned enough to have learned that the hardest thing about any political campaign is how to win without proving that you are unworthy of winning.

—Adlai Stevenson

SEVEN

"IT'S TIME FOR A GREAT CHANGE"

THE MEMO is the consultant's proof of life. In an industry full of blow-hards and hot-air merchants, the memorandum is the difference between bluster and a plan.

In 1989, the Sawyer Miller Group wrote a particularly long, grandiose memo for the novelist Mario Vargas Llosa. It was titled "Peru: The Liberal Mandate." The men from Sawyer Miller by then served up memos like pizza—same base, slightly different toppings. There was the standard, three-step timetable to victory: first connect with the voter; then take out the opposition; finally, create a sense of inevitable victory. There was the dogmatic section on the need for military-style organization. There was the firm's famously frank assessment of the candidate's vulnerabilities. And, almost as an afterthought, there was a warning: "Momentum is a dangerous thing."

Mario Vargas Llosa hardly seemed to need their advice. He had, at the very least, a fifty-point lead over any of his nearest rivals. (The numbers varied wildly: one showed him standing at 82 percent in the polls; others had him backed by half the electorate and enjoying a thirty-percentage-point lead. Either way, he was way out yonder in front.) He was Peru's most famous son, the fêted author of such esteemed works as *The Time of the Hero, The Notebooks of Don Rigoberto*, and *Aunt Julia and the Scriptwriter*. He was the only Peruvian to have achieved worldwide renown, he had millions of dollars at his disposal, he had overwhelming public support, and he had no credible opponent. What could possibly go wrong?

DAVID SAWYER, of course, had seen a shock upset to a sure thing before. Back in 1983 he had been called to Chicago to help Jane Byrne, the mayor, win reelection. She was the city's first female mayor—at the time, the only woman to have been elected to run one of America's big cities— and she had a huge lead over her challengers.

In Chicago, a Democratic town, the chief hurdle was getting past the party primary. Byrne looked set to see off the young Richard M. Daley, the son of Richard J. Daley who had served as mayor for a historic six terms, lorded over Cook County politics, and died in office in 1976. There was another Democratic candidate, but people didn't pay him that much attention. His name was Harold Washington. He was black. It was amazing enough that Chicago had elected a woman. But a black mayor? A few months out from the primary, the polls showed Byrne twenty-one points ahead of Daley. Sawyer saw his job, as he often did, as little more than nannying his candidate to victory. Sawyer and his firm were squarely behind Byrne's progressive agenda and they looked to add, quite literally, style. He provided wardrobe advice to clients like Byrne, taking them to be dressed on Fifth Avenue. (He took the men to Dunhill.)

When a new ream of statistics came through one evening in late 1982, the Sawyer Miller people got together in the boardroom. They brought in expensive port and some cigars and, as things wore on, they ordered in Chinese food. Dick Dresner, a formidable quantitative analyst of the polls, pored over a sheaf of computer paper containing the latest numbers from Chicago and then gave an impromptu forty-five-minute presentation on the breakdown of the Chicago vote. He set out the path to victory and predicted that Jane Byrne would be reelected. Bob Perkins, Sawyer's first Republican recruit, remembers being impressed by Dresner's lucidity and certainty.

It was getting late, and the team took a break. Then Ned Kennan offered his analysis. He hadn't really analyzed the polls, but he had been to Chicago, conducted some focus groups, and had had a few long conversations. "Politics is interesting to the white guys of Chicago," he said. "But to the black guys, it's religion. Harold Washington has got religion. He's going to win it, and there's nothing you can do about it." At the time, Perkins remembers, Washington was at six points in the polls.

David Sawyer went to Chicago and told Byrne that Harold Washington looked like more of a threat than they first thought. "His exact words were: 'He is beginning to show movement,' " Byrne remembers. " 'He is beginning to develop a movement.' " It was becoming a three-way race. Sawyer's solution was to take down Daley. Byrne remembers being angry. It was Christmastime. They were six weeks away from the primary. She had worked for Daley's father and did not want to attack the son. She felt let down by her consultants: "The whole campaign up until then had been to ignore Daley." Sawyer argued that Daley was down; it was the time to kick him. Byrne was reluctant, and hesitated. Harold Washington surged: he pulled in 37 percent of the vote; Byrne got 33 percent; Daley got 30 percent.

Harold Washington came from nowhere and won. So, when Sawyer's protégés headed to Peru in 1989 to prepare for the presidential election the following April, they knew all too well that "Momentum is a dangerous thing."

Still, the team that landed in Lima—Peter Schechter, Ed Reilly, Barry French, and Mark Malloch Brown—knew a fair bit about winning, too. In the couple of short years after the triumph in the Philippines, Latin America had become a showcase for Sawyer Miller's talents.

The whole team was fresh from their storied success in Chile. Schechter arrived in Lima on the heels of victory in Ecuador. Almost as soon as he joined the firm in 1987, he had been sent down to rent an apartment in Quito. Shuttling back and forth between the United States and Ecuador for six months, he cut the candidate's commercials, reengineered the campaign organization, and shaped the political message so as to help Rodrigo Borja, who had run and lost twice before, win the presidency in 1988. In Bolivia, Mark Malloch Brown—aided and abetted by Ed Reilly and Rob Shepardson, another new hire—had just marched his underdog candidate, Gonzalo Sánchez de Lozada, to first place in the polls. ("Goni" came from third to first to win the election, but the two leading parties formed a coalition to keep him out of the presidency. He ran again in 1993 and won.) Better known for being finance minister than for who he was, he unsurprisingly started out trailing far behind. Sawyer Miller sought to give him personality: he was rebranded publicly as Goni; he was encouraged to cut ties with his party, he launched a series of negative ads attacking his opponents for their part in Bolivia's struggle with hyperinflation; and he posed as a modern, independent-minded man, much in the mold of Wallace Wilkinson of Kentucky: Sawyer Miller filmed Goni tapping away at a computer (years later, Goni revealed he was only playing Pac-Man) and then walking over to a window to look out on a street of smiling, hopeful children. It was classic Sawyer Miller stuff—and it worked: Goni won the election in 1989, even though, under Bolivia's arcane election rules, the Senate was able to keep him out of the presidential palace for a further four years. When he ran again, twice, he won, on both occasions using American consultants.

Not only did Goni's success serve as an advertisement for Sawyer Miller, but the Bolivian himself helped open the door in Peru. As he said, "Sawyer Miller changed Bolivian and Latin American politics, because I recommended them to Vargas Llosa in Peru and a couple of other candidates. It was really the application of their technology. If you have a good product you can sell it well; if you don't have a good product, nobody can sell it . . . They gave the message and we stayed on message."

When Malloch Brown went to pitch his services to Mario Vargas Llosa, who, like Gonzalo Sánchez de Lozada, also wanted to impose the shock therapy of market liberalism on a failing economy, he marshaled Goni to help make his case. During the presentation, a call came from neighboring Bolivia: "Goni told Mario that the politics of conviction would be enhanced by a scientific campaign; that polling and television could be deployed to strengthen the argument for economic reform," Malloch Brown recalled in an article written after the election. "Mario . . . seemed intrigued by our black arts and was determined to make his campaign as modern as he hoped his presidency would be."

MARIO VARGAS LLOSA'S seemingly inevitable journey to the presidency began in 1987, on a beach. He was on vacation, listening to the radio, when he heard President Alan García announce his plan to nationalize the banks. For Vargas Llosa, as allergic to extensions of state power as reformed socialists tend to be, this was crossing a red line. As far as he was concerned, the banks were the wells of capitalism. García's plan would poison them. More government intervention would mean just more corruption and less growth, a bigger state and a weaker economy. The morning after the radio announcement, he recalls in his memoirs, Vargas Llosa took a run along the beach at Punta Sal, escorted by his wife and a flock of gannets. "Once more in its history, Peru has taken yet another step backward toward barbarism," he remembers telling her.

A group of like-minded free-market liberals quickly gathered to take

García on. Businessmen and artists, they met in Vargas Llosa's home in Barranco, an artsy district of Lima that sits on the cliffs beneath the Peruvian capital's low gray skies and looks out over the vast, dark waters of the Pacific. Within weeks, they had channeled their anger into a start-up political movement. They arranged their first rally to be held in Plaza San Martín, in Lima.

Crowds of mostly middle-class Peruvians flocked in the thousands, carrying banners that read, "No to García," "We don't want to be like Cuba," "Hitler No, Liberty Yes." Vargas Llosa spoke: "Official propaganda said only four bankers and a handful of preppies would come to the Plaza San Martín tonight. And from this platform I see a sea of heads lost in the night and reply: I wish there were this many bankers in Peru." The crowd laughed. "Because then our country would be a prosperous country with work and riches, not the poor, backward country that it is!" The crowd filled the square and, time and again, called out for Mario. The right in Peru suddenly seemed to have rediscovered its voice. The Liberty Movement had a message and a messenger. Mario had set aside his pen and picked up the megaphone. Unspoken though it was, the expectation that Mario Vargas Llosa would run for president took hold that night.

After the rally, one journalist remarked to one of Vargas Llosa's aides, "You have a big problem. You've been born backward. What you've done in the Plaza San Martín is the way candidates should finish—not begin." Others had more serious misgivings. Patricia, Vargas Llosa's wife, counseled him against running, worried about their safety. So, too, did the writer Octavio Paz, who warned that intellectuals had tried before to unravel a nation's problems and failed. Mario Vargas Llosa, both in conversation and in his memoir of the campaign, *El Pez en el Agua* (*A Fish in the Water*), also recalls his reservations about giving up the writer's life, the sacrifice of books that would go unread, the loss of stories and essays that would go unwritten. Jeff Daeschner, who reconstructs Vargas Llosa's presidential bid step by step in his book *The War of the End of Democracy*— the title is a play on Vargas Llosa's own book *The War of the End of the World*—suggests the novelist doth protest too much: Vargas Llosa had long harbored discreet ambitions of high office.

Mario and Patricia were still arguing over the possibility of a presidential run in the summer of 1988 when they had dinner with their cousins in Zurich. (The Vargas Llosas were in that class of cosmopolitan Peruvians who enjoyed spending long stretches in the capitals of Europe: Lon-

don, Paris, Madrid, and, occasionally, Zurich.) Freddy Cooper Llosa, an
architect in Lima who was Mario's cousin and would become his campaign manager, was quoted as remembering: "He made a very eloquent
description to his wife about why he was involving himself in politics,
about his idea of life as an adventure . . . He could not very well withdraw—not so much because of moral reasons—but because there was a
challenge there, which was what literature was all about." Whether it was
a sense of moral obligation or literary adventurism or simply ambition
that propelled Vargas Llosa to run, run he did, declaring his candidacy on
June 4, 1989.

Vargas Llosa was an admirer of Margaret Thatcher. Like so many other
devout believers in the free market, he had started out on the left and, in
early middle age, swung to the right. He hoped to emulate the Thatcher
revolution, in Peru, to make Peru, he said, the Switzerland of Latin America; the land of the Incas, a country of bankers. His program would be
radical and aggressive, axing state jobs and privatizing state-held indus-
tries. As a first step to replicating the Thatcher government, he sought to
import her advisers.

Tim Bell, at the advertising firm Saatchi and Saatchi, had been at the
heart of Thatcher's winning team in 1979. Ever since, he had been approached by an extraordinary array of politicians looking to replicate her
success. He had become the only British election adviser to work abroad,
the United Kingdom's own version of Sawyer Miller and Black, Manafort
and Stone all rolled into one. He was soon working in Malta, Jamaica,
France, and Sweden, and, by the late 1980s, in Chile, on the opposite side
from the Sawyer Miller men. Even Lee Kwan Yew, the Singaporean leader,
sought his advice: when Bell pointed out that this was probably unneces-
sary, as there was only one person in the Singaporean opposition,
he remembers Lee's response: "One too many." Bell liked to work for conservative politicians, women and men who stood up to socialism and
what he saw as the public servitude caused by state dependency. Over
time, this visceral opposition to the left has meant that Bell has gone to
work for very controversial figures on the right: Pinochet in Chile, F. W.
de Klerk in South Africa. When Vargas Llosa approached Saatchi and
Saatchi, Tim Bell said he was happy to help but could not get involved on
the ground. Among other things, he did not want to send people to Peru,
alarmed as he was by the reports of terrorist attacks conducted by the
Shining Path guerrillas. (With hindsight, this is ironic: Bell's firm was one

of the first to put people in Baghdad on a political consulting contract for the U.S.-led coalition in Iraq.) All this meant that Bell had only ever committed to keeping in touch with the Vargas Llosa campaign by phone. And without a presence in Peru, he was pretty soon edged aside by the consultants who were there, the men from Sawyer Miller.

Mark Malloch Brown pitched himself and the services of the firm as the ticket to help make the bitter Thatcherite medicine go down. He went to Lima thinking, as he later wrote, that "we could do for Mario what Thatcher's consultants had done for her: take the hard edge off a radical program for economic recovery."

The Vargas Llosa camp was suspicious of Sawyer Miller. "We hesitated before contracting a North American company, assuming that it would rely on highly emotive images rather than ideas," Alvaro Vargas Llosa, Mario's twenty-three-year-old son and the campaign's press officer, later recalled. They did not want an election of colors and feelings. Their obsession was "pedagogy": Mario Vargas Llosa wanted to show his country a better way, to teach Peru a lesson. "We did not want to win an election with a sensationalist campaign. To our surprise, however, the gringos from Sawyer Miller turned out to share our temperament. They had succeeded with Corazon Aquino's campaign in the Philippines, the 'No' campaign in Chile, Sánchez de Lozada in Bolivia . . . and Virgilio Barco in Colombia. Moreover, the representative of the Sawyer Miller team turned out to be English, Mark Malloch Brown." (In fact, Malloch Brown's family was South African, but after years working for *The Economist* on St. James, he struck the Peruvians as being as English as marmalade.)

For their part, the men from Sawyer Miller were soon at odds with the Mario Vargas Llosa camp. Their first—and enduring—concern was the candidate's relationship with the political establishment. Vargas Llosa had chosen to forge an alliance—FREDEMO, the Democratic Front—with the grandees of Peruvian politics. It quickly proved to be a mistake. His own party, the Liberty Movement, was new, an upstart party made up of people fed up with politics as usual. His allies in FREDEMO, the Popular Action and Popular Christian parties, were part of the old, discredited machine.

Mario Vargas Llosa soon found himself involved in just the kind of backroom horse trading that had destroyed public faith in politicians. It was, in fact, precisely the politics of the smoke-filled room that he was supposed to be standing against. The two big parties, the Popular Action

Party and the Popular Christian Party, offered him a deal: if he backed their candidates in the mayoral election, they would back him in the presidential race. The first round of negotiation did not go well. Vargas Llosa sought to act as the mediator of an agreement, but it quickly broke down. The novelist felt humiliated and infuriated. It was his first intimate exposure to the petty venality of Peruvian politics, and he was disgusted by it. He resigned his candidacy. Three weeks after starting his race for the presidency, he had dropped out and returned to life as a writer.

Malloch Brown thought that the resignation was a masterstroke, a brilliant breach with the political establishment. The best thing Vargas Llosa could do was tout his new-broom credentials by making clear that he was an outsider, severed of all ties to Peru's ineffectual old-party hacks. Malloch Brown, Reilly, and Schecter had been vehemently against the bargain with the big parties over the mayoral election. To them, it would communicate to voters that there was no difference between Mario Vargas Llosa and what he stood against. He was propelled by Peruvian hopes that he was antipolitical, anti-machine. And yet the carve-up over the mayoral contest was an archly political deal, a piece of pure machine politics. Mark Malloch Brown made the case against cutting a deal. "I urged him: 'Don't sign up again. You could do much better with a message and an organization of volunteers.' " Malloch Brown remembers, "I was utterly dismissive of the whole [FREDEMO] organization." Indeed, everyone around Vargas Llosa was urging him not to get back into bed with the Popular Action and the Popular Christian parties.

The Sawyer Miller men had a well-worn explanation for why Mario Vargas Llosa should steer clear of the established parties of Peru, a theory they clumsily dubbed the "moral-political axis." And by now the Sawyer Miller consultants had seen the moral-political trade-off at work on campaign after campaign in America. They each had their own examples. Jack Leslie, who was then president of Sawyer Miller, had learned this lesson the hard way on the Hunt-Helms race. In 1984, he helped Jim Hunt, a Democrat, run against the High Church conservative Jesse Helms for the Senate seat in North Carolina. Helms instinctively understood that people might not always like his views, but they liked the fact that he was seen as a "moral" politician, a man who stuck to his guns. He ended every campaign ad—and the North Carolina Senate race of 1984 broke all records for the volume of political commercials cut and aired—with the same question: "Where do you stand, Jim?" Again and again and again:

"Where do you stand, Jim? Where do you stand, Jim?" The implication, of course, was that Jim Hunt was political and inconstant; by contrast, you might not always agree with Jesse Helms, but, by God, you knew where he stood. Ronald Reagan took the same tack with Walter Mondale. George W. Bush did the same to "flip-flopping" John Kerry. They positioned themselves as moral candidates, their opponents as political. The Bush White House was quite open about it: Karl Rove liked to say that the greatest asset of his candidate, Bush, was that he was a man who meant what he said and said what he meant.

Alvaro Vargas Llosa did not have Sawyer Miller's experience in North Carolina, but he understood clearly that his father needed to stand as a moral figure, a man who renounced political expediency. As he put it, "We knew very well that if we had broken the alliance after my father's resignation . . . the election was won. But . . . my father was against any disloyal gesture."

The candidate still believed in the mysterious power of the party. They would, he thought, get him ballot access, disseminate his message, and marshal their votes in his favor. They were lead by the grand old men of Peruvian politics, and, the men from Sawyer Miller discovered, Vargas Llosa very much sought their approval. "In the end, Mario was unable to resist the urge," judged Schechter. "My view is that he became drunk on the notion that he was hobnobbing with these political wolves. He so criticized them, but in the end he wanted to be like them. They were the symbol of Peruvian elites."

Vargas Llosa signed back up with the alliance of big, powerful political parties, cutting a deal on the mayoral election. For all his ironic detachment as writer on the follies of life in Peru, he was still a boy from a broken, middle-class family, born in a provincial town. He behaved like a man who mocks the country club his whole life only because he wants so badly to belong. And, in signing up with the old, established parties, he squandered his biggest selling point to voters: the promise of change. In Reilly's view, it was all over not long after they began: "Peru was lost when Mario Vargas Llosa decided that . . . they had to do a deal with the big political parties. We argued against it, but we lost that argument and the campaign was lost. We created the vacuum on the side of change."

Sawyer Miller's men forever chafed against the party machine. Once Vargas Llosa signed back up with Luis Bedoya Reyes and Fernando Belaunde Terry, the two heads of the big political parties, the American consultants had to swallow it. But they advised him to keep the party men on the outside. "There is no reason why the public front of FREDEMO needs to tie up the operational management of your campaign," Sawyer Miller urged Vargas Llosa in their memo. He had become a "hostage," they said. The alliance, FREDEMO—the Democratic Front—looked more and more like a "retirement home for old politicians and committee men." The big parties were not going to deliver their side of the bargain, namely national organization, political savvy, and a bankable get-out-the-vote operation. Mario Vargas Llosa would have a much more powerful message standing alone. He had forfeited that. But the next best thing was a small, loyal cadre of staff around him, keeping the campaign independent of traditional political shenanigans. "In a campaign," the Sawyer Miller memo said, "control cannot be compromised by courtesies."

The result was that Mario Vargas Llosa was being pulled this way and that, tugged one direction by his foreign advisers, another by his home-grown political allies. And as much as the gringo consultants were trying surreptitiously to edge out the seasoned party apparatchiks, the old Peruvian foxes nodded in agreement with the Sawyer Miller men when they were in Lima, but then ignored their advice and carried on regardless as soon as the latter got on the plane back to New York.

Vargas Llosa's closest advisers were his family. Patricia, his formidable wife, effectively controlled his diary and, by extension, the campaign schedule. Alvaro, his son, who had toyed with magazine work in his teens and stiffened his conservative beliefs with a few years' study at the London School of Economics in the heyday of Margaret Thatcher's Britain, was appointed press secretary. The Sawyer Miller men considered him a precocious know-it-all and dubbed him "the child prince." He generated strong feelings: many people admired him; he had developed a reputation as one of the young Turks of Peruvian liberalism. Many in the Peruvian press corps, though, loathed him. Half the journalists covering the campaign, Alvaro said over breakfast at his home in Washington years later, "hated my guts." When asked whether this was because he was the son of the candidate or a cocky twenty-three-year-old, he said, "Probably both. I had access to the candidate . . . so I could do my job. But I was not a subdued, gray bureaucrat. I was a political fighter."

Lucho, a cousin who had had some limited success shooting commercials in Los Angeles, was brought in to make the campaign ads. Roxana, Lucho's wife, sang the campaign song. Freddy Cooper Llosa was the campaign manager. They were known inside the campaign as the Royal Family, an inner circle even closer than Mario's kitchen cabinet. They were all white. And, according to Peter Schechter, their combined political experience was "zip." Vargas Llosa's court bore a slight resemblance to the Sun King's, a place that revolved around a brilliant man prone to rashness, who could be swayed this way and that by quarreling advisers and relatives unversed in the affairs of state.

The appearance on television one evening of what became known as the "pissing monkey ad" epitomized the organizational chaos—not to mention the whimsy and arrogance—of the Vargas Llosa campaign. In the ad a monkey dressed in the typical clothes of a Peruvian bureaucrat—a white shirt, a red tie, and gray pants—starts prancing about on a desk. "Today great experts make great decisions," the narrator says. The monkey chomps on some fruit. "Workers dedicated to helping their country." The monkey receives a handful of money. "Men of incorruptible morals." The monkey stands on the desk and jibbers, then he sticks out his bum at the camera. "Who know how to face problems." The monkey defecates on the desk. "And always worry about those below." The FREDEMO logo comes up on-screen. "It's time for a great change."

There had been no wide consultation on the advertisement. There was no strategic purpose behind it, no target audience, no process for its approval, and no plan for its broadcast. It had its origins in a tortoise commercial shot by Daniel Winitzky, one of the campaign's young advertising guys. The earlier ad involved a tortoise walking into a glass wall; the tagline was, "We'll be able to advance when we change direction." Vargas Llosa really liked it. So, as Winitzky himself was quoted as saying, "It was only natural that from there we would choose an animal for every issue." The ad guys went to the zoo to brainstorm. When they shot the monkey ad, the toilet scene was unscripted but they thought it was hilarious and included the footage. When Freddy Cooper popped round to Mario's house one Saturday night and showed him the commercial, he laughed out loud and gave it the go-ahead. As a follow-up, Winitzky had already lined up a pig, which was to be dressed as a civil servant.

Few people other than Mario Vargas Llosa, however, thought the monkey ad was funny. The leading newspaper deemed it in bad taste, a disappointment coming from a party that was supposed to be led by an artist. To the many darker-skinned Peruvians, it seemed to be a white man's joke, a condescending laugh at the "apes." Worse still, well over half a million civil servants in Peru had been insulted, and those monkeys all had votes. The FREDEMO campaign immediately sought to pull the ad. But, Ed Reilly remembers, Mario's opponents had the last laugh: "We couldn't get it off the air. We got it off the commercial stations. But Alan García [the president and Mario Vargas Llosa's staunch opponent] kept it on state television all the way through the campaign." The monkey ad was special, one of those few pieces of political propaganda that do more for the opposition than for the candidate.

Other commercials were just ineffectual: Lucho, for example, amassed hundreds of people on a hillside outside Lima to sing the FREDEMO song. It was a big production and it looked lovely, but the men from Sawyer Miller could not, for the life of them, see its strategic purpose.

Mario's ads were just a fraction of the problem. His fellow FREDEMO candidates running for the Peruvian parliament blitzed the airwaves with political ads, one shriller, clunkier, and more mawkish than the next. One candidate's eyes brimmed with tears, another claimed a special connection with the Pope. Alberto Massa, an obese candidate for the lower house, ran an ad that showed him looking at a narrow chair in parliament and asking, "Will I get in?" As Daeschner reported later, Massa then sat down in a chair specially made to accommodate his girth. "With a little help from my friends, I think I'll get in." He didn't get in. But he did contribute to what Peruvians saw as obscene expenditure on advertising.

Peruvians working on the minimum wage at the time were earning just over two dollars a day. Peru's leading newspaper, *Caretas*, reported that four of FREDEMO's most profligate candidates had spent on average of $207,000 in two months, when they could legally earn just $162,000 over their five years in the Senate. Over the course of the election campaign, FREDEMO spent $12.3 million. Peru's social democratic party, APRA, the next biggest spender, spent a fifth of that, $2.7 million. FREDEMO advertisements played one after another after another, seemingly around the clock, becoming fodder for Peru's pundits and funnymen and incontrovertible evidence of the corruption of politics. Many people were disgusted; many just switched off.

When Mario Vargas Llosa called on the candidates in his FREDEMO alliance to curb the advertising, they paid him no heed. A week before the election, he was reduced to making a public apology. He seemed like an ineffectual leader at the helm of a party of plutocrats. Kurt Schultze-Rhonhof, a Lima businessman asked to work on the radical reform plan that would serve as the road map for the Vargas Llosa government, remembers, "The campaign was a terribly poorly structured ego trip for each and every candidate, who individually promoted his image." He watched the competition for money and airtime with growing despair. "Obviously, it alienated the electorate to whom they should have appealed."

The campaign was as disciplined as a toddler's tea party. Mark Malloch Brown described the process: "Decisions would be taken; campaign plans agreed to; ads written and scheduled; Mario's trips planned. Then my colleagues and I would leave, and Mario, who had been the fiercest advocate of strategic campaigning, would be the first to break ranks and go chasing after the day's ephemeral issue." Vargas Llosa and his family took pride in this impulsiveness. The election was an intellectual, even an artistic, adventure for them. They were thrilled by their own spur-of-the-moment ideas, convinced that politics meant going with the gut. "On dozens of occasions," recalled Alvaro, "our own impulses led the campaign along twists and turns far from the preestablished plan." Malloch Brown tried to point out that Margaret Thatcher was never so wayward. She stuck to her message. "Political communication is two things: definition and repetition," Malloch Brown later reflected. Mario kept moving on to the next thing. "Mrs. Thatcher made dullness a virtue; she never tired of saying the same thing." Vargas Llosa neither wanted nor tried to repeat himself.

The first step in the program laid out in the Sawyer Miller memo involved, as it almost always did, making a connection with ordinary people. This came particularly hard to Mario Vargas Llosa, because he did not seem to like them. Miguel Cruchaga, a senior campaign aide, was later quoted describing life on the campaign trail with Mario: "You say to him, 'Listen, Mario, it's six o'clock, maybe we can use our time to go to the market, there are many more people in the market. If you go to the market as a surprise, there's no danger that anything will happen to you and we can make a few more votes.'

"Then he would turn to me and say: 'Is that really necessary?'

" 'Well, it's not really necessary, but you know, every vote would count.'

"And Vargas Llosa would say, 'You know, I'm a little behind on my reading. I would much rather go back home.'" On the road, he preferred to eat alone. He detested dinners with the local political bosses. "They were all cut from the same cloth by the same tailor . . . they had all changed ideologies the way one changes one's shirt," he wrote in his memoir. "I would even go so far as to swear that they all looked alike, with their tight suits, their little de rigueur moustaches and their thunderous, saccharine, high-flown eloquence."

Sawyer Miller wanted to do what they had always tried to do from Kevin White's campaign in Boston through to Goni's run for the presidency in Bolivia: show that the candidate cares for people like you. And in his speeches, the novelist knew how to play to the heartstrings of Peruvians. He hit all the emotional notes. "I understand," Vargas Llosa began.

> I am running for President because I have come face-to-face with the Peruvian condition. I cannot pass it any more. Our country is falling apart and the most extreme images of a novelist's imagination have become our reality. When I see the little children running loose in the streets while their mothers queue for kerosene and bread; when I see their older brothers turning into the delinquent street children of our cities because our government cannot give them a decent schooling; when I see their fathers worn down by the constant struggle of making ends meet as inflation undermines their wages and their savings; when I see us cowed by a terrorism and violence that meets no resistance from our government; then I know the time has come to lay down the writer's pen and come home. To play my part in bringing the change that ends this nightmare.

Despite the words of solidarity with the Peruvian poor, however, Vargas Llosa always looked uncomfortable when it came to physical contact with the people in the shantytowns around Lima or with the peasants up in the Andean villages. His reluctance to press the flesh prompted Salvador Palomino, a former president of the South American Indian Council, to conclude, "I think that deep down, Vargas Llosa is a racist señor." Whatever the candidate's inner instincts, his outward show was distant, even disdainful. "Sending Mario's wife and her friends in their Chanel dresses into the barrios was not exactly what I'd call a grassroots movement." The huge security detail that accompanied him only helped to reinforce that gulf between the candidate and the voters. Alvaro Vargas Llosa says the campaign did not see the race problem it had until too late: "My mother and a team of a few dozen ladies were incredibly courageous and devoted their entire time to doing pilot programs in shanty towns . . . They were doing the right thing, but they were not the right faces. They had this original sin in their blood." On one occasion in February, the producers of a campaign ad mocked up a slum in Mario's back garden. A *New York Times* reporter noted that they laid out reed mats, battered pots and pans, and brought in a dirty Indian child. The cameraman framed the shots so as to avoid the swimming pool.

Mario always felt the pull of his private study. He made a point of reserving a couple of hours each morning to maintain his regimen of reading, making sure that even in the frenzy of the election campaign the time to read and reflect on the works of Karl Popper was sacrosanct. Who could blame him for taking a little respite: it was hard to be paranoid about losing when the polls showed that more than 50 percent of people supported him.

One occasion, in particular, demonstrated how disconnected the campaign had become. The Vargas Llosa team had gone out for dinner at the Libertador, an expensive but ugly modern hotel overlooking the Lima golf club. The dining room was almost empty, and the waiters handily outnumbered the guests. It was one of the weeks that Ed Reilly was in town and he asked the campaign team about the Shining Path, or Sendero Luminoso, the communist terrorist group founded by Abimael Guzmán, otherwise known as Presidente Gonzalo. The Shining Path had taken control of larger and larger tracts of the Andean highlands and, over the previous decade, peppered the capital with occasional car bombings and attacks on electricity transmission towers. The group seemed to lurk in the background of the 1990 election argument, but Vargas Llosa's campaign hands assured Reilly that the Shining Path was an irrelevance: " 'This is an Indian thing, going on in the hills.' " At almost that exact moment, there was an explosion and the lights went out. The Shining Path had blown up the electricity works.

Peter Schechter remembers the whole Peru experience as "traumatic." Like Malloch Brown, he had come with high hopes. Peter had a Peruvian girlfriend at the time, who had introduced him to a great crowd in Lima and, anyway, he loved Mario Vargas Llosa's novels. Yet he remembers it dawning on him gradually that Vargas Llosa did not much care for the general public. "It became increasingly apparent to me . . . that we had a huge asset that was slowly burning away. That, in the end, Mario represented the worst of Peruvian elites. [That he was] racist. He didn't like the smell of people. He was unable to touch people." Schechter's judgment, as he freely admits, is tainted; he had a nuclear argument with Vargas Llosa over his relationship with the traditional parties of the Peruvian right and was thrown off the campaign and sent home.

Vargas Llosa seemed able to afford all these mishaps and squabbles because he had no credible opponent. There was Alfonso Barrantes Lingán, a former mayor of Lima and socialist popular among the poor, who nicknamed him Frejolito, Little Beanie. But Barrantes Lingán did not start to fire up his campaign until February, by which time it was too late. Luis Alva Castro was the candidate of the ruling party, APRA, but he was in even worse shape. There was bad blood between him and Alan García, the president, and his support was weak within his own party, let alone the country at large. When Schechter was sent packing, Vargas Llosa was still more than thirty points ahead of his nearest rival. The only person who looked able to derail his bid for the presidency was the candidate himself.

As if on cue, he did just that. He delivered a speech to the annual conference of Peru's business community and announced two phases of shock therapy for Peru's economy. First, he would lift market controls on prices in order to stabilize the currency, which meant the cost of food and gas was bound to go through the roof. Then he said he would aim to quadruple tax income, slash import tariffs, and privatize swathes of government industry. He would bring Peru's nearly 3,000 percent inflation rate under control and make it possible, once again, to borrow and trade abroad. Peru's chief executives gave him a standing ovation. The Peruvian people, though, were alarmed, if not bewildered. In the *War of the End of Democracy*, Jeff Daeschner notes that "a significant proportion of the population mistook Vargas Llosa's proposal to reduce the size of the state as a plan to give away part of Peru's national territory." President Alan García, who was not running but was determined to stop Vargas Llosa from winning, taunted him. He warned Peruvians that half a million government workers would lose their jobs. A furious Vargas Llosa held a press conference, denying there were plans for such sweeping job cuts. But he said he could not give an exact number of people who would be made unemployed because "I don't know how many civil servants I would have to fire to make our administration efficient."

Pedagogy, as Alvaro said, was Vargas Llosa's obsession. He was a famed writer who wanted to educate the people of Peru. He presented an unvarnished version of his economic reform plan and, not surprisingly, people were alarmed. They feared for their jobs; they were afraid they would lose free education; they feared they would not be able to afford the staples of daily life. The García government cultivated these fears, but it was Mario who had planted them. Ed Reilly thought Vargas Llosa was arrogant. Malloch Brown thought he was being naive: "His political approach was much too rigid. He had this poorly understood Thatcherite thinking. He thought he could promise pain to the electorate." As people heard more about his plans, the polls showed support slipping away.

In March, little over a month before polling day, Ed Reilly heard about another candidate in the race. "I remember getting a call from Barry French," he said years later, referring to a Sawyer Miller man on his first campaign overseas. "He said, 'Hey, there is a guy going around on the back of a flatbed truck giving people potatoes. And they are calling him the Chinito, the little Chinaman.'" Daeschner noted in his book that Miguel Cruchaga, a leading Liberty figure and himself standing for the Senate, had had a similar experience a few weeks earlier, in the car park of the Lima airport. The man at the tollbooth had been told Cruchaga was a Liberty candidate. "Well, we're going to vote for the Chino," the parking lot attendant said, defiantly. Cruchaga answered: "What Chino?" Much the same happened to Hernando de Soto, the Peruvian economist. "You know how when you walk into a cloud of mosquitoes you hear nothing but the buzzing?" he told *The New Yorker* magazine a few months later. "That's how I heard the name of the next President in the streets. Everywhere, it was 'Fujimori, Fujimori, Fujimori.'"

Alberto Fujimori was the son of Japanese immigrants who left Kumamoto and settled in Lima in the 1930s. He had studied hard to become an agricultural engineer, then secured a place teaching mathematics at the National Agricultural University and risen to become the dean of the college. He had dipped into the limelight in the late 1980s, during a two-year stint hosting a television talk show called *Concertando*. He even got himself a nickname: Señor Concertando, Mr. Consensus-building. And if the FREDEMO alliance failed to take Fujimori's presidential campaign seriously from the outset, they could hardly be blamed. Nor had he. Fujimori established his political party, Cambio 90, in order to give voice to businessmen, professionals, and academics like him who felt shut out by the Peruvian ruling classes. The aim was to get Cambio 90 candidates into parliament. He registered himself as a candidate for the presidency, he told his colleagues, to garner more attention for his run for the Senate. (In Peru, it was possible to stand for both a seat in parliament and for president.) Less than two months before the election, the public opinion research barely registered Fujimori—he was lumped in with about ten other also-rans, crank candidates such as Brother Ezekiel, who claimed to be a modern-day biblical prophet. Neither Ezekiel nor Fujimori seemed to have a prayer.

The Cambio 90 campaign was a do-it-yourself affair. Fujimori decided against getting professional assistance, for the simple reason that he didn't have the money. He chose his own campaign slogan: "Honesty. Technology. Work." He started out with his own makeshift polling: he hired ten young boys to run around in the local neighborhoods and find out how many people had heard of him. He tapped into the protestant evangelical church, a network of passionate advocates for change who proved effective in spreading the Cambio 90 message. He balked at any heavy expenditure, telling reporters afterward that he had had to sell one of his pickup trucks and a tractor to pay for his advertising. While FREDEMO spent $12 million on advertising, Cambio 90 said it spent just over $120,000.

For months, he passed unnoticed. He held his first rally in February, an outdoor barbecue washed down with jugs of Pisco Sour. He made a trip to the small jungle town of Tarapoto just a few weeks before the election. In one farcical episode, he got himself filmed on the balcony of a hotel laying out his grand plan to rebuild Peru's infrastructure and lift up the country's poor. It was a rousing speech that made for great campaign footage. The fact that the streets below the balcony were empty did not matter. They were not caught on film. On the way back, Fujimori and his colleague stopped in the snack bar at the regional airport. In the time that they had a cup of coffee and waited for their commercial flight back to Lima, Vargas Llosa's entourage landed in a private jet, was convoyed into town to make a speech, came back, and flew off.

"Engineer Fujimori," as his aides respectfully called him, was not a charismatic politician but a stern, serious, self-disciplined man. He was not an electric orator, but was comfortable squatting on a stool in the marketplace and talking politics over rice and beans with ordinary voters. His campaign's most memorable extravagance was getting a big red tractor and driving into the barrios on a trailer hitched up behind it. Fujimori filled the vacuum left by Vargas Llosa, meeting the demand for an anti-politician that the novelist had met back in 1987 but had forfeited as he fell into the arms of the political establishment. Fujimori was an outsider.

By his very appearance, he captured the sense of exclusion that so many poor, dark-skinned Peruvians harbored against the wealthier European whites. The *cholos*, as the indigenous peoples of Peru who lived up in the Andean villages and decrepit Lima suburbs were disparagingly known, saw in this *nissei*—a second-generation Japanese immigrant—someone like them: brown, honest, and forgotten. Vargas Llosa, by contrast, seemed ever more the European aristocrat. (The fact that Fujimori was Japanese and far less "Peruvian" helped him in another way—many Peruvians liked to think that if the country went bankrupt, Tokyo would bail them out.)

With little over a fortnight to go before the elections, Sawyer Miller and the people at Liberty headquarters began to get nervous about Fujimori's momentum. They commissioned a poll from the barrios of Lima. The findings were worse than they expected, showing Fujimori rising as quickly and unstoppably as floodwater. Suddenly, he was out of the low single digits and running second in Lima at 20 percent. Alvaro Vargas Llosa recalled in his own account of the elections that sense of foreboding. "In a few hours, as if by magic, without anyone having suspected or predicted it, a candidate of Japanese origin that all of us had thought was swimming with Brother Ezekiel in the depths of oblivion and public ignorance . . . began to eat up immense margins of the capital's electorate." A few days later they got the results of a national survey. More dispiriting still, it showed that the Fujimori phenomenon was not limited to the capital. He was catching fire across the country.

Vargas Llosa had pledged to visit every department in the country. It was a classic campaign mistake: Richard Nixon had made just the same sort of fine-sounding, self-defeating pledge in 1960. It was intended to demonstrate a national leader's care for every corner of the country, but in campaign terms, it meant neglecting crucial constituencies and swing states that needed multiple visits. Nixon exhausted himself traveling the fifty states. Worse, he wasted time on votes already in the bag. Mario did the same. The problem was that Vargas Llosa liked crisscrossing the country and speaking to big crowds in municipal squares in provincial towns because it accorded with his notion of being a politician. In his generally diplomatic account of Peru 1990 that he wrote for *Granta*, Mark Malloch Brown betrays his exasperation in the final days of the campaign. Mario was off romancing the nation, he writes, charming them with stories of how he dreamed of growing up to be a matador. Meanwhile, "our poll

numbers screamed a warning: return to Lima and campaign in every bar-
rio to stop the rot in the fragile urban vote."

In the days before the vote, the Sawyer Miller team grew increasingly
agitated. Everyone tried to downplay the alarm, but there was a pervasive
fear in the Vargas Llosa camp. The latest polls showed that Fujimori was
doing well not just in Lima but across the country. He had jumped from
nothing to 6 percent in the polls. "My father was in Cuzco," Alvaro Vargas
Llosa remembered. "Mark called and said, 'I am worried. I have never
seen anything like this. He seems to be jumping up in the C and D segments of the population. You need to call your father and tell him to cancel the rally in Cuzco and come home.' " The rally in Cuzco, high up in
the Andes, had taken a long time to organize. It had been a difficult project for the Vargas Llosa campaign to pull off in the heart of the power
base of the Incas, and it had taken a huge effort to fill the square. Alvaro
continued: "Mark said cancel and come home. So I called my father and
told him that we thought he should cancel the rally and come home." Vargas Llosa replied: "Are you out of your mind?" He did the rally in Cuzco
and came back the following day. It became very clear very quickly that
Fujimori had the momentum. The lower and middle classes of Peru had
never really identified with Vargas Llosa. They had been waiting for
someone else to emerge. At the last moment, he did.

As things came to a close, it was clear that Sawyer Miller was shouting
from the sidelines, not managing the game. Malloch Brown wanted Vargas Llosa to demand that FREDEMO candidates withdraw their television ads, an attempt to start a fight with the political establishment and
regain some of the antipolitician, outsider kudos Mario had had back in
1987. He wanted the candidate to spend more time on TV and radio;
Mario still preferred his rallies. The triumphant two-minute advertisement Mario's cousin Lucho put together, which involved his wife singing
a ballad to Peru, made the Sawyer Miller men cringe: it showed Mario
among a multitude of whites.

From the outset, Mario Vargas Llosa had sought to win in the first
round of the Peruvian elections. This meant he needed to win more than
50 percent of the vote. Anything below that and he would be forced into a
second round, a run-off. On the morning of April 8, he and his wife went
to vote and then retired to a suite on the nineteenth floor of the Sheraton.
The FREDEMO campaign had booked several floors of the plush Lima
hotel. Mark Malloch Brown was stationed on the eighteenth floor, having

established a computer bank to crunch the numbers as the exit polls came in. The first results came in at about lunchtime and showed Vargas Llosa at about 40 percent, Fujimori at 25 percent. Malloch Brown thought this wasn't too bad, that Vargas Llosa might pick up a few points as the day wore on. With 45 percent of the vote, he could claim victory. But with each passing hour, Vargas Llosa's tally seemed to slip. By the time he appeared before the press at seven that evening, it seemed that he had just 35 percent of the vote and Fujimori 30 percent. (In fact, the final tally showed him getting just 28 percent of the vote, and Fujimori winning 24 percent.) Vargas Llosa told the assembled journalists that the country had given its endorsement to the liberal agenda. He asked Fujimori to join him for an unconditional dialogue, an invitation to cut a deal. Vargas Llosa had not gotten the mandate he felt he needed to push through a radical reform agenda, so he wanted to offer Fujimori the presidency in return for a promise that he push through free-market reforms. The press then showered Vargas Llosa with questions. He answered the first one not in Spanish but in French. It seemed as if he couldn't get out of Peru quickly enough.

But politics dragged two more humiliating months out of Mario Vargas Llosa. Although on the night of the first-round elections he wanted to quit, he was pressed to fight on and win the second round. The FREDEMO alliance urged him to stay in, as did many of his friends. (Much to his delight, the Catholic Church, which had for years bristled at Vargas Llosa's public atheism, also pleaded with him to stay in the race. Fujimori was allied with the evangelicals, and when given the choice, the Catholic establishment preferred a godless president to a Protestant-friendly one.) The consultants urged Vargas Llosa to go negative, and although he never attacked Fujimori and Cambio 90 as aggressively as they would have liked, the campaign took a much nastier turn. The FREDEMO researchers sought to expose Fujimori's secret ties with the government. They exposed his claims to being a penniless university professor as fraudulent, uncovering a sizable property empire. But even as things got dirtier, the dynamic did not change. The writer could not reverse the engineer's momentum. On June 10, the day of the run-off election, Fujimori wiped the floor with Vargas Llosa. Alberto got 56.5 percent of the vote, Mario 34 percent. Vargas Llosa got on a plane two days later to go to a literary event in France. "I expect that his immediate return to the writer's life was a relief," Malloch Brown concluded. "Yet nobody, least of all someone as self-disciplined as Mario, experiences a futile effort without anger."

IF THE DEBACLE in Peru angered Vargas Llosa, it made a laughingstock of Sawyer Miller. Mark Malloch Brown had really wanted Peru. "The pay in Bolivia was pretty terrible. I saw Peru as a chance to prove to my partners that we could make money in this business. The ultimate campaign." On paper, the 1990 election in Peru promised to be everything the men from Sawyer Miller could wish for. A glamorous candidate, the novelist Mario Vargas Llosa; a country in desperate straits, crippled by skyrocketing inflation, and cut off from world capital; a business community willing to throw millions of dollars at the campaign and its consultants; and polls that had Mario way out in the lead. But it was a case of "Be careful what you wish for." Mark Malloch Brown's hopes of glory—a sequel to the Philippines—had been dashed, and instead he had found himself in a grand, theatrical embarrassment played out in slow motion and to a global audience. For Sawyer Miller, Peru took some of the sheen off the whole idea of running political campaigns across the planet. After all, some of the partners in New York had been pointing out that politics, particularly international politics, was a loss leader. It took up a lot of time and paid badly, but at least it was supposed to provide some good publicity for the firm.

Not Peru. Vargas Llosa's defeat was snatched from the jaws of victory, the kind of failure that journalists could not help but savor: a novelist undone by an agronomist, a man of letters beaten by a number cruncher, the celebrity sunk by the ordinary. "The saga of the unravelling of his candidacy, and his spectacular defeat by a complete political novice, is extraordinary," wrote Alma Guillermoprieto a few months later, "and all the more so because the strength of feeling against the elegant writer and his neoconservative political program might have been foreseen by someone who understands Peru as well as his novels suggest that he does . . . (The novelist's campaign, which included the pricey services of Sawyer Miller, a New York–based political consulting firm, is believed to have cost around ten million dollars.)"

The blame game that followed resembled a drunken gathering of amateur knife throwers. Everyone ended up a little wounded. The Sawyer Miller advisers were criticized for adding to Vargas Llosa's preppy entourage: even before the arrival of Mark Malloch Brown and his colleagues, FREDEMO looked like a group run by white snobs—Peruvians with European names who had homes in Lima, New York, or Madrid. After the event, the men from Sawyer Miller were blamed for being foreign, deaf to the stirrings in Lima's shantytowns and Andean mountain villages, deaf to the subtle but insistent argument between the races in Peru. Instead, it was said, the gringos relied too much on polls, which were a new and rough science in Peru in 1990. Pollsters did not penetrate far into the Lima slums; they liked to contact people by telephone, skewing their sample toward richer voters; they preferred to collect information in the daytime, missing out on working-class men who were at their jobs. Miguel Cruchaga made the simple complaint that the election required an instinctive understanding of the social and historic forces roiling Peru: "One thing is Britain and another thing is Peru. Bring a British comedian to Peru and see if he can make anyone laugh here—it doesn't work that way." Politics is like comedy or cooking, he said, it conforms to local tastes.

Sawyer Miller also got the flak for failing to impose discipline on the campaign. Peruvians, such as Kurt Schultze-Rhonhof who had worked on Vargas Llosa's plan for government, looked on in despair as chaos ruled. "The Vargas Llosa campaign was lost by the campaigners, not won by Fujimori . . . This was, to some extent, coordinated by Sawyer Miller. They were the professionals, they were supposed to give advice." The disorganization meant that Sawyer Miller's meticulous plan—"Peru: the Liberal Mandate"—was never really acted upon. It was like the old story of the football coach who tells his team before they go out to play, "The bad news is they're better than us on paper. The good news is we're playing on grass." Sawyer Miller's strategy made winning sense on paper; unfortunately, they were playing on grass.

With the benefit of fifteen years to get over the deeply wounding experience of the campaign, Alvaro Vargas Llosa gave an evenhanded judgment of Sawyer Miller's work: "When they came to the campaign, we were winning the election. When they left, we lost. We were at 50 percent when they came in and we lost the election. This is something that wounded their pride. But to be fair, they were right about many things." If anything, he told me, the Vargas Llosa campaign did not listen enough.

The Sawyer Miller men, of course, tossed their own daggers, mostly in the direction of Mario Vargas Llosa. Ed Reilly ended up infuriated by the novelist, not simply by his insistence throughout the campaign on having time to reread his favorite authors—Malraux, Melville, Faulkner—but also because he made it so clear that he considered the literary life superior to politics: "He just was not serious about it. He was approaching it as a creative project. There was a level of vanity to all this that was incredibly destructive. There was a lack of seriousness." (Vargas Llosa more or less admits as much, acknowledging that his policy priorities were, perhaps, subordinate to "the adventure, the illusion of living an experience full of excitement and risk. Of writing the great novel in real life.") Schechter still seethes when talking about the Peru campaign. He still remembers it as painful. As much as he loves Vargas Llosa's books, he recalls Mario as "one of the most despicable human beings I have ever met."

Mark Malloch Brown judged that when Mario took off his novelist's glasses, he somehow lost sight of the racial and class strains in Peru to which he was so alert as a writer. Vargas Llosa disdained the white wealthy classes in his prose, but in politics he came to represent them. "He was much more in love with upper-class Peruvian society than I realized," Malloch Brown said. He became, according to Malloch Brown, the class enemy of the poor, a white man surrounded by bodyguards, well-dressed businessmen, and their wives in European fashions, driven in an armor-plated car, and literally out of touch with common Peruvians.

Mario Vargas Llosa has rejected the allegations of racism and pointed out that a pale-faced redhead won the race for the Lima mayoralty just a few months before the presidential election. "The decisive factor in the election was not skin color—neither mine nor Fujimori's." He acknowledges, though, that the alliance with the old political parties served him badly, because it tarnished him as an "old pol" and failed to deliver the national infrastructure he hoped for. He admits to a certain naïveté—"it was ingenuous on my part to believe that Peruvians would vote for ideas," particularly ones that promised such pain. In the end, though, Mario Vargas Llosa blamed the inherent evils of politics. He notes, with a certain pride, that Mark Malloch Brown once told him that he was the "worst candidate he had ever worked with." In his memoir, Vargas Llosa's judgment on the whole episode is condensed in a quotation lifted from Max Weber's seminal lecture "Politics as a Vocation":

> Primitive Christians also knew very explicitly that the world is ruled
> by demons and that anyone who becomes involved in politics, that is

to say, anyone who agrees to use power and violence as means, has sealed a pact with the devil, so that it is no longer true that in his activity the good produces only good and the bad bad, but that the contrary frequently happens. Anyone who does not see this is a child, politically speaking.

THE HUMBLING OF SAWYER MILLER in Peru was the firm's first real embarrassment abroad. There were more to come. In 1992, Sawyer Miller was identified in a report titled "The Torturer's Lobby," published by a Washington think tank. The paper fingered a handful of companies for taking money from countries with records of serious human rights abuses: Sawyer Miller was one of them, tarred by its lucrative work for the government of Colombia.

The firm earned more from Colombia over the years than from any other single foreign government account. It was a big part of Sawyer Miller's international business. And after all the campaigns where the impact of political consultants ended up a moot point, the countries where the American advisers lurked in the shadows and were then airbrushed from history, and all the elections where the firm fought and lost, Colombia was one indisputable example of how Sawyer Miller could have a direct and dramatic effect on both policy and politics.

When the Colombians came to Sawyer Miller in the mid-1980s, their country was seen in the United States as a narco-state, a government in the pocket of the cocaine cartels and a country getting rich off America's weakness for drugs. The government was desperate to transform that image, to get Colombia known for its spectacular scenery, its long history of democracy, its low inflation, its beautiful flowers, its great shrimp. The men from Sawyer Miller told the Colombians that they would never be heard on any other subject until they addressed the issue of drugs. They commissioned a national poll on U.S. attitudes toward Colombia and found that 70 percent of Americans would be willing to ban Colombian coffee as punishment for the country's harboring the drug industry.

That single piece of polling convinced then-President Virgilio Barco that the gringos were right: it kick-started a long, lucrative project for Sawyer Miller, which ran through four elections and three different presidents. The firm advised Colombia that if it wanted to move from being seen as a villain to being seen as a hero, it needed to pass through an in-

termediate stage: it needed to show the world that it, too, was a victim of
the drugs. Colombia was presented as the front line in America's war on
drugs. Scott Miller devised a television advertising campaign that reeled
off the names of Colombians—policemen, judges, and journalists—killed
in the drug war. The footage, the music, and the simple description of
them as "heroes" was heart-wrenching stuff and epitomized Sawyer
Miller's talent for image-remaking, using the modern media to erase international boundaries.

Written discreetly into the contract that the Colombian government
struck with the firm to provide polling and media strategy for the country in the United States was money for the firm to do political work inside
Colombia itself. The men from Sawyer Miller not only helped draft
Colombian foreign policy but also worked on domestic political strategies for a string of presidents. "It was a very satisfying relationship for the
consultants. We really were deeply in to two adminstrations in particular—Barco and Gaviria," says Peter Schechter. "We made money on
Colombia. They paid relatively on time. It was a very rewarding relationship, financially, with friendships and with real successes in helping the
client . . . What happened after a while was that people realized that we
could get it wrong. Then they realized that Latin Americans could do it,
too. But for a while we had the monopoly—we Americans and, in Latin
America, we at Sawyer Miller." For nearly a decade, nowhere was that monopoly more closely held or more rewarding than in Colombia.

But Sawyer Miller's work in Colombia raised a lot of concerns outside
the office—and inside, too. Some employees were embarrassed about the
involvement in Colombia, particularly given its record on human rights.
Time and again, Jack Leslie, who was in charge of the Colombia account,
had to defend the firm's relationship with Bogotá—he would point out
that Colombia was the only country in Latin America where there was
civilian control of the military, that Sawyer Miller had been hired precisely to disprove the prejudice that all Colombians were drug barons.
And there was also the small matter that Colombia was delivering millions of dollars in revenue to the firm.

Around the same time, Sawyer Miller went to work in Russia to make
the case for capitalism. The contract came from the U.S. government, part
of an aid effort to advance Russia's privatization program. Sawyer Miller
got paid $7 million to put together an ad campaign about the joys of pri-
vatization. By 1994, the firm's name was on the front of *The Wall Street*

Journal, under the headline "Helping Ourselves: U.S. Aid to Russia Is Quite a Windfall—For U.S. Consultants." A few months later, things got worse when it emerged that Sawyer Miller's ads for a political party in Russia had been recut. These were ads made by Sawyer Miller but paid for by the U.S. government. In effect, American taxpayers were subsidizing a Russian political party—without knowing it.

The firm's work abroad had often flirted with trouble. It was hard to keep the halo on straight when getting paid hundreds of thousands of dollars, in used, greasy bills handed out from the bottom of a Nigerian government official's desk. It was hard to claim to be on the side of the angels when polling for a Sudanese dictator—for him, a vanity exercise in the trappings of democracy; for them, a well-remunerated adventure to Khartoum. Frankly, it was hard to claim an ennobling mission abroad when the firm had links with people like Noriega in Panama.

But it was not moral compromises abroad that would prove the undoing of Sawyer Miller. It was money. All the while that Mark Malloch Brown et al. were making the news on the international campaign trail, the real business of Sawyer Miller had become business. David Sawyer had set out to make some real, reliable money serving chief executives, pitching what he called the "political model": the idea was simply that whatever your line of work, you are in a campaign—vying for the support of the consumer, going negative on the opposition, preempting investor rebellions, pitching your story to the public. Miller expanded on the idea, helping to persuade businesses to see themselves as either incumbents or insurgents, the establishment under threat or the guerrillas seeking power. And then along came a cadre of consultants—Harris Diamond, Jack Leslie, and others—who proved able to work the corporate clientele better than either Sawyer or Miller. They discovered that business was not only as political as politics, but that it paid better, too.

EIGHT

"WHAT IS A JUNK BOND?"

DAVID SAWYER, the great preacher of corporate democracy, was never at ease in the boardroom. It wasn't his natural habitat. He was more comfortable behind a camera on the campaign trail or, better yet, sitting in a red leather armchair in the Coach Room of the Knickerbocker Club. Nonetheless, he was drawn to the executive suite. Politics was an irregular business, and almost from the start, he had yearned for the thick, steady income stream of a corporate client base.

As with so much else, he could see the logic of applying the political model to business, but he looked to recruit other people to make it happen. It wasn't straightforward, as Bob Perkins, a Republican and the first person Sawyer hired to establish his corporate practice in 1981, remembered: "David and Scott were a little bit ahead of the curve. Political consultants hadn't become rock stars yet. Nobody in business thought that the political world had anything to do with them." Sawyer's vision was to become a new kind of consultancy. Sawyer Miller would be to communication strategy what McKinsey was to management systems. It seemed so obvious to David Sawyer that businessmen were on the campaign trail every day. They were struggling to get elected and reelected—with their customers, their shareholders, their staff—every day. The information revolution was going to have an inevitable impact on corporate America and Sawyer was convinced that a political communications firm, a new kind of "strategic think tank" as he called it, would be indispensable to CEOs. Sawyer Miller promised to attack a corporate perception problem as if the firm were part of a campaign—with a political orientation, a bias for action, and a faith in poll-based strategy.

In the early days, though, it was slow going: Perkins stayed for a couple of years. After him came Harry Clark, also a Republican. "We were the first firm trying to take the political model into business," Clark remembered. They started to work for Brown and Williamson Tobacco. "We never really ramped it the way we wanted to." And having arrived in 1983, Clark, too, was soon gone, setting up his own firm in the Sawyer Miller mold.

Then Sawyer drafted Oren Kramer, a young Democrat from the Carter White House who had worked on domestic policy. In the absence of anyone with any specialist knowledge of the subject, he was handed the financial services portfolio. "Nobody else knew anything about financial services," Kramer explains. "Think about it: We were Democrats." Kramer started to make inroads into Wall Street.

Unsurprisingly, the corporate clients that came to Sawyer Miller were companies in crisis. When E. F. Hutton, the great American brokerage firm, was investigated for fraud in the mid-1980s, they came to Sawyer Miller. Kramer spent the best part of a year trying to encourage Hutton's top management to understand the politics at play in Washington. The administration had its own political troubles, and it suited the Justice Department to be seen getting tough on a rogue American stockbroker. In short, Kramer tried to get E. F. Hutton to treat its financial problem like a political scandal—i.e., get everything out in front of the public and get it out quickly. As anyone who has spent longer than a guided tour around Washington will tell you, the cover-up is usually more damaging than the crime. Kramer's advice to Hutton was tell the public everything you know, immediately and however bad: "Get it out there and get it behind you." In 1985, the firm entered a guilty plea to two thousand counts of mail and wire fraud, and soon after, the century-old financial conglomerate was broken up and sold off. Still, Sawyer Miller could not help boasting of its involvement in the saga. It told a trade journal about its work for the firm, and the news appeared under the headline "When Sawyer Miller Talks, E. F. Hutton Listens."

Drexel Burnham Lambert signed up the firm when the first of its bankers was arrested on insider trading charges in 1986. Over the next five years, its relationship with Drexel defined Sawyer Miller in the corporate world as much as the Philippines had made its name in international politics.

Drexel proved to be the Icarus of investment banking firms. It popularized the junk bond business, generated heart-stopping profits, and, in the process, became a byword for Wall Street greed: in 1986, the year the indictments for fraud and insider trading began, the firm reported earnings of half a billion dollars; the following year Michael Milken, the firm's star trader, who made Drexel's market in junk bonds, earned half a billion dollars in executive compensation.

David Sawyer had been introduced to Drexel by Skip Stein, an old friend who served as an informal adviser, professional matchmaker, and accidental provider of glamour to the firm. Stein was the son of a fabled donor to the Democratic Party and was on the way to becoming a very successful, if unsung, entrepreneur in the financial services business. He was also one of the more sought-after bachelors in New York: people in the office said he had gone out with Jackie Onassis, Linda Eastman (later McCartney), Mia Farrow, and Susan Sarandon. He was what the people at Sawyer Miller called "a friend of the firm," and he knew everybody. From David Sawyer's earliest days, when Skip put the young, wannabe political consultant in touch with Senator Tom Eagleton, Skip Stein had ushered clients in the firm's direction.

Scott Miller also had his own personal introduction to Drexel. After the breakup of his first marriage—an eighteen-month relationship that Miller likes to refer to as his "practice marriage"—he also made a go of it for a few years as a New York bachelor, providing the political junkies at Sawyer Miller with something else to talk about, namely, his girlfriends. Then he met Denise. He was working for Gary Hart at the time, flying from San Diego to Chicago: he was in seat 3A; she was in 3B. (It would be nice to think that there was something about altitude that opened a valve in the Sawyer Miller heart—Scott finding his wife on a plane, Peter Schechter falling for a stewardess on the Eastern Airlines flight to Ecuador, Iris Sawyer meeting Tom Kempner on the way to Los Angeles, Mark Malloch Brown and Trish trusting the secret of their clandestine romance only with Charlie Whitehouse, the firm's travel agent who booked their airline tickets. The fact was, romance happened on the road because the Sawyer Miller crew spent so much time there.) Denise was to prove the great love of Miller's life, his wife and the mother of his two sons. She also happened to be a physical fitness instructor to some of the wealthiest and best-known people in New York: one of her clients was the wife of Leon Black, the head of mergers and acquisitions at Drexel.

In the course of things, Miller was introduced to Milken, who, knowing his audience, pitched the argument between Drexel and the authorities as a battle between the new and the old. He gave Miller an impassioned speech about how junk bonds were all about the democratization of capital, how the old Wall Street white-shoe firms had long controlled capital, and how they scorned and feared the power accumulated by an upstart like Milken. Junk bonds were financing the corporate raiders who were challenging the corporate establishment on Wall Street and in Middle America. The white shoes, Milken said, liked to pour scorn on him and his work: "Junk is for Jews," they said. Miller was convinced—or he convinced himself—that Drexel's case fitted the Sawyer Miller profile, that the bank was another insurgent being suffocated by the incumbents. It also helped that Drexel was paying Sawyer Miller an enormous amount of money.

In 1989, Rudy Giuliani, then a federal prosecutor working in New York, indicted Milken on ninety-eight counts of racketeering and fraud. Drexel felt that it and its business were fundamentally misunderstood. Scott Miller was soon spending more time on the scandal at Drexel than on any other client project. Sawyer Miller's job was to leave the court case to the lawyers, but to turn public opinion around. The junk bond business had become associated in the public eye with the savings and loan crisis. Sawyer Miller tried to disassociate the two. As far as the public was concerned, Milken, the "Junk Bond King," embodied the clever chicanery of bankers on Wall Street. Sawyer Miller tried to depersonalize things. Rather, it pressed Frederick Joseph, Drexel's CEO, to get the bad news out, all of it, and early. The firm tried to explain the Drexel business: Miller wrote a two-page advertisement that they placed in *The Wall Street Journal* headlined "What Is a Junk Bond?" It was held up by the advertising industry as the best-read ad in the history of newspapers.

Drexel's reliance on Sawyer Miller consumed more and more of the firm's time. After the Milken indictment, Scott Miller was called down to the bank's head office at 60 Broad Street and asked to become president of Drexel Burnham. By then, it was more important for Drexel to have an adman who knew how to communicate as the face of the bank than a financier who knew how to add. Miller pointed out that he and David Sawyer had a firm of their own that they were trying to build into a going concern. In response, Drexel offered to buy Sawyer Miller. Scott remembers returning to the office in Midtown that day, avoiding the gaze of Mandy Grunwald, not quite believing that he was in talks about selling out to a bank. He needn't have worried: Fred Joseph and Leon Black's ad-

visers went away and did their sums and came back with an offer of just
$5 million for Sawyer Miller. In one sense, this was a relief: Miller knew he
would have struggled to persuade the rest of the firm to agree to a Drexel
Burnham buyout. Then again, it was upsetting that Drexel, which had
earned a name for itself paying $200 million over the odds for almost any
available asset in America, thought Sawyer Miller was worth only $5 mil-
lion. The firm had generated revenues of just under $10 million in 1989,
but, it seemed, Sawyer and Miller had less of a business than they
thought.

Milken eventually entered a guilty plea to six securities and reporting
felonies and went to prison for nearly two years. Drexel collapsed into
bankruptcy in 1990. But Sawyer Miller had established itself as a firm
willing to represent companies with unsavory issues and to advise far-
flung political candidates.

When one of Goldman Sachs's partners, Bob Freeman, was indicted in
1987 for insider trading, the investment bank called on Sawyer Miller.
Robert Rubin, who would go on to be the chairman of Goldman and later
a U.S. treasury secretary, was a friend of David Sawyer's. He brought him
in to advise on handling the Freeman indictment. (The Goldman Sachs
partner eventually pleaded guilty to the felony.) Rubin was one of the
early adopters on Wall Street, one of the first to see the crossover in communications between politics and business, something that was later reinforced by his own time in Washington. "People who have had experience
of the public domain from a political perspective," he explained, "are
much more sophisticated."

American Express, a longtime client, was fighting an everyday election
against the bank cards Visa and Mastercard. Rob Shepardson said that
Sawyer Miller followed an old political maxim when working for Amex:
the first thing you do when a fire starts in your house is not get a bucket
of water and put it out; you start a fire in your neighbor's house. For
Amex, Sawyer Miller helped devise a campaign to expose the costs in-
curred by people using credit cards like Visa. They sought to drum up
grassroots opposition to the 19 percent interest charges and prompted
Capitol Hill to examine Visa's business practices. "It was all a holding operation to push back against the bank cards until Amex got its value
proposition right," Shepardson remembers. "It was a classic Sawyer Miller
thing. Our application of the political model was almost direct."

Sawyer's most significant recruit into the corporate practice was Harris Diamond. Like so many of the others, he joined after a long, pestering courtship. Almost every Sunday night, just after *60 Minutes* finished airing, the phone would go at Diamond's home and it would be David Sawyer, badgering and flattering him to join the firm. Sawyer once booked a seat on a plane next to Diamond, bending his ear for the whole flight about how he had to join Sawyer Miller. Diamond, a Democrat, had experience from a host of U.S. political campaigns around the country. His political values were forged in the George McGovern campaign of 1972—he wanted to open up the party to gays, blacks, and Latinos and move it beyond its core base of white workers and unions. He was also keenly attuned to the revolution in leadership being wrought, unannounced, by the Reagan presidency. Sawyer sensed in Diamond a man who instinctively understood that Reagan's impact was seeping into the American boardroom. Diamond, Sawyer felt, would finally be able to translate Sawyer's vision of electronic democracy in corporate America into a substantial business for Sawyer Miller.

After joining in 1987, Harris Diamond took charge of the Wall Street clients, and sure enough, he was very soon billing more than any other partner, in fact, more than many of the other partners combined. He treated a corporate crisis—an impending bankruptcy, a leveraged buyout, an ethical scandal—like a political crisis, presenting companies to their employees, shareholders, and customers as a collection of values and dreams, much like a candidate. He told the magazine *Manhattan Inc.* that a manager can take a company and "redo it on a cost-factor basis and slash and cut, but if he's not successful and communicating that this company is now valuable, working, able to work well, then I don't care how well he made the books, he's lost his customers, he's lost his suppliers, he's probably lost his employees." Sawyer Miller started selling campaign teams for corporate clients: Diamond would establish a kitchen cabinet inside the company that included the chief executive and a handful of others, and together they would hammer out strategy; Ned Kennan and Ed Reilly would run a series of focus groups on the company's negatives and test reactions to proposed messages.

By 1990, corporate clients accounted for the vast majority of the business. This was not just a measure of Diamond's aptitude for selling the political model into the boardroom or of his appetite for work: it was, also, where the money was. And unlike Perkins, Clark, and Kramer, who had come before him, Diamond's timing was right. In the late 1980s, corporate America was beset by litigation, and the air was thick with an impending recession. Businesses in trouble knew they needed political communication. Through the 1980s, Sawyer Miller had worked for Frank Lorenzo, who built up and bankrupted Continental Airlines, fighting the unions and the press with equal relish. A court eventually ruled him "unfit" to run his business, and Barbara Walters on ABC television declared him "the most hated man in America."

Little wonder that Sawyer Miller had become the first stop for companies with an image problem. These included KKR, the private equity firm immortalized in *Barbarians at the Gate*, the book about the buyout of RJR Nabisco in 1989; BAT, the tobacco company with investments in apartheid South Africa, trying to buy up insurance businesses in the United States; Charter Medical, which became involved in a scandal in the psychiatric health business over charges of aggressive marketing; Resorts International, the Atlantic City casino business, as it teetered into chapter 11 bankruptcy; and, similarly, 7-Eleven's holding company, as it meandered through its leveraged buyout and then in and out of bankruptcy. When a chief executive visited the offices of Sawyer Miller, it was more than likely he was about to hit the front page of *The New York Times*—for all the wrong reasons.

Sawyer Miller, unlike its clients, was beginning to get good press. It was 1990, and the firm was finally getting the plaudits for its part in the communications revolution. Under the headline "The Global Spin Doctor," *Manhattan Inc.* marveled that "David Sawyer has operatives advising leaders and CEOs all over the globe. And now, as empires fall, Sawyer is using polling, media techniques and connections to build his own." John Scanlon, New York's best-known, long-lunching, hard-drinking PR man, was quoted saying, "There's virtually not a major national or international client they are not involved with." The company itself was described as a "central microchip in the global brain center of New York." Maura Sheehy, the author of the *Manhattan Inc.* piece, concluded, "A network linking multinational corporations and governments, covering the world, and all the wires lead to an office on 60th Street, on the East Side of Manhattan: the scope of [David Sawyer's] vision is enormous. So is the opportunity for profit, both for his clients and for Sawyer himself. Since his beginnings in politics, Sawyer has made his living on his reputation as a visionary. He's marketed himself as being ahead of his time. In the past couple of years, the world has changed. David Sawyer's time has arrived."

In fact, the opposite was true. Sawyer Miller's vision was coming together, but the firm was just beginning to tear itself apart.

Behind the good press, the booming success of the corporate practice was deeply divisive. The young men and women who had joined the firm in the mid-1980s—idealists who thought Sawyer Miller was the place to practice politics by modern means—had started to question whether the firm was losing its magic. They had joined when the big names on the client roster were Daniel Patrick Moynihan and Corazon Aquino, but by 1990 they were spending more and more of their time working for Drexel Burnham Lambert, British American Tobacco, and the government of Colombia. David Sawyer may have always aspired to building a multinational corporation in his own name, but he had recruited a cadre of clever, antiestablishment, creative people on the promise of changing the world through electronic democracy, not selling canny PR to thoughtless big businesses and dubious foreign governments. To them, it seemed like a betrayal. "It was frustrating, but it was also incredibly sad," remembered Peter Schechter. "This place had lost its intellectual soul. From a place born of a love of politics, the only thing that mattered was money. The only thing that counted was who would bring in the most. It was all about the billings."

SCOTT MILLER was the first to go. From almost the moment he joined, he had had a rumbling but gentlemanly argument with David Sawyer over the size of the firm. Miller had been the boy wonder of McCann Erickson and learned at a young age that life in a large corporation did not suit him. He associated big with mediocre and he did not like the internal politics or the predictability of a large organization. As Sawyer continued his relentless hiring of young talent and big names from Washington and Madison Avenue, Miller grew disenchanted. Sawyer's attempt to hire Davis Weinstock, one of the best-paid PR men in America, was just one example of the low-burn disagreement that Miller had with the founder of the firm. Sawyer seemed to be hiring people at whim who were dragging the firm in directions it did not want to—or should not—go. Miller's dream was that the firm would remain a sparky little hothouse of about half a dozen charismatic partners who dispensed brilliant strategic advice to corporate chieftains and political candidates and farmed out the boring humdrum work—the PR functions, the marketing work, the ad production—to others. Sawyer Miller would be the hub; other businesses could serve as the spokes. PR, as practiced by someone like Weinstock, was not what Sawyer Miller was meant to be about. But the firm now numbered more than a hundred people. Miller had lost that argument with David Sawyer.

Just as important, Miller was losing his zest for politics. In 1988, he went off to be the media director for Michael Dukakis's doomed effort to wrest back the White House for the Democrats. It was a dispiriting experience. Miller's vivid memory of the campaign was standing by a coffee machine with Dukakis in a recording studio in Hell's Kitchen in New York City. It was October, just weeks before Election Day, and the campaign team was panicking. Roger Ailes, the young TV producer who had worked for Nixon in 1968 and would go on to create the Fox News network for Rupert Murdoch in the 1990s, was having a devil of a good time making ads for George H. W. Bush. He simply used and reused the image of Dukakis popping out of the top of a tank, a wonky smile on his face, a wobbly helmet on his head. "On the whole," Dukakis confided to Miller, "I wish I'd never gotten into the tank." The Dukakis campaign's only response was to lambaste the Bush team for resorting to low, negative advertising—a desperate and cheap shot from a bunch of well-worn political advertisers who had all, at some point, profited from going negative. It was not the only campaign Miller fought and lost in 1988. His first presidential candidate, Joe Biden, dropped out; Dick Gephardt failed to make it through; Bill Gray lost his race for the Senate seat in Vermont.

By then, Miller was back working with Sergio Zyman, the former marketing director of Coke, who occasionally parked himself at Sawyer Miller. Scott and Sergio were also doing marketing work for companies like Miller Brewing. This was the kind of corporate work Miller believed in. Harris Diamond, he thought, was turning the firm into a bunch of corporate ambulance chasers, taking on crisis communications work for any and every kind company in a car crash. And so, one day in 1989, Miller told David Sawyer he was leaving. He worked out the terms with Jack Leslie, who by then was the president of Sawyer Miller and in charge of hiring, firing, and the general running of the place. Miller would be able to take his clients with him—companies such as Coke, Miller, and Apple—and the company would buy out his 35 percent share for a dollar. Leslie typed up an agreement and reached into his wallet and handed him a dollar bill.

The partnership of David Sawyer and Scott Miller, not quite a decade old, now lived on in name only. It was the first real blow to morale. Scott Miller had been an aloof and distant figure all along but revered as something of a god in the firm. He had been the creative inspiration of the place, and with him gone, it seemed to have lost some of its verve, its wit, and, some even said, a little of its genius.

Mandy Grunwald was the next to leave. Her exit marked not just the departure of the longest-serving member of staff but a more fundamental change at Sawyer Miller: Mandy left the firm because the firm decided to abandon U.S. politics.

By the late 1980s, many of the senior partners at Sawyer Miller had grown weary of politics. This was not just because Michael Dukakis had added to their long list of defeats—although that did not help. The disenchantment with politics went deeper. "The nature of the campaigns started to wear you down. They really became slugfests," said Jack Leslie, who had been with Sawyer Miller since 1983. David Sawyer, according to his old friend Jane Hartley, felt much the same way: "I think he was totally disgusted with domestic politics. It had become a mudfest." Harris Diamond, who had joined the firm in 1987, says, "The political world went a little bit off the rails with respect to negative advertising and negative campaigning. It also became the politics of personality." There was an irony to all this, of course: these guys had helped make it that way. Back in the early 1970s, Sawyer and his first partner, Maurice Sonnenberg, had joked that the only really true campaign was a negative one. In the mid-1980s, Leslie had fought for Jim Hunt in North Carolina, waging what was until that point the most expensive and, arguably, the nastiest Senate campaign. But the very techniques Sawyer Miller pioneered now seemed distasteful and extreme to many there. The disillusionment was also practical: the young men who had joined the firm in the mid-1980s now had wives and, in some cases, children. "You couldn't go off for two months and live above pizza parlors someplace," said Leslie.

The growth of the corporate practice fomented an argument about the politics business. It was a growing disagreement over whether to get out of politics to focus on business or to continue trying to do both. For the partners who had given their young working lives to the firm, people who had worked hundred-hour weeks through their twenties and thirties and sacrificed their love lives, their weekends, and their beauty sleep in the service of the Sawyer Miller vision, this was a battle for the heart of the firm. It was an argument between their first love, politics, and the much more financially rewarding relationship they had discovered with business.

By the end of the 1980s, this was no longer an argument that rumbled quietly in the background, but an ever more overt tug-of-war. Robert Mead, who joined in 1989, was brought in by Harris Diamond: "One of my primary responsibilities was to change the firm, to make it a corporate firm," he says. His arrival came "toward the tail end of the romantic era of swashbuckling international campaigns. From that point forward, we made our money on the corporate side. Harris and I built the corporate side."

Mandy Grunwald was increasingly disgusted by the corporate work that was financing Sawyer Miller. As difficult and prickly as she could be, Grunwald was seen as the moral conscience of the firm. She was the one who, when she heard that the firm had taken on work for a big tobacco company or read a report of human rights' abuses in Colombia, would walk into David Sawyer's office and ask, "Aren't we supposed to be on the side of the good guys?" Now the firm was putting the best possible spin on the insider trading scandal at Drexel and, at the same time, devising strategies for Democrats taking a stand against income inequality, white-collar crime, and those workers who lost their jobs thanks to junk bond–financed leveraged buyouts. She thought Sawyer Miller wanted to have its cake and eat it, too.

More than that, Grunwald embodied the argument for staying in politics. Not only was it the only part of Sawyer Miller's work that she really cared about but, she made the case, without politics the firm would have nothing to sell. It had garnered its tactical wisdom, its understanding of new technologies, and its strategic foresight from the campaign trail. It recruited brilliant young people from politics. Without a foot in the political world, she argued, it would lose its foothold in business.

But she lost the argument to Harris Diamond and Jack Leslie, who, with the backing of David Sawyer, Ed Reilly, and Mark Malloch Brown, decided that the future of the business was with business. Political candidates, they argued, were costing the firm corporate accounts. The political consultancy business had mushroomed since the mid-1980s, adding to the competition for candidates and squeezing fees. David Sawyer was still seen as one of the doyens of Democratic political consulting, but inside the firm, they all knew he had long been overtaken by a new crop of rising stars. It was a Republican age, and the Republican consultants—Stu Spencer, Richard Wirthlin, and the extraordinary Lee Atwater—were the doyens of the day. Anyway, in Harris Diamond's judgment, political consulting was a nice way for one man to make a good living, but it all hinged on the individual relationship with the political candidate. It was the equivalent of working as a butler for hire, always contingent on the one-on-one dealings with the lord of the political manor. It never offered opportunities of scale. Corporate PR, on the other hand, promised to be a big business. Diamond and Leslie, in particular, wanted Sawyer Miller to leave the campaign trail and follow the money. As Diamond explained fifteen years later, "The issue was could you do politics and the corporate world at the same time? . . . My sense was you couldn't do both."

They had sought a compromise solution when they discussed hiring James Carville to set up a separate political firm, a sister company to do campaigns. But the courtship of Carville backfired badly. He said no and Mandy was furious at having been overlooked. Disillusioned with the direction of the firm and insulted by the way she had been treated, Grunwald left Sawyer Miller and never looked back. She became the director of advertising for Bill Clinton in the 1992 campaign, finally getting to work for a Democrat who would make it all the way to the White House. Looking back on the departure from Sawyer Miller, she said, "The firm itself had succumbed to corporate forces of its own. It had sold out—not its politics, but any politics—and lost its life."

If the cultural revolution under way at Sawyer Miller was signaled by the departure of Mandy Grunwald, it was sealed by the arrival of Ed Rollins. His recruitment was David Sawyer's last big hiring decision and, given the Democratic heritage of the firm, it was extraordinary: Rollins had been the national campaign director for Ronald Reagan in 1984, helping the president win forty-nine states and utterly humiliate the Sawyer Miller candidate, Walter Mondale. Therefore, not only was he the most important Republican recruit in the history of David Sawyer's occasional but largely unsuccessful attempts to draft political talent from across the aisle, but his hiring sealed the end of Sawyer Miller's involvement in U.S. domestic politics. No Democrat would sign up a firm that employed Rollins; no Republican would hire a company headed by Sawyer. Rollins joined the firm in 1990 to help apply political techniques to corporate challenges, consolidating the idea that the business world was now the main client, not U.S. political parties.

In physical as well as partisan terms, Rollins seemed to tear the firm apart: as the young consultants working at 14 East Sixtieth Street saw it, he expanded the power, cost, and gravitas of the D.C. office. Mark Malloch Brown moved to Washington at that time. With Rollins—and a couple of the Republicans he brought with him—now working down in Washington, it was unclear whether the hub of Sawyer Miller was New York or D.C. (Ironically, within a span of about six months, Rollins, the man they had seen as a "vicious and unwanted Republican," came to be seen as the soul of Sawyer Miller—the only partner still unadulteratedly in love with politics, the only guy who would answer things honestly [in a firm of swirling revolutions and conspiracies], the only partner willing to consider changes and improvements, the one old hand still interested in mentoring younger professionals.)

The remaining partners at Sawyer Miller hoped that even without an involvement in politics they could continue to do distinctive work, applying the political model to commercial situations. They would continue to work international political campaigns and they would do more than corporate PR in the United States; they would provide what they called communications strategy. The new recruits, though, felt as though the firm was changing beneath their feet. Mark Longabaugh, an eager young Democrat who loved campaigning and would end up running for Congress, said of those times, "Right as I got there, they made a decision to get out of politics. It was greed . . . The corporate practice had become so lucrative. They didn't want the Democratic background of the firm interfering with the management of their corporate practice." There was, of course, an absurd inversion to all this. "The firm itself was tired of politics, seeing nothing but the sex appeal of corporate clients. And the corporate clients saw in Sawyer Miller the sex appeal of politics."

Ned Kennan saw little left in the firm that made him feel proud, let alone sexy. He and David Sawyer had first worked together in 1975. Ever since, Kennan's company—KRC Research and Consulting—had been Sawyer's preferred polling outfit. It had taken more than a decade and fundamental reform of the KRC business by Ed Reilly, but finally Sawyer Miller merged with KRC in 1989. Within little over a year, Ned decided he wanted to leave.

Kennan loved the mass psychology of politics. He relished the opportunity to delve into a cognitive exploration of another country. When Sawyer Miller was contracted to work for the government of Poland in

1990, to advise on the implementation of an economic reform program, Kennan immersed himself in the poets and composers, the painters and legends, of Poland. As always, he was fascinated by the role of the mother in the family there, the nature of bonds between brothers and sisters, parents and children. He once described the kinds of questions he asked in focus groups: "If the situation you are in, in Poland, were music, what kind of music would it be? What composer? Why? If the situation you are in were a car, what kind of car? If food, what kind of food? If a poem, which poem?"

He would go on: "Who is the finance minister most similar to in your family? In your family who is most like him?"

And if they said: "Well, he reminds me of my grandfather," then Kennan would ask: "Why? What did you think about your grandfather?"

"Well, I didn't actually know him because I lived in Warsaw and he was far away."

"Was he your maternal or paternal grandfather?"

"Maternal."

"What did your father think of him?"

"He never really liked him."

"Why?"

Kennan's point was this: "We find that what people think is secondary in importance to how people think. What people think, in our opinion, the what, should be viewed as a vehicle that schleps—scientific language—that schleps the how."

Kennan had wanted to build a successful research company but he wanted, more than that, to be entertained, even enlightened, by the work he did. He told his clients that if they were looking for objective evaluation, they should go somewhere else. He told customers that the research he did was not for them but for himself. It was a means for him to understand the world better, to see more of it. What he was getting to see in the changing Sawyer Miller was a world he did not like.

One day in 1991, Kennan joined his partners for a Sawyer Miller board meeting held in the Rainbow Room, the grand Art Deco restaurant and ballroom at the top of a building in Rockefeller Center. Before things got going, Ned said he wanted to say something: "I'm resigning," he told them. He said he felt they had started to prostitute themselves. He said he was not enjoying looking at himself in the mirror in the mornings. He stood up and left. David Sawyer chased him down the hall, imploring him to stay, fearing that he would be all the more exposed to the designs of his ambitious young partners without his oldest friend in the business. "David, get out," Ned told him. "Those guys are making this a different company. You are going to die soon. Get out, David. I am your friend and I love you, but I can't stand it."

There were, indeed, discreet discussions under way to move David Sawyer out of the business. For more than a year, the four young partners—Harris Diamond, Jack Leslie, Mark Malloch Brown, and Ed Reilly—had been nursing their frustration with David Sawyer. He would pay lip service to the notion of a partnership—the idea of a shared say in the firm's direction—and then, without consulting them, promptly go out and sign up some big political name on a $10,000-a-month deal. The "ten-a-month guys," as Harris and Jack called them, tended to be too grand to solicit new business and had to be paid for out of the money that people like Harris and Jack were bringing in. Nor was Sawyer very good at lavishing praise or attention on his staff. Like a suitor who woos with more ardor than he loves, he would not leave you alone when trying to recruit you, then became a little neglectful once he had you inside the firm. He could also be immensely irritating, full of brilliant ideas but then failing to follow through.

"It came in waves," according to Mark Malloch Brown. "There was for a long time this feeling that he was not pulling his weight. The guy wasn't letting go of the reins. He still used the firm as an extension of his personal bank account. His finances were the firm's finances. He started getting detached from his ability to operate in the market. There was a very fine line between really clever strategy and dumb bullshit at Sawyer Miller. As he got disengaged from the business, David drifted into that second category." It all got increasingly tetchy. The firm brought in a management guru to advise them on how to deal with growth, but the relationship with Sawyer had broken down. By 1990, Malloch Brown said, "The firm had outgrown David. To be honest, David's manner got under my skin."

More practically, Sawyer was not bringing in the money. Jack and Harris, Ed and Mark were. One evening in 1990, over dinner at the Petrossian Restaurant—the best, indeed, the only place in New York to eat caviar on banquettes upholstered in silver mink—the four men discussed a plan to take control of Sawyer Miller. They put a proposal to David Sawyer that they would replace the current ownership structure—he had the vast majority of the business and, in effect, total control—and they would all become equal partners.

Sawyer went away for his Christmas holidays. He consulted his friends and sounded out other potential buyers of the firm, then came back to them at the beginning of 1991 and told them he was already a man in his fifties; a few years later he would want to retire and sell out of the business anyway. So, rather than go through two rounds of negotiation, he wanted to sell them the whole of the business immediately.

Office politics is, of course, even more dispiriting than national politics. It can be just as dirty and more petty. There was a year of wrangling between Sawyer and the Four Musketeers, as their underlings dubbed them, a year of gamesmanship and small-time power plays, snide remarks and whispered speculation. Everyone has a slightly different version of the threats and counterthreats. The offices at East Sixtieth Street no longer buzzed with excitement about what the firm was doing in the world, but with gossip, much of it misinformed, about what was happening inside the firm. It was said that the four men were pushing the founder out by telling him they would walk with their clients unless he handed over control of the company. Others said that Sawyer was trying to outmaneuver them, suggesting they expand the partnership to bring in more of the younger employees. Others had heard that Diamond and Leslie already had plans to sell the business as soon as they bought it off Sawyer. They all speculated as to what Harris and Jack, who came into work together each morning on the train from Westport, Connecticut, were plotting over their copies of *The Wall Street Journal.* The junior consultants in the business all had their lines of loyalty, whether to Sawyer or, more likely, to one of the four active partners. And yet, they too felt turned over. Harris, Jack, Ed, and Mark were getting ownership of the firm; the next generation—people such as Rob Shepardson, Lenny Stern, and Peter Schechter, who were just five or so years younger—were getting nothing.

Behind the poisonous office gossip, the negotiations were, indeed, mean. In hindsight, both sides were unreasonable. Sawyer was stuck in the founder's trap, feeling that, because he had created and built the company, they owed him more than they did. His lawyers stickled over not only price but every last privilege of executive life: ongoing office assistants to be paid for by Sawyer Miller, membships at the Knickerbocker and the New York Athletic clubs to be paid for by Sawyer Miller, travel expenses to be paid for by Sawyer Miller, and continued ownership of the company phone number. The four young partners, on the other hand, had not bought out a business before and, as they admitted years later, they behaved badly. They were driven, as much as anything, by the fact that they were all relatively newly married and were starting families and wanted stable, substantial incomes and a share of the business. They badgered Sawyer, then froze him out. Harris Diamond was the point man in the negotiations with Sawyer. "We broke china," he recalled, uncomfortably. With a hint of regret he acknowledged that there had been youthfulness, impetuousness, and an excess of ambition in the four who wrested control of the company. He and David, he said, "had been close. In the end, we weren't close. It was an awful year. We did it right to the extent that we could. We kept it among the five of us. But it was awful." Mark Malloch Brown still feels a certain level of remorse: "One thing I want to be clear about is that whatever the difficulties, they did not justify the way we treated him. I really, really feel bad about the way we treated him."

The tension and the anger, of course, were felt by everyone. One Sawyer Miller staffer says the place became "a shark tank." Another says, "They isolated him, they threatened to leave, they made ultimatums. They forced him to do this deal. They forced him to acquiesce." A third says, "David was devastated . . . those guys seemed to come in the darkness of night and take the firm over. David felt betrayed by those four people." The staffer remembers coming in one day and seeing Sawyer sitting behind his big black desk, energetic and well-dressed as ever, yet ignored by the people whirring around him. He had been bought out for $4 million, with a potential earn-out of $9 million. Still, it was pathetic, as if David Sawyer, like King Lear, was ending his days in office but not in power, stripped of his authority by a younger, hungry generation.

In the eyes of many who had worked at the firm and loved the place, the four partners' purchase of Sawyer Miller took on the quality of a morality play. They saw David Sawyer, the old man, being squeezed out by four ambitious operatives, whom he himself had hired, who destroyed a place that served democracy's cause and turned it into a PR factory to make money. Ed Reilly, one of the four, acknowledges that there was sizzle and swagger to Sawyer Miller, partly a product of David Sawyer's personality, partly the result of the high-profile work the firm did, and partly because it was staffed by a group of people prone to storytelling and myth-making—even about themselves. The decision to buy out Sawyer certainly robbed the firm of some of that pizzazz. Yet Reilly rejects those who cast the buyout as the triumph of Mammon over God, the notion that there was "this idealistic, cause-driven political consulting firm that sells itself to the Madison Avenue advertising agency and loses its soul. The idea that we were doing the Lord's work and now we are not. We were rarely doing the Lord's work. We were involved in competitive fights. On a few occasions, the competitive fights had a huge moral consequence to them, as in the Philippines. But the bread and butter of the firm was competitive challenges in U.S. domestic politics, where the consequences were pretty narrow or where it was one set of shareholders versus another [set of] shareholders . . . That is who we were."

After they bought out David Sawyer, they were not even that. The most promising younger consultants at Sawyer Miller had already departed en masse: Shepardson and Stern left to set up their own firm, taking the legendary adman and recent recruit to the firm, David McCall, with them; Peter Schechter, along with another recent hire, Charlie Leonard, headed off to set up their own firm, too.

Within a few months of completing the deal with Sawyer, the four partners who had bought Sawyer Miller from David Sawyer sold it into a merger with the public relations arm of Bozell, the advertising firm. For Malloch Brown and Reilly, this proved an unhappy experience. The Sawyer Miller spirit was subsumed by the Madison Avenue culture. There was much less discussion and none of the old bull sessions. It was all much more hierarchical, much more like the companies and bureaucracies that people like Malloch Brown and others used to enjoy sneering at back in the day at Sawyer Miller. The combined firm went by the acronym BSMG, and to some of the old Sawyer Miller hands, the new name seemed apt: they felt they were peddling overpriced and underresearched BS.

Within little over a year, Malloch Brown moved to Washington and, soon after that, landed a job at the World Bank. Reilly saw out his five-year contract and then headed off to set up his own business. Only Harris Diamond and Jack Leslie persevered. Between them, they took the rump of Sawyer Miller and went on merging it with other agencies and reversing it into other companies until they had built the biggest public relations company in the world: Weber Shandwick.

←——→

DAVID SAWYER'S HISTORY as a businessman was, in one sense, classically tragic. The firm, built on his talent, charm, and boundless self-belief, floundered on his own failure. For twenty years, Sawyer had peddled a vision of a world in which electronic democracy forced a dialogue with the people. It was a dialogue he struggled to have within his own little company. He was terrific at hiring people, but he had a hard time keeping them. He was great at dispensing strategic advice but could not, ultimately, divine a strategy that would satisfy his people and create a long-term future for his company.

Worse, the 1990s were cruel, personally as well as professionally, for David Sawyer. He had in the mid-1980s finally found a love that put him at peace. Nell McFarland made him, as many attest, obviously happy. Soon after their marriage, they adopted a baby boy. Luke, their child, was David's unbridled delight. Sawyer telephoned a string of people from the West Coast the morning Luke was adopted, beside himself with joy and ecstatic at the discovery of fatherhood. For a few years, Nell, David, and Luke, as well as Nell's two sons from her earlier marriage, Andrew and Gavin, shared a rich life together: they summered in the Hamptons, sailing on the yacht David shared with ABC news anchor Peter Jennings; they chartered a boat to sail around the Greek islands; they visited the Galápagos Islands; they holidayed in the Bahamas. After he was edged aside from Sawyer Miller, David sought to expand the G7 Group, a side business he had set up that provided information about the inner thinking of government to big Wall Street financial institutions with vast stakes in the movement of interest rates or the reform of tax policy.

In the early 1990s, Nell was diagnosed with cancer. The treatment was a long and vicious ordeal. David cared dutifully for her, but he returned from holiday just after New Year in 1995, and he was clearly out of sorts. His face was blotchy. He was more than unusually forgetful. He was having dizzy spells. He was treated for a problem in his inner ear. A few months went by and things worsened. He was diagnosed with an inoperable tumor. He deteriorated very quickly, becoming incoherent and confused. Yet, as his friend Jane Hartley remembers, he remained unfailingly polite. It was as if even the cancer could not kill his class.

David Sawyer died on July 2, 1995, in New York Hospital. He was fifty-nine. The funeral was held at the Dune Church, overlooking the sea in the Hamptons. A few days later, Daniel Patrick Moynihan stood up on the floor of the U.S. Senate to mourn the passing of "a pioneer in the field of political consulting, a brilliant analyst, and a dear friend." Sawyer, who first worked for Moynihan in 1982 and on every one of his campaigns since, "helped to open up the governments of Eastern Europe and Latin America by introducing mass communication into their electoral processes," Moynihan said.

Nell had seemed to be in remission as David weakened. But the week of his funeral, she caught the flu. Within ten days, she, too, was dead. Luke, then just seven years old, had lost both parents in little over a fortnight. His future was put in the hands of David Sawyer's lawyer, Bill Zabel. Although David and Nell had suggested that an old family friend become guardian of the child, his stepbrothers, Andrew and Gavin, stepped in. And, despite their painful divorce, Nell's ex-husband, financier Alan McFarland, and his wife, K.T., took Luke in. He grew up as one of the three McFarland boys.

NINE

"QUIT AND MOVE"

IN 1979, MARGARET THATCHER was seeking to become Britain's first female prime minister. The Conservative Party leader recruited a team of young advertising hotshots to help propel her to Downing Street. They came up with a now iconic billboard campaign. It showed a snaking queue of unemployed workers accompanied by a joyless pun: "Labour isn't working." Less well remembered is her opponent James Callaghan's retort to the marketing industry's encroachment on politics: "I don't intend to end this campaign packaged like cornflakes. I shall continue to be myself." He did. And he lost.

The 1980s—Sawyer Miller's heady decade—cemented spin's triumph over unvarnished politics. The firm's worldwide success was symptomatic of an unloved but seemingly inescapable fact of modern political life: style's trumping of substance. The icing seemed to matter as much as, if not more than, the cake. The campaign ads consumed more time, money, and thought than the party manifesto. The communications director became more important than the policy adviser. In some cases, he became more valued than the politician himself: in 2007, the Conservative Party in Britain hired a spin doctor and agreed to pay him two and a half times the salary of David Cameron, the party leader.

The irony of this was that in its early days, the men and women who joined Sawyer Miller believed they would be part of a positive revolution. They saw themselves as harbingers of a direct, unencumbered dialogue between the government and the governed, between the powerful and the people. They believed they were part of an unstoppable crusade for change, one that would break the stranglehold of the political establishment and blow away the old party bosses, the stuffy politics of the country club, and the stitched-up deals in smoky union halls. They thought that, in conquering the new media, they could deliver fresh ideas and new faces directly into the homes of ordinary people. They saw television as a potential slingshot for Davids challenging government Goliaths everywhere. They believed that they were agents of a newer, truer, healthier democracy.

As David Sawyer put it, "Something is happening in politics called the electronic democracy. And something is happening in the world, and it ain't politics in any form known before, and it's gonna change everything. Everything has to be reinspected. What was generally thought of as a powerful medium, isn't. It's not television; it's people."

And yet, within little more than a dozen years, Sawyer Miller had made the journey from the idealistic to the banal. The alpha dogs faded from view, not because they failed in their political machinations but because they succeeded in a more mundane enterprise. Today, Jack Leslie and Harris Diamond sit in adjoining offices overlooking Fifth Avenue in New York, running a corporation with more than three thousand employees. The firm that was once Sawyer Miller is now Weber Shandwick. It has a client roster that would have made David Sawyer's eyes water, but not the sweeping political ambition that made him proud. Harris Diamond's explanation: "We were more comfortable and more desirous of pursuing our vocation in the corporate world."

By the late 1990s, the firm was almost unrecognizable. The four men who had wrested control of the firm—Jack Leslie, Harris Diamond, Mark Malloch Brown, and Ed Reilly—had gone their separate ways. They had won their bruising battle with David Sawyer, but the team broke up almost as soon as it won the prize. Mark Malloch Brown left the firm in 1994. He understood the financial argument for focusing on corporate PR, but he was not much interested in it. He headed to the World Bank and a new career as consigliere—part father confessor, part professional hit man—to a string of the world's most powerful and controversial men: James Wolfensohn, the World Bank president; George Soros, the hedge fund billionaire; and Kofi Annan, the secretary-general of the United Nations. Ed Reilly fumed quietly as the firm succumbed to the forces of Madison Avenue, surrendering, as he saw it, Sawyer Miller's old sense of itself as an ideas factory and becoming, instead, a provider of press releases to big U.S. corporations. He worked out his contract and then, in 1997, set out to build his own strategic communications firm in the

Sawyer Miller mold, working both for Wall Street and Democratic presidential contenders such as Dick Gephardt.

To many of the young politicos who joined the firm believing its hype about technology's capacity to enliven public debate and empower the people, Sawyer Miller had traded in a political adventure for a bankable business. They understood the unignorable fact that political consulting is an unstable commercial enterprise, but they didn't like it. So, as the corporate PR business grew, the partnership broke up, the staff scattered, and the alumni of Sawyer Miller fanned out to work in politics and businesses across America.

The firm's legacy was the globalization of politics, a host of copycat companies of globetrotting political consultants—and lingering bitterness.

THE SAWYER MILLER GROUP had a lasting impact on the world because their craft worked. It did not guarantee success, but it improved the odds. And so, while some of the men from Sawyer Miller retired to a life of part-time consulting and plenty of horse riding, many of the Sawyer Miller alumni stuck with the firm's vision. The older generation may have had enough of five-star hotels in far-flung capitals, clandestine meetings with presidential candidates in private homes, political advertisements in languages they did not understand, and a lot of waiting around; but the younger guys did not.

Peter Schechter, for example, headed off with Bob Chlopak and Charlie Leonard, two of David Sawyer's latter-day recruits to the firm. Together, the three men set up a Washington consulting firm that employed fifty people working on domestic issues such as the Clinton health-care reform plan and foreign elections across Latin America and the former USSR. Schechter and Leonard were the Americans drafted to do debate prep in English with Ernesto Zedillo, the Mexican presidential candidate, on the eve of the country's first presidential debate, in May 1994. "Zedillo was a very unimpressive candidate," says Schechter. "He turned out to be a much more impressive president." Dick Dresner, the pollster whom Sawyer used in campaigns from Chicago to Costa Rica, conquered the Eastern bloc. His most famous candidate was Boris Yeltsin, whom he took on in 1996 when the incumbent had worse public approval numbers than Stalin: "In the United States, you'd advise a pol with those kinds of numbers to get another occupation." Yeltsin, with the help of Dresner and his colleagues from California, won.

Rob Shepardson and Lenny Stern, best friends who had joined Sawyer Miller in the late 1980s, set up their own company, SS+K. Headquartered on Wall Street, its offices are the ultimate in postmodern corporate chic: they feel like one large loft apartment. SS+K, more than any of the other businesses spawned by the Sawyer Miller alumni, is the spiritual successor of the original firm. It is not an advertising agency or a public relations business, but a strategic consultancy, selling ideas, images, and messages for a communications age being remade by the Internet. Their clients range from Delta Airlines to Barack Obama to cyclist Lance Armstrong, who hired SS+K to help fight the public battle against cancer. (Those little yellow bracelets that read "Live Strong" were developed by Nike in conjunction with SS+K: more than sixty million were sold in just two years.)

By the late 1990s, a whole host of American political consultants were doing what Sawyer Miller had done, but reaching into ever more far-flung territories, in countries new to competitive elections, such as Russia and Hungary; countries with a long democratic tradition, such as Britain; and countries demonstrating that democracy and Islam can coexist, such as Turkey and Indonesia. The industry that followed in the wake of Sawyer Miller was as individualist and unstructured as the original firm, a coincidence of one-man bands, short-lived partnerships, and niche firms fronted by charismatic egotists, often with special ties to specific countries. Still, they added up to an accidental democracy corps, an inchoate cadre of American professionals who practiced a common political language from Albania to Azerbaijan. They represented one of the many sinews of a growing globalization, the embodiment of a modern Babel in politics.

Across the aisle from Sawyer Miller, as it were, was a whole Republican lineage to the global campaign business. Conservative political consultants were fueled by the same mixture of off-year restlessness, political adventurism, ideological ambition, and the profit motive. To be sure, Republicans were more homebound than the Democrats. One reason was that, in David's Sawyer's day, they were winning at home. Another was that the Democrats were by temperament more internationalist, worldlier, more prone to holiday in France than in Wyoming. That said, Roger Ailes, whose political work stretched from Richard Nixon to George

H. W. Bush, was himself a prolific operator abroad. Paul Manafort, who had worked on the Marcos account against Sawyer Miller's team when it campaigned for Cory Aquino, has made a worldwide business catering to political elites. He and his partner, Rick Davis, have worked Somalia, Kenya, Georgia, Angola, Russia, and more. Just before he headed off to another foreign election, this time in Montenegro in 2006, Davis explained the continuing growth of the business: "There is a booming democracy trend . . . [and] it has felt like U.S. policy. If the United States says you have got to have a democracy, the first thing they say is okay, find us someone who knows something about that."

But that's only the half of it. The real money, he continued, comes from the business opportunities that arise after victory. "We're more in the deal business. The thing I love is that the political elites and the economic elites in every other country but the United States of America are the same. So, if you go to Nigeria or Kenya or Ukraine or any place, the people who are the elected officials and running the elections are the richest people in the country, who own all the assets."

Conservative consultants in the Bush years have had a field day, and nowhere more so than in Ukraine. Davis said that he and Manafort had people on both sides of the election working for Viktor Yuschenko and Viktor Yanukovytch. Dick Morris worked there for Yuschenko. So did Frank Luntz. They were all American conservatives, doing the same as Sawyer Miller's men had done for years, taking a wealth of experience gained on the U.S. campaign trail and putting it to work in less sophisticated, less competitive democracies. They were there aiming to make fifty thousand dollars a month and advance the conservative cause along the way.

American consultants have already worked in more than half the countries of the world, but they are now reaching into further-flung markets. Greg Minjack, for example, developed his advisory skills working for Bush's adman Mark McKinnon, who in turn was an apprentice to David Sawyer. In 1999, Minjack was part of the team working for Mesut Yilmaz and the Motherland Party in Turkey. Since then, Americans have taken up commissions advising candidates in Lebanon, the Palestinian territories, and Indonesia. Minjack himself is operating in more and more fledgling Muslim democracies. "Albania—that is the most secular of Islamic places I have ever been. I enjoyed Azerbaijan. I really wanted to play in Kyrgyzstan," he says. "I am still trying to crack Kazakhstan and Uzbekistan."

Farther east are billions of people yet to see American political technologies and tactics at work. Their time will come—and soon. American political consultants are beginning to seep into Asia. They have made their mark in the Philippines, South Korea, and Indonesia. Many consultants have followed the path beaten by the Sawyer Miller Group to Manila; David Morey and Joel McCleary opened the way to Seoul; Rob Allyn, who worked for Vicente Fox in Mexico and sought to get a Haitian American millionaire elected president in Port-au-Prince, was the first Texan to run a campaign in Jakarta. Americans are now seeking to sell their wares in other markets. Doug Turner, a young consultant from New Mexico, is trying to make his way in Japan, a project he himself describes as "an experiment." Still, he says his work for the Democratic Party of Japan has taught him that "Japan is a huge, huge market. It is an extraordinarily unsophisticated political market place. It is in the Dark Ages." And then, of course, there is mainland China. One day it, too, shall be a democracy and, unfeasible as this seems today, a market of continental proportions for American political consultants.

The history of America's influence in the political back rooms and campaign headquarters of the world is not over, perhaps not even past its peak. American consultants sometimes complain that business is not what it once was. Some say international advisory work was a geographical accident, a U.S. bonanza that spilled largely into neighboring Latin America. Others suggest it was a short-lived function of the information revolution in the 1980s and 1990s, as Americans exported their understanding of television before politicians elsewhere really got it. More still point out that the Americans have been supplanted, replaced by a homegrown generation of consultants in every democracy in the world. And there is some truth to all of that. But the onward march of America's political professionals—a global conquest not of America's political spirit nor certainly its political structures but its political style—continues. Looking ahead at Asia and the Muslim world, America's political consultants have some of their most testing and potentially lucrative work ahead of them.

One result of this global political integration will be homogeneity. As politicians around the world find themselves hiring the same advisers to deal with broadly the same public policy issues—rising health-care costs, competitive standards in public education, immigration, terrorism, and global warming—they will find themselves delivering the same political prescriptions in broadly similar terms.

Silvio Berlusconi campaigned for power in Italy in 2001 with a manifesto titled "Contract with the Italian People," which was drawn up by Frank Luntz, the Republican political consultant who helped draft Newt Gingrich's "Contract with America" in 1994. Likewise, when *The Guardian* newspaper invited Joe Klein, the U.S. journalist who so closely chronicled the Clinton presidency, to catalog the differences between a British and American election, he conceded that they are disarmingly similar: "Clinton announced his version of the third way in 1991 with three words: Opportunity, Responsibility and Community . . . Imagine my surprise when, visiting England in 1997, I found Tony Blair blithely gadding out and repeating the mantra—Opportunity, Responsibility and Community—as if he had invented it." Like stowaways in the hold, American political ideas have arrived quietly in the company of American political tacticians. One of the paradoxes of globalization is that it has made an unprecedented range of stuff available to an extraordinary number of people, but the laws of economics—particularly the logic of scale—has meant that multinational companies have concentrated consumer tastes on a narrowing menu of products and services. More people eat, wear, and do the same things than ever before. Globalization has homogenized the consumer. It is likely to do the same to the voter.

The disappointment for the men from Sawyer Miller was that they had envisaged new technologies widening the public's choice. Instead, they found that politics and politicians were converging. Increasingly, they would hear that Republican or Democrat, Conservative or Labour, Christian Democrat or Socialist, one is as bad as the other. One measure of their disillusion was the number of Sawyer Miller men who leapt on the bandwagon of outsider candidates, such as Ross Perot. Another was how many quit the campaign trail altogether.

To be sure, the hand-wringing can be overdone. As unfashionable as it is to say, spin is not, in and of itself, a sin. There is something Luddite about the popular tendency to bemoan modern, media-savvy politics and remember with misplaced nostalgia a lost age of intelligent public debate. To rail against focus groups and polling, artful speechwriters and rapid rebuttal, targeted messaging and expensive advertising, is to wish that politics can live out of time. The politician who eschews spin is as self-denying as the farmer who shuns fertilizer. The critical lesson—the redeeming moral, if you like—in this tale of arch-pragmatism is that the messenger is the man. The key test for anyone in communications is not what you do but whom you do it for.

Nonetheless, the men from Sawyer Miller came to feel partly responsible for the public's disillusion with politics, aware that even as democracy triumphed around the world, people were shunning the ballot box in the millions. They understood, more keenly than most, that the flip side of freedom is the business of politics. They had seen from the inside out that the professionalization of politics had not ennobled it.

Scott Miller's exit from politics came in the form of a Dear John letter. It was 1991, America was tipping into recession, the Bush administration was sending troops into the Gulf, and Dick Gephardt, then the leader of the House, had asked Miller to prepare a strategy for renewal for Democrats looking at their election plans for the coming year. Miller's memo read: "Quit and move. Quit. Washington is a place with hundreds of good people with fine values and strong beliefs. But these good people swim in a fetid pool of bad business-as-usual. Of cynicism. Of suspicion of those they were meant to serve. All of us in America, and certainly those good hundreds, deserve a new start." Democrats should admit the sordid little fact that they want so badly to beat the Republican administration that they will say or do what's bad for America to get there. They secretly hope for millions more unemployed, thousands of body bags coming back from the deserts of Iraq. They should admit it, quit, and move. "Move back to the communities where you serve but do not live . . . Volunteer with the PTA and the local rescue squad. Have fun. Go to Disney World. Fix the roof. Fight with the boss for a raise. Get a life."

Miller's farewell note was not just another act of defiance by a restless malcontent. It was a statement of profound disillusion with politics and politicians, Democrats and Republicans alike. What made him so bitter was that he was as much disgusted with himself as with them. "I felt this sense of guilt that we had helped make politics more crass," he says, looking back. "The political campaign that we developed was the candidate as icon, the negative as truth. What we found at Sawyer Miller was that as soon as a political market had TV, there was no stopping electronic democracy. That was really positive. But there was no stopping the negatives either: the abuses of free information, the abuses of the ability to create emotional responses on television." Like millions and millions of other Americans fed up with politics, Miller was slinking out of the public square. He had bought himself a bright white clapboard house on a few acres of land in New Canaan, Connecticut, and retreated to the company of his young wife, their newborn son, and his boneheaded Hungarian sheepdog, Duke. Unlike other disaffected voters who tuned out of the national debate in the 1990s, Miller had not watched television's debasement of politics from the couch. He had been part of it.

"I am appalled by our legacy," says Mark Malloch Brown. Sawyer Miller pioneered American political consulting around the world, but, he argues, the industry that the firm inspired has since abandoned its faith in local research. Instead, American political consultants today hawk last year's campaign trail wisdoms around the world. "I see it as a complete vulgarization of what we sought to do . . . it moved much more in the direction of vanity consulting on both sides: the candidate wanted the consultant named in *Time* magazine; the consultant wanting to decorate his CV between elections in the United States."

Peter Schechter still loves politics, believes in the ballot box, and has faith that good leaders can improve people's lives. Yet, he says, "I have probably convinced every politician that I have ever worked for to go negative at some point." The men from Sawyer Miller knew they were party to a decline in the national conversation, a less meaningful politics, a politics of sound bites and slurs, personalities not policies, image and a lack of imagination.

For his part, Ned Kennan retreated to a home in the low hills of Massachusetts, where he found comfort in Buddhism, his two Sharpeis, and a quieter, more ruminitive life. Looking back, he says, "The enormous number of political consultants and spin masters and advisers have reduced leaders in their countries to a bunch of puppets. They try to create the candidate, rather than get the candidate to elevate the values he or she has and get them to reach the general public. People are being made."

EPILOGUE: "VOTE DIFFERENT"

IN THE SPRING OF 2007, a remake of the famous 1984 Apple ad appeared on the Web, showing scenes from the original TV commercial interwoven with contemporary footage of Senator Hillary Clinton. In the original Apple spot, people march like brainless drones, mesmerized by the flat, unrelenting monologue of their leader. In the updated version, the Big Brother figure is Clinton: "One month ago, I began a conversation with all of you and, so far, we haven't stopped talking. And that's really good," she echoes, over the sound of stomping feet and computerized Klaxons. "I intend to keep telling you exactly where I stand on all the issues." The viewer sees rows of men, heads shaved and minds numbed, sitting in the thrall of the vast black-and-white screen as it pumps them with more party propaganda. Then, just as she did in the TV ad that aired in the middle of the Super Bowl in 1984, a woman in a white T-shirt and orange shorts comes running into the industrial auditorium and hurls a hammer at the screen. It—and, with it, the face of Hillary Clinton—explodes into countless pieces of white light, freeing the men from their mental slavery. "Vote Different," as the 2007 Internet ad was called, concluded: "On 14th January, the Democratic primary will begin. And you'll see that 2008 won't be like '1984.' BarackObama.com."

The ad was not, in fact, made by the Obama campaign but by someone calling himself Parkridge47. And for weeks, as the numbers of people who downloaded the ad from YouTube grew from the thousands into the hundreds of thousands and then the millions, no one knew who Parkridge47 was. Eventually, he was tracked down by a blogger, who identified him as Philip de Vellis, a strategist at an Internet consulting firm and a former field operative for the 2004 Kerry-Edwards campaign in

Ohio. Mr. de Vellis explained: "I was motivated to make the ad because I was frustrated at politicians in general and the way they are using video right now. They are treating it just like they are using TV: to broadcast online. I wanted to make a statement that you have to do more than that. You have to interact with your audience out there. A pretend conversation is not enough." He said he had put together the new and old footage over a couple of days, posted it online, and anonymously tipped off a few bloggers. The video went viral and, within a few months had been downloaded by more than three million people. The medium, de Vellis said, was not only the message but the means of mass communication. "I think this really opens the opportunity for citizen ads," he concluded. "People like me who have something to say: Come out and say it." *The San Francisco Chronicle* called the "Vote Different" ad "a watershed moment in the 21st century media and political advertising."

It also marked an unintentional and indirect reunion of Sawyer Miller clients and candidates, a "mash-up," to use the jargon of the Web, of the firm's past, present, and future. The spot was a reworking of an advertisment that epitomized the strategic work Scott Miller had done for Apple. It was an attack on Hillary Clinton, the candidate being advised by Mandy Grunwald. And it was a plug for the candidate whom Rob Shepardson and Lenny Stern were helping, Barack Obama. To be clear, de Vellis himself had no connection with Sawyer Miller. (He was soon snapped up by a Washington political consulting firm, but it had no ties to SMG.) But in his description of the citizenry being empowered by a new medium and his call for a new kind of connection between politicians and their audience, he sounded like the David Sawyer of his day.

For politics stands at the threshold of a revolution set to be wrought by another technology: the Internet. And, with a slightly different cast and an entirely new medium, the Sawyer Miller story is about to repeat itself.

In early 2006, Stan Greenberg's polling firm was hired to run public opinion surveys in the mountain kingdom of Nepal. These were turbulent times in the little landlocked nation in the Himalayas. The king had dissolved parliament; the Maoist rebels were at war with the monarchy; the people, furious at the food shortages and fed up with royal tyranny, were coming out in their thousands onto the streets of Kathmandu. Amid the turmoil, one of the pollsters working on the Greenberg project was kidnapped. He was a Nepali, working for the local firm the Americans had contracted to do legwork up over the passes and into the villages high in the mountains. When he was taken, he was written off as dead. More than thirteen thousand people have died in Nepal's civil war, and the hapless pollster looked set to become another faceless victim, murdered for the crime of wielding a clipboard. But then the Maoist rebels issued a ransom demand. They were holding him hostage, they said. In return for his freedom, they wanted the polling data. "It was very interesting," Jeremy Rosner, Greenberg's partner, said, reflecting on the incident. "What's the currency of the world now? It's not gold, it's data. It's the information." (The Maoist rebels and the pollsters struck a deal that secured the researcher's release: the insurgents got copies of the poll findings, but not the raw numbers, nor exclusive rights to the data.)

The Maoists of Nepal are not the only ones fixated on personal data. America's professional political class has become obsessed with voter profiling. If politics was recast in the last thirty years by television, it will be remade once again by the Internet—more precisely, by the database.

Until a few years ago, voter databases were haphazard and casual, like shopping lists on crumpled pieces of paper. The political parties absent-mindedly quilted together voter registration lists, which provided patchy and rudimentary information. In the late 1990s, however, a new arms race began in democratic politics, led, as ever, by the parties in America. The Republicans and the Democrats started to compete to compile ever more sophisticated files on each of America's 168 million registered voters. The Republicans built their own information bank, called Voter Vault; the Democrats built theirs, DataMart. A host of private-sector and not-for-profit groups also started collecting information in vast databases that serve as the equivalent of a high-school yearbook for the voting population of the United States.

The key fact is this: these days, just a few votes count. Political parties are chasing an ever smaller sliver of the electorate. The Democrats and the Republicans are neck and neck. They do not hope for landslide victories but a win by a percentage point or two. There is, therefore, a higher premium on reaching a smaller number of swing voters. Success hinges on effective communication with two specific audiences: undecided voters and lazy partisans—the people in the middle need to be wooed; the people on your side need to be ferried to the polls. In order to win, politicians do not need to speak to the country at large but to find those few million Americans who matter. New technologies suddenly give politicians the potential to do just that.

Constructing a voter profile is complicated and inexact, requiring reams of data and very clever computer models to make sense of it all. It involves using official banks of information, such as census data, and mining the surprisingly rich seams made available by the marketing industry: magazine subscriber lists, hunting and fishing licence lists, all-terrain vehicle user clubs, mortgage data and credit card information, charitable giving lists, cable subscription plans. At first glance, the result is a hodgepodge of random information: home ownership; length of residency; number of children; length of commute; early or late Internet adopter; health concerns; estimated annual income; WeightWatchers membership; gym user or regular yoga practitioner; gun owner, fly fisherman; Harley-Davidson enthusiast; subscriber to the Atkins Diet.

None of this information alone is likely to tell you if an American will vote Republican or Democratic. Certainly, some things pretty reliably predict political behavior: church attendance, income, whether you own or rent a house, ethnicity, and your past voting record. Sure, too, are some quirks of consumerism: a driver of a Lincoln Mercury is more likely to vote Republican than a driver of a Volvo; Absolut vodka drinkers trend Democratic, unlike Bud Light drinkers. But the real value in all these different subscriber lists and user clubs comes when hundreds of data points are combined, when the information fields are aligned on a giant spreadsheet and the separate details about one individual are layered one upon another. Then, rather like a screen print, a distinct image becomes clear.

Now, on the Internet, people are even more revealing when they type in what they are looking for on Google; they declare their interests and values, their hopes and fears. The search engine forecasts that in a few years it will be able to put together user profiles that identify an individual's professional ambitions and private aspirations. Political professionals are only just beginning to imagine the political uses of knowing the electorate, voter by voter, in such detail.

The cheerleaders for database politics cast it as a means of creating a renewed intimacy in public life, reconnecting individuals and officials. Ed Gillespie, then-chairman of the Republican National Committee, liked to compare new targeting technologies to what Abraham Lincoln did in the nineteenth century, when he would visit the local courthouse in Illinois and scour the lists for neighbors registered to vote. Simon Rosenberg, the president of the New Democrat Network, which seeks to harness progressives to the power of new media, says, "All of this allows politicians to come to voters in ways that are more germane to their lives." As Joe Trippi, who managed the 2004 Howard Dean campaign—widely seen as the first mainstream attempt to ignite the electorate online—puts it, "Technology has generated a new means for citizens to reconnect. This is a revolution of a different sort—a digital reawakening of democracy—a gradual transformation that requires no act of parliament or constitutional amendment. Politics is not changing; the tools of democracy are being reforged. People are being put back into the process."

It all sounds exciting and wonderful and alarmingly like David Sawyer's predictions a generation ago, of a world remade by real-time information. In their early days, the men from Sawyer Miller invested similar hopes in television as people such as Joe Trippi now do in a "digital reawakening of democracy." The new medium, they promised back in the 1970s, would usher in more direct dialogue, a more inclusive democracy, a more cerebral and personal debate. But the men from Sawyer Miller saw so many of those dreams turn to ashes. It is little wonder that they predict that this next wave of digital democracy will come to be mastered and managed by the professional political classes, too. Ed Reilly says the unfolding transformation of politics from the television age to the new media age is underestimated by everyone: "Instead of using the platforms to spread your message, there are now platforms which mean you can reach people with their message. Broadcast, you can reach every individual with *your* message; narrowcast, you can reach them with *theirs*."

Buying data, processing it, and delivering the kind of narrowband messages that appeal to slivers of the electorate—demographic segment by demographic segment, economic class by economic class, wedge issue by wedge issue—is going to be enormously expensive. Harris Diamond says that if the world has gasped at inflation in politics, it has seen nothing yet. "The next twenty to thirty years, you are going to see a consolidation of politicians with access to a large amount of money. We have always said that money is the mother's milk of politics. That is going to be true in the UK, in France, and certainly in Latin America. It is going to take incredible wealth. It looks like we're headed toward an oligopoly. It used to be a monopoly of party bosses, now it is an oligopoly of the professional political class."

The age of the image-maker is being eclipsed by the era of the niche marketer. The David Sawyers of the political world have been overtaken by the Karl Roves. Sawyer instinctively understood the politics of television: public opinion research, message discipline, and image management. Rove is pioneering the politics of the database: microsegmentation, tailored messaging, direct communication, and planned personal contact.

The political tides have all but erased the names of David Sawyer and Scott Miller, as each new election season sweeps in another backroom boy genius—James Carville, Dick Morris, Karl Rove—to be hailed as the unseen mastermind of politics. But even in the fickle, forgetful world of politics, the men from Sawyer Miller are worth remembering. They were the Manhattan Project of the lowbrow science of politics, a small but extraordinary group of people who took American-style campaigning into new realms. They helped create an industry that continues to change the world, a professional political class reaching into new corners of the globe, new areas of business, and, now, a new, unfolding era of communication revolutionized by the Internet. The world is now moving into the second generation of what David Sawyer liked to call electronic democracy. The work of the alpha dogs has only just begun.

A NOTE ON SOURCES

ACKNOWLEDGMENTS

INDEX

A NOTE ON SOURCES

The chief sources for this book are the subjects of it, the alpha dogs themselves. Even in the best of circumstances, this makes for partial history and muddled anecdotes. Memories can be twisted—and that's for those who are still able to remember. And, of course, these are not the best of circumstances: this is a book about political consultants, people whose profession it is to turn ideas into dramas, arcane policies into grand narratives, bland technocrats into charismatic titans. Still, the men and women who worked at the Sawyer Miller Group have heard enough—indeed, told enough—tall tales from the campaign trail that I found their recollections pretty reliable. Many not just made themselves available for interview but also provided files of old memos, strategy papers, and scribbled notes, as well as reels of Sawyer Miller political and corporate ads. I tried to cross-check one person's version with another's and, where I had two or more people in the room telling a version of events that was consistent, I wrote it without attribution. If I have had only one person's account to go on or if I've relayed a point of view, then I've tried to make clear who said what when. (A handful of old alumni asked to speak anonymously.)

The book was based on about two hundred interviews, but a couple dozen people were really central to telling the story of the firm. They were: Scott Miller, Ned Kennan, Joel McCleary, Ed Reilly, Mark Malloch Brown, Jack Leslie, Harris Diamond, Mandy Grunwald, Peter Schechter, Rob Shepardson, Lenny Stern, David Morey, Mark McKinnon, Robert Mead, Bob Keefe, Micho Spring, Joey Shawcross, James Carville, Dick Dresner, Robert Shrum, Iris Sawyer, Joe Napolitan, Skip Stein, Robert Rubin, Tim Bell, Richard Wirthlin, Jane Byrne, Diego Arria, Shimon Peres, Cesar Gaviria, and Gonzalo Sánchez de Lozada.

Although this book tells a pretty fresh piece of history, it had the benefit of relying on what is already a huge amount of election literature. There is a small but growing library of books on political consultants. For people interested in the subject, the following books represent a selective but very useful bibliography: *Public Opinion*, by Walter Lippmann (1922); *The Rise of Political Consul-*

tants, by Larry Sabato (1981); *The Selling of the President, 1968,* by Joe McGinnis (1970); *Candidates, Consultants, and Campaigns: The Style and Substance of American Electioneering,* by Frank Luntz (1988); and *Politics Lost,* by Joe Klein (2006).

The chapter on Boston was helped by *Style Versus Substance: Boston, Kevin White, and the Politics of Illusion,* by George V. Higgins (1984). The account of Sawyer's work in Venezuela was assisted by *Competitive Elections in Developing Countries,* edited by Myron Weiner and Ergun Ozbudun (1987); *Electoral Mobilization and Public Opinion—The Venezuelan Campaign of 1973,* by John D. Martz and Enrique A. Baloyra (1976); *Venezuela at the Polls,* edited by Howard R. Penniman (1980). The most useful factual histories that helped inform the Israel chapter were *Politics in Israel,* edited by Asher Arian; and *The Election in Israel* series, which Arian also edited, starting in 1973 and ending in 2001. The Coke chapter benefited from a reading of *I'd Like the World to Buy a Coke: The Life and Leadership of Roberto Goizueta,* by David Greising (1999); *The Other Guy Blinked: How Pepsi Won the Cola Wars,* by Roger Enrico and Jesse Kornbluth (1987); *Blink: The Power of Thinking Without Thinking,* by Malcolm Gladwell (2005); and *The Predators' Ball: The Inside Story of Drexel Burnham and the Rise of the Junk Bond Raiders,* by Connie Bruck (1989). *Waltzing with a Dictator: The Marcoses and the Making of American Policy,* by Raymond Bonner (1987); *People Power: An Eyewitness History: The Philippine Revolution of 1986,* edited by Monina Allarey Mercado; and *In Our Image: America's Empire in the Philippines,* by Stanley Karnow (1990), were essential in helping put the Philippines chapter together. The Peru story leaned on Mario Vargas Llosa's own account, *A Fish in the Water* (1994); the 1991 volume of *Granta* that included essays by both Mark Malloch Brown ("The Consultant") and Alvaro Vargas Llosa ("The Press Officer"); and *The War of the End of Democracy: Mario Vargas Llosa vs. Alberto Fujimori,* by Jeff Daeschner (1993). The book also had the benefit of the first draft of David Sawyer and Scott Miller's proposal for a book they proved too busy to write, called *Changing Channels,* as well as Miller's 2004 book, written with David Morey, *The Underdog Advantage.*

Magazine and newspaper articles were even more useful. The archives of *The Wall Street Journal, The New York Times, The Times* (London), and *Time* magazine were particularly helpful, but among the hundreds of articles culled for this book, a couple in particular are worth mentioning: Maura Sheehy's piece on Sawyer Miller, "The Global Spin Doctor," in *Manhattan, Inc.* magazine in 1990; and Sidney Blumenthal's story on Scott Miller and the John Glenn campaign, "Glenn Is It!" in *The New Republic* in 1983.

ACKNOWLEDGMENTS

It would be nice to thank a long list of people for their help with this book and then, as tradition requires, insist that the mistakes are all my own. But the flaws would not be there if the book had never been written and, frankly, that would not have happened if it had not been for the patience, inspiration, and generosity of family and friends.

When I lived in Washington, D.C., my cousin Thomas Harding pressed me to think more deeply about politics and to then do more than just talk about it—to write a book. My colleagues in the Washington bureau of the *Financial Times* made it possible for me to get up close and personal with American politics on the campaign trail, while keeping in mind an audience beyond America. As well as thanking Ted Alden, Holly Yeager, Demetri Sevastopulo, Josh Chaffin, Stephanie Kirchgaessner, Guy Dinmore, Alan Beattie, Andrew Balls, Patti Waldmeir, Jurek Martin, Ayda Harding, and, of course, Nancy McCord, I'd like to thank Andrew Gowers, the former editor of the *Financial Times*, who sent me to Washington. Lionel Barber, the former U.S. editor and now editor of the *Financial Times*, has taught me more than I'd like to admit about journalistic values, political judgment, and storytelling. I am enormously grateful to him.

It was Andrew Wylie, my agent and, undoubtedly, the alpha dog of modern publishing, who was the most instrumental figure in helping me to write the book. He cheerfully batted away ideas that weren't any good and then put his considerable enthusiasm to work in support of the Sawyer Miller story. Sarah Chalfant, his colleague and a great addition to the literary scene in London, has been a huge help since I moved back here. Eric Chinski has been my editor at Farrar, Straus and Giroux and, in his own gentle and thoughtful way, my teacher. When he signed me up, I knew a little about writing 650-word articles, but nothing about 100,000-word books. He took a bunch of postcards and helped me turn them into a story. Gena Hamshaw, who works with Eric, has shown grace, persistence, and endless good humor, as I've missed deadlines in the publishing process.

Robert Thomson not only brought me to *The Times*, but was generous enough to give me the time to finish the book before I got here. Both at the *Financial Times* and at *The Times*, he was an inspirational editor. It is not his style to teach people and yet I have learned so much from him about language, ideas, and, most of all, people. And I'm hugely grateful to Jackie Stradling, who kept the news at bay long enough for me to finish the book.

Above all, though, I would like to thank my friends and family. My mother and father, Zumbs and Robert, and Leo and Eve have been the people who encouraged and supported me through the time when I wrote this book. I cannot thank them enough.

I wrote most of this book while living in a little house in Wiltshire. It didn't have a television, so when I wanted to go and watch something I went to see friends down the road who have a TV. One evening, I went over there and met Kate. She introduced herself as a book doctor, someone who helps people whose work needs surgery. She turned the book—and my life—around.

INDEX

ABC, 76, 115, 130, 202, 214
Abrams, Robert, 97
Acción Democrática party, Venezuelan, 43–44, 46, 50, 52
Ad Age, 72
Adams, John, 100
Adams, John Quincy, 40
advertising industry, 19, 24, 89, 199; consumer research and, 24–25; Miller in, 24–26, 38; "Vote Different" ad and, 225–26
Agnew, Spiro, 57
Aguilar, Pedro Pablo, 52
AIDS, 74
Ailes, Roger, 79, 204, 219–20
Albania, 219, 220
Ali, Muhammad, 72, 74
Allen, Woody, 32
Allende, Salvador, 153
Allyn, Rob, 221
alpha dogs: Kennan on, 11; schools of, 78
Alva Castro, Luis, 184
Ameche, Don, 32
American Association of Political Consultants, 55
American Express, 200
Amir, Yigal, 95

Angola, 220
Annan, Kofi, 125, 217
Apple Computer, 6, 65–66, 74, 204, 225, 226
APRA, 180, 184
Aquino, Benigno "Ninoy," 117–18, 122, 131
Aquino, Corazon, 3, 115, 118, 140, 141, 145, 153, 154–55, 175, 203, 220; campaign of, 130–31, 134–37, 138; *New York Times* interview fiasco and, 124–25, 127, 128; as presidential candidate, 122–24; *see also* Philippines, election of 1986 in
Arad, Eyal, 91–92, 95, 97
Arafat, Yasser, 98
Argentina, 5, 46, 114, 150, 160
Arias, Oscar, 4
Arizona, 37
Armstrong, Lance, 219
Arria, Diego, 51–52, 55
Asia Society, 118
AT&T, 74
Atwater, Lee, 207
Aunt Julia and the Scriptwriter (Vargas Llosa), 169
Austria, 154

Avedon, Richard, 27
Azerbaijan, 219, 220

Babbitt, Bruce, 37
Bailey, Douglas, 41
Baloyra, Enrique A., 48, 53
BarackObama.com, 225
Barak, Ehud, 101, 103–105, 106
Barbarians at the Gate (Burrough and Helyar), 202
Barco, Virgilio, 175, 193, 194
Barnes, Fred, 119
Barnicle, Mike, 33
Barrantes Lingán, Alfonso, 184
Baxter, Leone Smith, 40
BBC, 7
Becket, Maria, 126
Beckley, John, 40
Bedoya Reyes, Luis, 177
Begin, Menachem, 85, 86–87, 88, 144
Bell, Tim, 160, 174–75
Ben-Gurion, David, 100
Berkshire Hathaway, 70
Berlusconi, Silvio, 7, 222
Betancourt, Rómulo, 42–43
Bickersons, The (radio show), 32
Biden, Joe, 65, 204
"Billie Jean" (song), 69
Black, Leon, 198, 199–200
Black, Manafort and Stone, 119, 121, 174
Blair, Tony, 7, 47, 101, 103, 107, 222
Blevis, Alan, 34
Blink (Gladwell), 79
Blumenthal, Sidney, 62
Bolivia, 3, 103, 141, 160, 175, 182, 190; 1989 election in, 171–72
Bonner, Raymond, 116
Borja, Rodrigo, 171
Boston, Mass.: 1979 election in, *see* Boston election of 1979; 1983 election in, 35–36

Boston, Mass., election of 1979 in, 15–17, 31–35, 51, 182; negative campaign strategy in, 31–33; results of, 34; White's governing style and, 20–22; White's image in, 33–34
Boston Globe, The, 33, 34, 36
Boston Herald, 36
Bosworth, Stephen, 136
Bowie, David, 150
Bozell, 213
Bradley, Bill, 135
Brando, Marlon, 27
Brazil, 46, 114, 160
Brezhnev, Leonid, 113, 122
Brinkley, David, 116, 118, 137
British American Tobacco (BAT), 202, 203
Bronfman, Charles, 86, 143
Bronfman, Edgar, 86, 143
Brown, Gordon, 102
Brown, John Y., 41
Brown and Williamson Tobacco, 197
Bryce, James, 53–54
BSMG, 213
Buddhism, 161, 163
Buffett, Warren, 69–70
Bush, George H. W., 77, 107, 204, 219–20
Bush, George W., 7, 8–9, 47, 51, 77–78, 98, 107, 150, 177
Byrne, Brendan, 41
Byrne, Jane, 37, 170–71

Caddell, Patrick, 55, 64–66, 72, 73
Caldera, Rafael, 43, 46, 47, 49, 50
California, 57, 134; 1934 election in, 40
Callaghan, James, 216
Cambio 90, 185–86, 189
Cameron, David, 7–8, 216
Campaigns, Inc., 40

Campbell, Don, 148

Canada, 92

C & C, 68

Cap and Gown, 26

Capote, Truman, 27

Carotas, 180

Carey, Hugh, 55

Carroll, Lewis, 67

Carson, Johnny, 84

Carter, Jimmy, 37, 57, 58–59, 62, 64–65, 122, 161

Carville, James, 48, 78, 101–106, 163–64, 207, 230

Castro, Fidel, 48, 69

Catholic Bishops Conference of the Philippines, 133

Catholic Church, 189

CBS, 82, 144

Central Intelligence Agency (CIA), 119–20, 121, 134–35

Challenger, 36

Chappaquiddick incident, 51

Charter Medical, 202

Cherry Coke, 69–70

Chiat, Jay, 66

Chicago Boys, 153

Chicago election of 1983, 170–71

Chile, 3, 150, 153–60, 171, 175

China, People's Republic of, 117, 221; Tibet and, 162–63

Chlopak, Bob, 218

Christian Democratic Party, Chilean, 156

Churchill, Winston, 72

Cicero, Quintus, 111

Clark, Harry, 139, 197, 201

Classic Coke, 76, 78

"Classification of Juvenile Delinquents Based on Their Psychological and Behavioural Attitudes" (Kennan), 18

Clinton, Bill, 10, 34, 75, 97, 102–103, 107, 164, 207, 218, 222; first inaugural address of, 75

Clinton, Hillary, 97; "Vote Different" ad and, 225–26

Clow, Lee, 66

CNN, 149

Coca-Cola, 6, 23, 25, 26, 34, 64, 80, 204; Classic Coke introduced by, 76; Mean Joe Greene ad of, 61–62; New Coke fiasco of, *see* New Coke; new products developed by, 69–70; Pepsi's rivalry with, 66–69

Coca-Cola Classic, 76

Cojuangco, Jose "Peping," 122–23, 127

Cojuangco family, 122, 131

Coke II, 79

Colombia, 3, 4–5, 7, 121, 141, 147, 150, 160, 175, 203; drugs issue and, 193–94

Columbus, Christopher, 43

COMELEC, 133–34

Common Cause Party, Venezuelan, 55

Concertando (television show), 185

Condor, Operation, 153

"Confessions of a Buddhist Political Junkie" (McCleary), 161

Congress, U.S., 118, 135; *see also* House of Representatives, U.S.; Senate, U.S.

Connecticut: 1974 election in, 29; 1980 election in, 37, 102

Connery, Sean, 150

Conservative Party, British, 7, 47, 92, 107, 216

Constitutional Tribunal, Chilean, 155

consumer democracy, 64, 80–81

Continental Airlines, 6, 202

Contract with America, 7, 146, 222

Contract with the Italian People, 222

Converse All-Stars, 25

Cooper Llosa, Freddy, 174, 178–79

Cosby, Bill, 68, 84

Costa Rica, 114, 160, 218; 1978 election in, 56

Cott, 68

Coury Torbay, José, 55–56
Cranston, Alan, 64, 135
Cronan, Trish, 147, 148, 198
Cruchaga, Miguel, 181, 185, 191
C-Span, 149
C-3PO, 151
Country Life, 166
Cuba, 48, 69
Cuomo, Mario, 59, 83
Curley, James Michael, 21
Czech Republic, 5

Daeschner, Jeff, 173, 180, 184
Daily Telegraph, The, 7
Dalai Lama, 3, 4, 139, 162
Daley, Richard J., 170
Daley, Richard M., 170–71
D'Amato, Alfonse, 97
DataMart, 227
Davis, Rick, 220
Davis, Sammy, Jr., 4
Dean, Howard, 229
Deardourff, John, 41, 55
Decima, 92
Defense Department, U.S., 121, 134
de Klerk, F. W., 174
DeLauro, Rosa, 102
Delaware Valley Mental Health
    Foundation, 28
Delta Airlines, 219
democracy, 6, 56, 138, 142, 158; con-
    sumer, 64, 80–81; digital, 228–30;
    electronic, 114, 201, 217, 223–24,
    230; Miller on, 152
Democracy in America (Tocqueville),
    53
Democratic Front, *see* FREDEMO
Democratic National Committee, 108
Democratic National Convention of
    1960, 27
Democratic National Convention of
    1968, 120

Democratic National Convention of
    1980, 37–38
Democratic National Convention of
    2004, 106
Democratic Party, Japanese, 221
Democratic Party, Michigan, 41
Democratic Party, U.S., 5, 21, 38, 44,
    57, 61, 65, 72, 102–103, 106, 114,
    153, 197, 206, 223, 227
Deri, Aryeh, 103
de Soto, Hernando, 185
de Vellis, Philip, 225–26
D. H. Sawyer and Associates, 29, 31,
    41, 109
Diamond, Harris, 90, 148, 164, 195,
    200–202, 204, 205, 206–207, 217,
    229; in Sawyer buyout, 210–13
Diana, Princess of Wales, 109
Dichter, Ernst, 20
Diet Coke, 69, 70, 73
digital democracy, 228–30
"direct cinema," 28
Dodd, Christopher, 37, 102
Dole, Bob, 97
"Dolphin and the Shark, The," 65–66
Dominican Republic, 46, 48, 114, 141
Donaldson, Sam, 115
"Do They Know It's Christmas?"
    (song), 150
Double Cola, 68
Doyle Dane Bernbach, 25
Dresner, Dick, 35, 170, 218–19
Drexel Burnham Lambert, 197–99,
    203, 206
Dromi, Uri, 100
Dukakis, Michael, 107–108, 204, 205
Duke (Miller's dog), 224

Eagleton, Thomas, 29, 198
Eban, Abba, 154
Economist, The, 125, 126, 127, 175
Economist Development Report, 125

Ecuador, 3, 7, 141, 160; 1988 election in, 171

Edwards, John, 225–26

E. F. Hutton, 197

Egypt, 85, 88

Eisenhower, Dwight D., 51, 73

Election Game—and How to Win It, The (Napolitan), 45

elections, U.S.: of 1796, 40; of 1800, 100; of 1824, 40; of 1922, 40; of 1936, 40–41; of 1960, 18, 44, 51, 82, 99, 187; of 1964, 25, 44; of 1968, 44–45, 79, 204; of 1972, 21, 29, 65, 97, 102, 201; of 1976, 41, 57, 62, 63, 64–65, 113; of 1980, 37–38, 44, 51, 56–58, 62, 63, 91, 102, 144, 145, 147; of 1982, 108, 113, 215; of 1984, 61–64, 65, 73, 82–85, 107–108, 113, 114, 144, 145, 156, 207, 225; of 1988, 65, 107–108, 204; of 1992, 77, 97, 103, 107, 164, 207; of 1994, 222; of 1996, 97; of 1999, 101; of 2000, 7, 9, 107; of 2004, 7, 8–9, 44, 98, 102, 106, 107, 225–26, 229; of 2008, 7, 97, 225–26

electronic democracy, 114, 201, 217, 223–24, 230

Emporia Gazette, The, 71

Enrico, Roger, 73, 78

Enrile, Juan Ponce, 137

Erving, Julius "Dr. J.," 25–26

Ese hombre de la cara (*This man isn't afraid to face you*) (television program), 51

Ethiopia, 150

Ezekiel, Brother, 186, 187

Ezrahi, Yaron, 105

Farrow, Mia, 198

Fernández, Lorenzo, 47, 48–52, 53, 55, 56, 63, 85

Fernández, Luis Mariano, 49

Finkelstein, Arthur, 96–97, 98, 100, 101, 103, 106

Flying Fortress, 65, 71–72

focus groups, 16, 18–19

Fonda, Jane, 151

Food and Drug Administration, U.S., 74

Foot, Michael, 144

Ford, Gerald, 41, 57

Fox, Vicente, 221

Fox News, 204

France, 45, 145, 174

FREDEMO (Democratic Front; Peru), 175–76, 178, 180, 185–86, 188, 189, 191

Freeman, Bob, 200

French, Barry, 171, 185

Friedman, Matthew, 138

Friedman, Milton, 153

Fujimori, Alberto, 185–89, 191, 192

Gaither, George, 52

Gallup, George W., 41

Gallup polls, 18, 19

Garbo, Greta, 165

García, Alan, 172–73, 180, 184

Garth, David, 41, 55, 86, 88

Gaviria, César, 194

Geertz, Clifford, 53

General Hospital (television show), 76

Georgia, 220

Gephardt, Dick, 204, 218, 223

Gere, Richard, 11, 150

Germany, 103

Ghana, 7

Gillespie, Ed, 228–29

Gingrich, Newt, 7, 146, 222

Giscard d'Estaing, Valéry, 45

Giuliani, Rudy, 199

Gladwell, Malcolm, 79

Glenn, John, 61–64, 82, 108, 143

Glick, Joe, 158

globalization, 7, 92, 122; information revolution and, 222–23; of politics, 7–8; SMG legacy and, 218–19

Goizueta, Roberto, 67, 69; New Coke project and, 70–73, 75–76, 77, 79

Goldman Sachs, 6, 147, 200

Goldwater, Barry, 25, 44, 55

Google, 228

Gould, Philip, 101, 107

Graham, Billy, 151

Granta, 187

Grasso, Ella, 29

Gray, Bill, 204

Great Britain, 7, 45, 46, 72, 86, 91, 92, 103, 178, 191; 1979 election in, 107, 160, 174, 216; 1983 election in, 144; 1988 election in, 107; 1992 election in, 47; 1997 election in, 101

Greece, 3, 114, 121, 126, 141, 150

Greenberg, Stan, 37, 101, 102–106, 226–27

Greene, Graham, 119

Greene, Mean Joe, 61–62

Gregg, Allan, 92

Greising, David, 70

Grunwald, Mandy, 10, 41, 59, 102, 146, 147, 150–51, 163, 164, 199, 226; leaves SMG, 205–207

G7 Group, 214

Guardian, The, 222

Guillermoprieto, Alma, 190

Guzmán, Abimael, 183

Habib, Philip, 134, 136

Habla el Presidente (*The President Speaks*) (television program), 46

Haiti, 221

Handbook for Electioneering (Cicero), 111

Hands Across America, 150–51

Hanna, Mark, 40

Hanwright, Joe, 34

Harley-Davidson, 80

Harper's, 166

Harris, Lou, 18

Harrisburg Pennsylvanian, 40

Hart, Gary, 64, 65, 74, 82, 198

Hart, Peter, 29

Hartley, Jane, 205, 214

Havel, Václav, 5

Hebron Accords, 105

Hecht, Haim, 103–104

Hellcats of the Navy (film), 63

Helms, Jesse, 147, 176–77

Hernández Colón, Rafael, 41–42, 56

Herrera Campins, Luis, 55

Higgins, George, 22

Hiriart, Lucia, 157

history, swarm theory of, 10

Hogan, Hulk, 74

Hoge, Warren, 124

Hollings, Ernest "Fritz," 64

Hope, Bob, 68, 84

House of Commons, British, 125

House of Representatives, U.S., 37, 44, 223

Huks, 119

human rights, 5, 193–94

Humphrey, Hubert, 44–45, 55, 120

Hungary, 141, 219

Hunt, Jim, 147, 176–77, 205

IBM, 65–66, 74

I'd Like the World to Buy a Coke (Greising), 70

Illinois, 29

Indonesia, 219, 220, 221

information revolution, 6, 221–22

In Our Image (Karnow), 120

Internet, 10, 219; digital democracy

and, 228–30; "Vote Different" ad on, 225–26; voter databases and, 227–28

intifada, 92–93, 95

Iraq, 88, 175, 223

Irgun, 92

Israel, 5, 6, 17–18, 72, 85, 113, 114, 138; Americanization of politics in, 88–93, 96, 98–101, 105–106; demographic revolution in, 87; elections as personality contests in, 100–101; election system reform in, 94; intifada and, 92–93; 1973 election in, 95; 1977 election in, 85–88, 90, 93, 94; 1981 election in, 88, 90, 93, 94, 107, 110, 144; 1984 election in, 90, 93, 94; 1988 election in, 93, 95; 1992 election in, 93, 94–95; 1996 election in, 93, 96–101, 104, 105; 1999 election in, 93, 94, 101, 103–105, 106; FLO recognized by, 95; Rabin assassination in, 95–96, 100, 105–106; split-ticket voting in, 101; television in politics of, 87–88, 97–99, 100; 2001 election in, 105; U.S. political consultants and, 86–89, 91–92

Israeli Defense Forces, 104

Italy, 7, 91; 2001 election in, 222

Jackson, Andrew, 40

Jackson, Henry "Scoop," 37, 63

Jackson, Jesse, 64, 151

Jackson, Michael, 69

Jamaica, 174

Japan, 117, 221

Jefferson, Thomas, 40, 100

Jennings, Peter, 132, 214

Jerusalem, The, 18

Jobs, Steve, 65, 66

Johnson, Lady Bird, 116

Johnson, Lyndon B., 22, 25, 41, 47, 116

Jones, Robert Trent, Jr., 122–23, 126–27, 135

Jordan, 18

Joseph, Frederick, 199–200

junk bonds, 197–98, 199

Justice Department, U.S., 197

Kansas Project, 71–72

Karnow, Stanley, 120, 137

Kazakhstan, 221

Keefe, Bob, 29

Kempner, Nan, 109, 165

Kempner, Tom, 109–10, 164–65, 198

Kennan, Ned, 11, 15–20, 23, 34, 35, 51, 60, 91, 148, 156–57, 158, 170, 201, 224; on alpha dogs as term, 11; background of, 16–18; leaves SMG, 208–10; as pollster, 17–20

Kennan Research and Consulting (KRC), 148–49, 156–57, 158, 208

Kennedy, John F., 18, 22, 23, 27, 44, 51, 65, 73, 79, 82, 99

Kennedy, Robert F., 29, 118

Kennedy, Ted, 37, 51, 63, 102, 144, 147

Kentucky, 147; 1987 election in, 101–102, 163–64

Kenya, 220

Keough, Don, 69–70, 76, 78–79

Kerry, John, 8–9, 98, 102, 104, 106, 177, 225–26

Kim Dae-Jung, 4, 144, 145–46

King, Coretta Scott, 151

Kinnock, Neil, 45

Kissinger, Henry, 116, 131

KKR, 147, 202

Klecanda, Pat, 147

Klein, Joe, 222

Knesset, Israel, 87, 89, 94, 101, 104

Knickerbocker Club, 39, 59, 80, 154, 196
Knight, Andrew, 126
Koch, Ed, 41, 55, 58
Koppel, Ted, 130
Korea, People's Democratic Republic of (North Korea), 117
Korea, Republic of (South Korea), 4, 117, 121, 142, 143–44, 221; 1992 election in, 145; 1997 election in, 145
Kragen, Ken, 150–51
Kramer, Oren, 59, 197, 201
Kyrgyzstan, 220–21

Labor Party, Israeli, 85–88, 90–91, 93, 94, 96, 101, 104–105
Labour Party, British, 7–8, 47; as New Labour, 101, 103, 107
Landon, Alf, 40–41
Landsmark, Ted, 21
Langford, Frances, 32
Lansdale, Ed, 119
Laurel, Salvador, 115
Laxalt, Paul, 116, 137–38
Leacock, Richard, 28
Lebanon, 104, 220
Lee Kwan Yew, 174
Lennox, Susan, *see* Sawyer, Iris Michaels
Leonard, Charlotte, 213, 218
Leone, Dick, 83
Leoni, Raúl, 43
Leslie, Jack, 147, 148, 150, 164, 176, 194, 195, 204–207, 217; in Sawyer buyout, 210–13
Liberty Movement, 173, 175, 187
Licht, Frank, 29
Lieberman, Seymour, 20
Likud party, Israeli, 85, 86–88, 90, 92, 93, 94–95, 98, 101
Lincoln, Abraham, 47, 228–29

Lindsay, John, 20
Lippmann, Walter, 40
Listerine, 19
Liston, Sonny, 63
Literary Digest, 40–41
Live Aid, 150
Llobet, Oswaldo, 55
Locsin, Teddy Boy, 131–32, 133, 134
Longabaugh, Mark, 208
Lorenzo, Frank, 202
Lucho (Vargas Llosa's cousin), 178, 180, 188
Lugar, Dick, 133, 136
Lumet, Sidney, 11
Luntz, Frank, 92, 220, 222
Lupton, Jack, 67, 72

Macapagal, Diosdado, 120
Machiavelli, Niccolò, vii
Macintosh computer, 66, 74
Macmillan, Harold, 104
Magnuson, Warren, 37
Magsaysay, Ramon, 119–20
Major, John, 7
Malloch Brown, Mark, 143, 147–48, 151–52, 162, 195, 198, 206, 208, 217; Aquino campaign and, 125–31, 133–36, 140–42; 1990 Peru election and, 171–72, 175, 181, 187–92; in Sawyer buyout, 210–13; on SMG's legacy, 224
Malta, 174
Manafort, Paul, 119, 138, 220
Mandela, Nelson, 103
Mandelson, Peter, 101
Manhattan Inc., 151–52, 201, 202
Manilow, Barry, 4
Mao Zedong, 28, 163
Marcos, Ferdinand, 45, 46, 145, 161, 220; in 1986 campaign, 124–25, 127–30, 134–38; snap election

decision of, 115–16; U.S.-Philippines relationship and, 116–19, 120

Marcos, Imelda, 116–18, 119, 120, 129, 136

Marti, John D., 18, 53

Massa, Alberto, 180

Mastercard, 200

McCain, John, 7

McCall, David, 213

McCann, H. K., 23

McCann Erickson, 23, 38, 39, 68, 71, 146, 203

McCartney, Linda Eastman, 198

McCleary, Joel, 57–59, 87, 108, 121, 122, 125, 132–36, 139, 141, 145, 150, 158, 161–63, 164, 221

McCoy, Alfred W., 128

McFarland, Alan, 215

McFarland, Andrew, 214–15

McFarland, Gavin, 214–15

McFarland, K. T., 215

McFarland, Nell Michel, *see* Sawyer, Nell Michel McFarland

McGinnis, Joe, 79–80

McGovern, George, 21, 64, 65, 102, 201

McKinley, William, 40, 47

McKinnon, Mark, 7, 11, 148, 220

McKinsey & Company, 147, 196

McLaughlin, John, 119

McLuhan, Marshall, 80, 86, 152

Mead, Katia, 148, 150

Mead, Robert, 148, 150, 206

"Meditations at Versailles" (Thackeray), 13

Mercury project, 61, 62

Mexico, 221; 1994 election in, 218

Michaels, Iris, *see* Sawyer, Iris Michaels

Michel, Clifford, 109

Milken, Michael, 198, 199–200

Miller, Denise, 198

Miller, Mrs. Alex, 41

Miller, Scott, 6–7, 41, 51, 60, 78, 107, 108, 113, 115, 124, 134–35, 139–40, 146–48, 194, 226; in advertising industry, 24–26, 38; Apple-IBM rivalry and, 65–66, background of, 23–26; Boston election of 1979 and, 22–23, 30–35; Coke-Pepsi rivalry and, 67–68, 71–73, 75–77; Cosby ad and, 68; on democracy, 152; Drexel account and, 198–200; farewell note of, 223; leaves SMG, 203–205; marriages of, 198; Mean Joe Greene ad of, 61–62; move the movable theory of, 77; 1984 election and, 107–108; 1984 Glenn campaign and, 61–64; 1984 Mondale campaign and, 82–85; office of, 149; Reagan ad and, 113–14; retirement of, 224; Sawyer's recruitment of, 26, 30, 37

Miller Brewing, 204

Miller Lite, 26

Minjack, Greg, 220

Ministry of Information, Philippines, 140

Monaco, 76

Mondale, Walter "Fritz," 61, 63, 64, 82–85, 107, 113, 144, 145, 156, 177, 207

Montenegro, 220

Morey, David, 4, 143–46, 221

Morris, Dick, 220, 230

Moscow Olympic of 1980, 143

Mossad, 16

Motherland Party, Turkey, 220

Moynihan, Daniel Patrick, 113–14, 203, 214–15

Mudd, Roger, 144

Mullins, Gay, 74

Murdoch, Rupert, 204

Mydans, Seth, 124

Nagourney, Adam, 103
Napolitan, Joe, 44, 45–46, 51, 55;
    Philippines assignment of, 120–
    21
National Security Council, 121
NBC Nightly News, 72
Nepal, 226–27
Netanyahu, Binyamin, 91, 95–101,
    104–105
New Coke, 70–75, 77–79; opposi-
    tion to, 74–75; rebranding of, 79;
    roll out of, 72–73
New Democratic Network, 229
New Frontier, 65
New Hampshire, 64, 156
New Labour, *see* Labour Party,
    British
New People's Army, 117, 124
New Republic, The, 62
Newsweek, 74
New Yorker, The, 185
New York State, 57, 59; 1994 election
    in, 97
New York Times, The, 72, 103, 124,
    129, 183, 202; Aquino interview
    fiasco and, 124–25, 127
Nicaragua, 135
Nietzsche, Friedrich, 18
Nigeria, 3, 7, 145, 161, 195, 220
Nightline, 130
Nike, 219
Niven, David, 38
Nixon, Pat, 116
Nixon, Richard M., 21, 22, 27, 51, 57,
    79, 82, 97, 99, 116, 120, 187, 204,
    219
Noriega, Manuel, 5, 161, 162,
    195
North Carolina, 205; 1984 election
    in, 147, 176–77
Notebooks of Don Rigoberto, The
    (Vargas Llosa), 169
Novak, Bob, 119, 131
Nunn, Sam, 135–36

Obama, Barack, 219, 225
Ogilvy, David, 24–25
Ohio, 9
Old Coke Drinkers of America, 74
Olympic Games of 1980, 143
Onassis, Jackie, 198
O'Neill, Tip, 151
Operation Condor, 153
Oslo peace process, 95
Osmeña, Sergio, Jr., 120
Other Voices (film), 28

Palestinian Liberation Organization
    (PLO), 95
Palomino, Salvador, 182
Panama, 5, 121, 122, 134, 141, 160,
    161, 162, 195
Paraguay, 160
Parkman, George, 35
Pataki, George, 97, 98
Paterno, Vicente, 123
Paz, Octavio, 173
Pemberton, "Doc," 69
Pennebaker, D. A., 28
Pennsylvania, 29, 148; 1970 election
    in, 29
Penthouse, 75
People Power (Paterno), 123
People Power revolution, 3, 116, 122,
    134, 143
Pepsi, 64, 66–69, 79; New Coke reac-
    tion of, 72–73, 77–78
Peres, Shimon, 4, 85, 90, 93–97, 99–
    101, 102, 144
Pérez, Carlos Andrés, 5, 47–48, 50,
    52, 53, 54, 55, 56
Perkins, Bob, 139, 170, 196–97, 201
Perot, Ross, 222
Peru, 3, 5, 141, 169, 172–74; 1990
    election in, *see* Peruvian election
    of 1990
Peru, election of 1990 in: advertising

in, 178–80; blame and criticism after, 190–92; British advisers and, 174–75; Catholic Church and, 189; cost of, 190; economic reform issue in, 184–85; excessive spending in, 180; Fujimori's campaign in, 185–88; monkey ad in, 179–80; opposition candidates in, 185–86; polling in, 186–87, 191; race problem in, 182–83, 192; results of, 189–90; SMG in, 171, 175, 176, 177–78; traditional parties in, 175–77, 184; Vargas Llosa's campaign in, 178–83, 186, 188, 191–92; Vargas Llosa's decision to run in, 172–74; Vargas Llosa's inner circle and, 178–79; Vargas Llosa's memoir of, 173, 192–93

"Peru: The Liberal Mandate" (SMG memorandum), 169

Pez en el Agua El (*A Fish in the Water*) (Vargas Llosa), 173, 192–93

Philippines, 3, 45, 115, 138, 139, 143, 150, 155, 159, 161, 171, 175, 213, 221; Aquino assassination in, 118; CIA and, 119–20, 121; 1969 election in, 120; 1978 election in, 117; 1981 election in, 117; 1986 election in, *see* Philippines, election of 1986 in; People Power revolution in, 3, 116, 122, 134, 143; U.S. relations with, 116–20

Philippines, election of 1986 in: American consultants and, 119–21, 122, 125–26; Aquino assassination and, 118; Aquino's campaign in, 130–32; fake medals controversy in, 128–29; negative campaigning in, 128; *New York Times* interview fiasco and, 122, 124–25, 127, 128; outcome controversy and, 133–37; Reagan White House and, 132–38; SMG and, 122, 125–

27, 131–32, 140–41; as Yellow Revolution, 130–31

Philippines Central Bank, 140

Philippines Coconut Authority, 140

Philippines Sugar Administration, 140

Piñerúa Ordaz, Luis, 55

Pinochet, Augusto, 3, 153, 155, 157–60, 174

Poland, 5, 86, 141, 208–209

political action system (PINS), 91

political consultants: conservative, 219–20; globalization of politics and, 7–8; information revolution and, 221–23; international reach of, 6–7, 219–22; as modern industry, 6–7; motivations of, 138–39; in 1972 Venezuelan election, 44–46; U.S. style of, 7–8

"Politics as a Vocation" (Weber), 192–93

polls, polling, 17–20, 103; development of, 18–19, 40–41; dial session technology and, 91–92; first, 40; focus groups and, 18–19; group psychology approach to, 19–20; in 1988 Chilean election, 156–57, 158; in 1990 Peruvian election, 186–87, 191; skewed sampling in, 41; straw-ballot technique of, 40–41; in 2006 Nepalese election, 226–27; wrong question in, 79

Popper, Karl, 183

Popular Action Party, Peru, 175–76

Popular Christian Party, Peru, 175–76

Portugal, 141, 150

Power (film), 11

President Speaks, The (*Habla el Presidente*) (television program), 46

Prince, The (Machiavelli), vii

Project Kansas, 71–72

Pryor, David, 76

Public Opinion (Lippmann), 40
Puerto Rico, 114; 1968 election in, 41–42; 1972 election in, 41–42

Queen, 166
Quirino, Elpidio, 119

Rabin, Yitzhak, 87, 94–96, 100; assassination of, 95–96, 100, 105–106
Radio Veritas, 135, 136–37
Ramos, Fidel, 137
Rather, Dan, 82
RC Cola, 68
Reagan, Nancy, 109, 116, 132–33, 136
Reagan, Ronald, 4, 22, 44, 47, 61, 62–63, 73–74, 82, 83, 91, 92, 107, 113, 144, 145, 151, 152, 177, 201; Marcos regime and, 118; 1986 Philippine election and, 132–38; and role of president, 80–81; Waldorf dinner speech of, 57–58
Reese, Matt, 44, 51, 52
"reframing," 92
Regan, Imelda, 136
Reilly, Ed, 148, 156–57, 158, 171, 176, 177, 180, 183, 185, 191–92, 201, 206, 217–18, 229; in Sawyer buyout, 210–13
religious right, 7
Republican National Committee, 228
Republican Party, U.S., 8, 44, 57, 77, 91, 118, 219, 223
Resorts International, 202
Retton, Mary Lou, 151
Rhode Island, 29
Richards, Ann, 98
Right Stuff, The (film), 62–63
Rise of Political Consultants, The (Sabato), 44

RJR Nabisco, 202
Rogers, Kenny, 151
Rolling Stones, 20–21
Rollins, Ed, 207–208
Rolls-Royce, 24–25
Romualdez, Benjamin, 120
Roosevelt, Franklin D., 41, 47
Rosenberg, Simon, 229
Rosenthal, Abe, 124
Rosner, Jeremy, 227
Rove, Karl, 8–9, 78, 91, 98, 177, 230
Roxana (Vargas Llosa's cousin), 178
Rubin, Robert, 200
Russia, 7, 141, 194, 220; 1996 election in, 218–19

Saatchi and Saatchi, 174
Sabato, Larry, 44
Sadat, Anwar, 88
Sadruddin Aga Khan, Prince, 76, 125–26
Safeway Select, 68–69
St. John, Pete, 150
Salas, Rafael, 130
Salvatierra, Rafael, 49, 52
Sam's Choice, 69
Sanchez de Lozada, Gonzalo, 103, 171–72, 175
San Francisco Chronicle, 226
San Jose Mercury News, 129
Sarandon, Susan, 198
Sawyer, David H., 4, 6–7, 8, 58, 90, 102, 106, 113, 114–15, 121, 138, 139–40, 146, 154, 162, 195, 203, 204, 205, 206–207, 220, 229; Aquino campaign and, 122–23, 125; background of, 11, 26–29; buyout of, 210–13; consumer democracy idea of, 80–81; corporate practice and, 196–97, 200–201; death of, 214–15; on electronic democracy, 217; failed

marriage of, 108–10; filmmaking career of, 26–29; first wedding of, 27–28; Glenn campaign and, 61–64; hirings outlook of, 147–48; Kennan's departure and, 209–10; Miller recruited by, 26, 30, 37; Mondale campaign and, 82–85; 1972 Venezuelan election and, 42–44, 46, 49–52, 54, 56; 1977 Israeli election and, 86–88; 1979 Boston election and, 22–23, 30–36; 1981 Israeli election and, 88–89; 1984 U.S. election and, 61–64, 82–85, 107–108; office of, 149; Peres's relationship with, 85; politics interest of, 28–30; post-SMG life of, 214; Puerto Rico election and, 41–42; South Korea account and, 143–44

Sawyer, Iris Michaels, 27–28, 36, 42, 54, 56, 108–10, 164–66, 198

Sawyer, Luke, 214–15

Sawyer, Nell Michel McFarland, 109–10, 164, 214–15

Sawyer Miller Group (SMG), 3, 41, 45, 63, 64, 90, 101, 107, 110, 113, 119, 146; Aquino campaign and, 122, 125–27, 131–33, 140–42; arms control issue and, 75–76; Bozell merger and, 213; business-politics factions of, 140; celebrities and, 150–52; Chilean election and, 153–55, 158–59; clients of, 4–6, 114–15, 139–42, 163, 196–203, 205–206; corporate practice of, 139–40, 163, 196–203, 205–206; creation of, 39–40; Drexel account and, 197–200; executive departures from, 146–48, 160–62, 164, 203–206; Flying Fortress adjunct of, 65, 71–72; globalization of politics and, 8; global reach of, 3–5; Grunwald's departure from, 205–206; Hands Across America

campaign and, 150–51; hirings of, 59–60, 146–48, 196–97; Human Rights issue and, 4–5, 193–94; international practice of, 141–42; Kennan's departure from, 208–10; KRC and, 148–49; legacy of, 218–24; Machismo culture of, 10–11; Miller's departure from, 203–205; 1989 Peruvian election and, 169–71, 175, 176–78, 187–88, 190–91; nuclear disarmament issue and, 126; office culture of, 148–49; offices of, 3–4, 114–15, 149–50; Philippine government business of, 140–41, 143–44; political culture created by, 5–6; Rollins' influence on, 207–208; Russian privatization campaign and, 194–95; Sawyer buyout and, 210–13; success of, 114–15; technology exploited by, 5–6, 9–10; in Torturers' Lobby report, 4–5, 193; U.S. intelligence services and, 121; values of, 152–53; Vargas Llosa memorandum of, 169–70, 178, 181

Scanlon, John, 202

Schechter, Peter, 148, 154–56, 158, 160, 171, 176, 177, 179, 183–84, 192, 198, 203, 211, 213, 218, 224

Schneiders, Greg, 63

Schroeder, Gerhard, 103

Schuller, Robert H., 151

Schultze-Rhonhof, Kurt, 180–81, 191

Schwartz, Tony, 25, 41

SDP, 125

Second Life of Susan Lennox, The (film), 165

Selling of the President, The (McGinnis), 79

Senate, Peruvian, 185–86

Senate, U.S., 37, 41, 44, 102, 113, 215

September 11, 2001 terrorist attacks, 106

7–Eleven, 202

Shagari, Shehu, 161
Shamir, Yitzhak, 90, 91, 92, 93–94
Shapp, Milton, 29
Sharon, Ariel, 91, 105
Sheeh, Maura, 202
Shepardson, Rob, 148, 171, 200, 211, 213, 219, 226
Shining Path guerrillas, 174, 183
Shrum, Bob, 38, 101, 102, 103–104, 106, 130
Shultz, George, 136, 137–38
Sin, Jaime Cardinal, 123, 137
Sinclair, Upton, 40
Singapore, 174
Six-Day War, 94
60 Minutes, 201
Smith, Alfred E., 56–57
Smith, Hanoch, 88
Smith, Joseph B., 119–20
Smith, Senator (hypothetical candidate), 65
Social Christian Party (COPEI), Venezuelan, 43–44, 46, 47, 49, 51, 52–53, 55
Soda Pop Dreams, 74
Solarz, Stephen, 129, 136, 142
Somalia, 220
Sonnenberg, Maurice, 29, 31–32, 205
Soros, George, 125, 153–54, 217
South Africa, 103, 202
South American Indian Council, 182
Southern Collegian, The, 24
Soviet Union, 46, 86, 113, 141, 218; collapse of, 114
Spain, 114, 141, 150
Spencer, Stuart, 134–36, 207
Spike (Miller's dog), 149
Spring, Micho, 22, 33
Squier, Bob, 41, 44–45, 50–51, 55, 120
SS+K, 219
Staebler, Neil, 41
State Department, U.S., 116, 118, 134, 136, 151

Stein, Skip, 197
Stern, Lenny, 148, 211, 213, 219, 226
Stern Gang, 92
Stevenson, Adlai, 27, 167
Strasberg, Lee, 27
Sudan, 121
Supreme Court, U.S., 107
swarm theory of history, 10
Sweden, 174
Swift Boat ads, 9
Switzerland, 125

Tatad, Francisco S., 127
Tatler, 166
technology, 5–6; *see also* Internet; television
television, 27, 82, 114, 229; impact of, 9–10; information revolution and, 221–23; in Israeli politics, 87–88, 97–100; Miller on, 38; Mondale's aversion to, 83–84; in 1972 Venezuelan election, 46, 50–51; in 1998 Chilean election, 159; Nixon-Kennedy debate and, 79, 99; power of, 5–6, 38, 144–45; style and substance in, 79–80
terrorism, 104, 106, 174, 183, 222
Terry, Fernando Belaunde, 177
Tet offensive, 36
Texas, 98, 150
Thackeray, W. M., 13
Thatcher, Margaret, 107, 144, 152, 160, 174, 175, 178, 181, 216
Theatre Intime, 26
Third Way, 103
This man isn't afraid to face you (Ese hombre de la cara) (television show), 51
This Week with David Brinkley, 115–16
Tibet, 3, 139, 162–63
Time, 46, 74, 86, 224

Time of the Hero, The (Vargas Llosa), 169

Timilty, Joe, 22, 31, 33–35

Titicut Follies (film), 28

Tocqueville, Alexis de, 53

Torturer's Lobby, 4–5, 193

Trippi, Joe, 229

Trujillo, Rafael, 48

Turkey, 219, 220

Turner, Doug, 221

Turner, Ted, 114

Ukraine, 220

United Kingdom, *see* Great Britain

United Nations, 51, 91, 113, 125, 154, 217

United Shoe Machinery Corporation, 26

USA for Africa, 150–51

Uzbekistan, 221

Valdes, Don Gabriel, 154, 156, 158

Valdes, Juan Gabriel, 153–54

Vargas Llosa, Alvaro, 175, 177, 178, 181, 188, 191

Vargas Llosa, Mario, 5, 189–90; campaign style of, 180–84, 186, 191–92; and decision to run, 172–74; fame of, 169; inner circle of, 178–79; SMG's memorandum to, 169–70, 178, 181; Thatcher as model for, 174–75; voters' estrangement from, 182–83; *see also* Peru, election of 1990 in

Vargas Llosa, Patricia, 173, 178

Venezuela, 5, 6, 85, 120, 138, 160; 1958 election in, 43; 1963 election in, 43; 1968 election in, 43, 46–47; 1972 election in, *see* Venezuela, election of 1972 in; 1978 election in, 54–55; two-party democracy of, 42–44

Venezuela, election of 1972 in, 42–53, 55–56; candidates in, 47–48; Fernández's campaign in, 47–52, 53; foreigner issue in, 52–53; Pérez's campaign in, 50–51; political consultants in, 44–46; political polarization in, 46–47; results of, 53; television and, 46, 50–51; two-party system and, 42–44; U.S. election system and, 44

Vermont, 204

Vietnam War, 21, 24, 36, 74, 117

Village Independent Democrats, 90

Village Voice, The, 129

Visa, 200

Vogue, 27

Volkswagen Beetle, 25

"Vote Different" ad, 225–26

Voter Vault, 227

Walesa, Lech, 4, 5

Wall Street Journal, The, 72, 74, 194–95, 199, 211

Walters, Barbara, 202

Waltzing with a Dictator (Bonner), 116

Wangyal, Geshe, 161

Warhol, Andy, 149

War of the End of Democracy, The (Daeschner), 173, 184

War of the End of the World, The (Vargas Llosa), 173

Washington, George, 40

Washington, Harold, 170–71

Washington state, 37

Watergate scandal, 74

"We Are the World" (song), 150–51

Weber, Max, 192–93

Weber Shandwick, 213, 217

Weinberger, Caspar, 136

Weinstock, Davis, 203–204
Wells, H. G., 43
Wells, Mary, 26
Wells, Rich, Greene, 26, 37
West Virginia, 44
Whitaker, Clem, 40
White, F. Clifton, 44, 55
White, Kevin H., 15–17, 30–34, 35, 37, 51, 182; governing style of, 20–22
White, William Allen, 71
Whitehouse, Charlie, 198
Whitman, Walt, 163
Wilkinson, Wallace G., 101–102, 163–64, 171
Will, George, 115
Williams, Robin, 151
Wilson, Woodrow, 47
Winfrey, Oprah, 151
Winitzky, Daniel, 179
Wirthlin, Richard, 72–73, 78, 91–92, 95–96, 98, 100, 106, 207
Wiseman, Frederick, 28
Wizard of Oz, The (film), 72

Wolfe, Tom, 62
Wolfensohn, James, 125, 217
Woodruff, Robert, 71
World Bank, 125, 213, 217
World War II, 18

Yale School of Organization and Management, 80
Yanukovytch, Viktor, 220
Yediot, 99
Yellow Revolution, 130–31
Yeltsin, Boris, 7, 218–19
Yilmaz, Mesut, 220
Yom Kippur War, 94, 95
YouTube, 225
Yuschenko, Viktor, 220

Zabel, Bill, 215
Zedillo, Ernesto, 218
Zyman, Sergio, 70, 71, 76, 204